Gift of The Editor

Aug 1959

An Introduction
to PASTORAL COUNSELING

Edited by WAYNE E. OATES

An
Introduction to
PASTORAL
COUNSELING

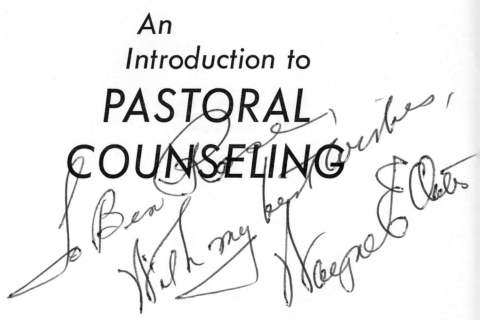

BROADMAN PRESS
Nashville, Tennessee

Library of Congress catalog card number 59–9688

Printed in the United States of America

Editor's Preface

Since 1944 a thorough-going curriculum in pastoral counseling has been incorporated in the program of all of the seminaries of the Southern Baptist Convention. A vital conversation has gone on among those of us teaching in this field in each of our seminaries. Many abiding insights have been brought to light in seminars and classes which all of us have conducted with theological students. Yet we have not had a common textbook which gathered these conceptions of the work of the pastoral counselor into one volume. We have been dependent upon continued repetition by word of mouth of many of our best understandings. For teaching purposes in our own classrooms, therefore, we have jointly agreed upon the imperative need for an introduction to pastoral counseling. Happily enough, Broadman Press, under the able direction of Dr. William Fallis, arrived at a similar conclusion at about the same time. Hence, we as professors of pastoral care in Southern, Southwestern, New Orleans, Golden Gate, and Southeastern Baptist Theological seminaries have brought to the reading public our combined discussions of pastoral counseling in this volume.

As we have worked at the task, we have been conscious of needs of persons far beyond our classrooms for such a volume as this. Working pastors have only recently had courses in pastoral counseling in their seminary training. Most of these courses have been instituted since the majority of pastors were in school. Consequently, such a volume as this is also intended to be a refresher course for these pastors. The conversations of the theological seminary classroom are brought to the pastor's study in these pages. The working hypotheses and the specific information and techniques are summarized in brief fashion here. Our fondest dream would be realized if the reader should conclude after reading the last page that counseling cannot be learned from a book. We hope that this book will motivate many pastors to seek clinically-supervised education in pastoral care in the programs being conducted by seminaries and hospitals.

Finally, we as seminary professors participate in a way that is richly meaningful to us in the Seminary Extension Department of our Convention. We are particularly anxious to reach the pastor who has never been to a seminary but who is taking full advantage of on-the-job training through the work of the Seminary Extension centers. We hope this book will be a road map for many a pilgrimage of these groups into the area of pastoral care and counseling.

In all of these groups—the beginning seminary student, the graduate of the seminary, and the pastor who has never been to a seminary—we find a common need to which this book is addressed. The pastor, regardless of his training, does not enjoy the privilege of electing whether or not he will counsel with his people. They inevitably bring their problems to him for his best guidance and wisest care. He cannot avoid this if he stays in the pastoral ministry. His choice is not between counseling or not counseling, but between counseling in a disciplined and skilled way and counseling in an undisciplined and unskilled way. The pages of this book are dedicated to the discipline and skill necessary for effective pastoral counseling in the role and function of the average pastor. Through the face-to-face encounter with desperate persons, this pastor as a minister of reconciliation has here both a widened and deepened channel for the communication of the good news of the Lord Jesus Christ to those who sit in regions of darkness and yearn for a great light.

Contents

Part I: Counseling in the Context of the Church . . 1

1. The Heritage of the Pastoral Counselor . . 3
   Albert L. Meiburg

2. The Pastoral Director as Counselor 19
   James Lyn Elder

3. The Purpose of the Church and Its Counseling
   Ministry. 28
   Samuel Southard

Part II: The Personhood of the Pastoral Counselor . . 39

4. The Emotional Health of the Pastoral Counselor 41
   Samuel Southard

5. The Attitudes of the Pastoral Counselor. . . 53
   James Lyn Elder

Part III: Pastoral Counseling: Its Process and Procedures 67

6. Making the Contact: Informal Pastoral
   Relationships 69
   Wayne E. Oates

7. Making the Contact: Pastoral Visitation and
   Counseling 81
   James Lyn Elder

8. Keeping Confidences in Pastoral Counseling . 87
   Wayne E. Oates

9. The Budgeting of Time in Pastoral Counseling   96
   John W. Drakeford

10. The Exploratory or Short-Term Interview . .   108
    Wayne E. Oates

11. The Process of Multiple-Interview Counseling.   117
    Richard K. Young

12. Recurrent Problems of Longer-Term
    Counseling   130
    Richard K. Young

13. The Pastor as a Marriage Counselor   151
    Samuel Southard

14. Calling in the Help of Other Counselors. . .   170
    A. Donald Bell

15. Ways to Learn Pastoral Counseling   185
    John W. Drakeford

Part IV: Pastoral Counseling and the Ministry of the
        Word of God in Christ   201
16. Pastoral Counseling and the Communication of
    the Gospel   203
    James Lyn Elder

17. Pastoral Counseling and the Experience of
    Prayer   211
    Wayne E. Oates

18. Pastoral Counseling and the Interpretation
    of Scripture.   222
    D. Allen Brabham

19. Pastoral Counseling and Christian Doctrine .   236
    Samuel Southard

Part V: Pastoral Counseling and the Educational Intentions of the Church. 251

20. Personality Development and Pastoral
Counseling 253
John M. Price

21. Pastoral Counseling and the Educational Ministry of the Church 269
Harold L. Rutledge

22. The Processes of Group Counseling 282
John M. Price

23. The Counselor Training of Prospective Group
Leaders 295
A. Donald Bell

24. Counseling the Discouraged Group Leader. . 309
A. Donald Bell

25. The Pastoral Counseling of Other Counselors . 318
Wayne E. Oates

Appendix: Standards for Clinical Pastoral Education . 325

About the Authors 329

Part I

Counseling in the Context
of the Church

Counseling of any kind is shaped and directed by the context in which it takes place. The native environment of pastoral counseling is the fellowship of believers, the gathered community of Christians, the church. This community of believers has throughout Christian history provided a royal priesthood of men and women of faith who have brought "the whole counsel of God" to bear upon the stresses and strains of needy people. Therefore, we want to see modern pastoral counseling as a "green twig" on the venerable bough of the concern of the churches for needy people in the times of their turning for help from others. Albert L. Meiburg discusses the pastor's heritage as a counselor.

The Christian community endows the counselor with a distinctively religious role as the "overseer of the flock." His work with individuals can never be removed from his responsibility as one into whose hands has been entrusted the care of the whole church as well as that particular individual. Therefore, James Lyn Elder will discuss the pastoral director as a counselor.

The underlying and overarching purposes of the church as a church give character and content to the counseling done by a pastor and other religious workers. These purposes, whether clearly perceived or vaguely felt, both stimulate and encourage or coerce and frustrate the work a pastoral counselor does with individuals. Samuel Southard, therefore, will explore the purpose of the church and its counseling ministry.

1. The Heritage of the
Pastoral Counselor

Albert L. Meiburg

When the pastor closes his study door and is alone with some person who has sought his help, he is engaged in one of the enduring functions of the Christian ministry. Because of the considerable popularity of pastoral counseling in recent years the impression may exist that this is merely a current vogue or fad. The pastor's work as a counselor will be enhanced if he knows something of his ancient heritage in his face-to-face ministry to his people.

The purpose of this chapter, then, is to sketch in broad outline the long and honorable tradition of the pastor as a "surgeon in the joining of broken souls." In order to establish as an anchor point a reasonably clear picture of the minister's unique role as a counselor, it is necessary to examine his heritage in Scripture, in Christian history, and during recent times.

An indication of the importance of counseling in ancient Judaism is seen from a study of the biblical words for counsel. Most frequently used is the Hebrew word *etsah*, which is used as a substantive at least eighty-four times in the Old Testament. It is also used as a verb, *yaatz*, twenty-three times in the sense of giving or receiving counsel, and from this root is derived the Hebrew word for counselor. These words may mean advice given or received, plans formed, or the ability to form plans, especially God's ability. Isaiah describes the Messiah as one upon whom rests the Spirit of the Lord, "the spirit of

3

counsel and might" (11:2), and names the Messiah "Wonderful Counselor" (9:6, RSV).

A second interesting Hebrew word which is translated in English as counsel is the word *sodh*, which has as its root meaning a couch, cushion, or pillow. From this is derived its use as meaning a sitting together or an assembly, either of friends talking intimately or of judges consulting together. For example, in Proverbs 15:22: "Without *counsel* purposes are disappointed: but in the multitude of counsellors they are established." *Sodh* is used to denote familiar conversation in some cases, as when the psalmist speaks of taking "sweet *counsel* together" with his close friends (55:14). *Sodh* is also used with the verb meaning to make naked or uncover to form the expression meaning to reveal a secret, as in Proverbs 11:13: "A talebearer *revealeth secrets:* but he that is of a faithful spirit concealeth the matter."

There are also certain biblical prototypes of the present-day pastoral counselor. In the time of the patriarchs, for example, disputes and problems were dealt with by the head of the family. During the Exodus and the wanderings, Moses was the outstanding figure. On one occasion at least, and probably more, the people stood about Moses all day long. Jethro, Moses' father-in-law, saw that this was too heavy a burden for one man and that Moses would wear himself and the people out. At Jethro's suggestion, Moses selected men who were experienced in handling problems in their own families and gave them the responsibility for small groups. Moses himself continued to consider the more difficult questions (Ex. 18:13–26).

In the time of the judges, Samuel was the outstanding counselor. He traveled on a circuit, hearing controversies, giving judgments, teaching, and counseling as the need arose. An indication of Samuel's effectiveness as a counselor is seen in Saul's desire to consult him which prompted him to request the witch at Endor to recall Samuel from the dead (1 Sam. 28:7–25).

Although the prophets were primarily speakers and not counselors in the usual sense of the word, one cannot read Jeremiah and Ezekiel without sensing that here were men of God who were particularly interested in things of the heart. It is not difficult to feel that either of these two men would have been able to lend a sympathetic ear to those who came to them with burdens.

The real incarnation of the pastor's ideal as a counselor may be seen in the New Testament in Jesus of Nazareth. Despite the brevity of the Gospel accounts, they give us an amazing record of One who had a unique insight into the needs and problems of people. Jesus himself "knew what was in man" (John 2:25). The dynamic of his life was a never-failing compassion. His ministry was a series of variations on the theme which rang forth in his inaugural address at Nazareth: "The Spirit of the Lord is upon me, because he hath anointed me to preach the gospel to the poor; he hath sent me to heal the brokenhearted, to preach deliverance to the captives, and recovering of sight to the blind, to set at liberty them that are bruised" (Luke 4:18).

In his ministry to individuals Jesus demonstrated sympathy, honesty, sincerity, and patience. He made no distinction between high and low, rich and poor, wise and simple. The taunt of his enemies, that he was a "friend of sinners," history has made a mark of honor.

Although Paul is usually thought of primarily as the great missionary, he was unsurpassed as a pastor. His letters are themselves a form of pastoral counseling and arose out of the practical problems which were laid at his door. These letters show that Paul was called on for help in cases involving quarrels between two Christians, interfaith marriages, divorce, illicit sexual relations, master-slave relations, and threatened schisms in the church as well as husband-wife and parent-child relationships.

The dynamic of Christian love as expressed in the early church unquestionably set in motion a concern for people that has been the motivating power behind pastoral counseling through centuries. Space does not permit here a detailed tracing of the history of pastoral counseling.[1] We must be content to choose for illustration several outstanding men, each prominent in his own period, because of their special attention to this phase of the ministry.

In the age of the Church Fathers, John Chrysostom showed a profound understanding of the work of the pastor. As the spiritual counselor to the citizens of a sophisticated capital, Chrysostom sought to modify the humiliating practice of public penance with its several stages of readmission to communion. He also felt that there must be some diversified therapy for sinners. On one occasion he said, "It is not right to take an absolute standard and fit the penalty to the exact measure of the offense, but it is right to aim at influencing the moral feelings of the offenders." [2] Chrysostom's *Treatise on the Priesthood* remains one of the classic treatments of pastoral responsibilities. In this writing he showed an awareness that "no one can, by compulsion, cure an unwilling man." [3]

Chrysostom thought of himself as a physician of the soul, dispensing medicines to those who voluntarily sought his help. In *On Penitence* he advised the priest to show charity to the sinner. "Urge him to show the wound to the priest; that is the part of one who cares for him, and provides for him, and is anxious on his behalf." [4]

Another great writing which gives the point of view of the Church Fathers on pastoral counseling is the work by Ambrose

---

[1] For detailed and systematic histories of pastoral care, see John T. McNeill, *A History of the Cure of Souls* (New York: Harper & Brothers, 1951); and Charles F. Kemp, *Physicians of the Soul* (New York: The Macmillan Company, 1947).

[2] *Treatise on the Priesthood,* cited by George H. Williams, "The Ministry in the Later Patristic Period," *The Ministry in Historical Perspectives,* ed. H. Richard Niebuhr and Daniel Day Williams (New York: Harper & Brothers, 1956), p. 70.

[3] *Ibid.*

[4] *On Penitence,* cited by Williams, *loc. cit.*

of Milan, *Three Books on the Duties of the Clergy*. In this famous work Ambrose described how the character of the "man of counsel" determines to a large extent whether or not people will seek his help: "We note therefore that in seeking for counsel, uprightness of life, excellence in virtues, habits of benevolence, and the charm of good nature have very great weight. Who seeks for a spring in the mud? Who wants to drink from muddy water?" [5] Again he asks, "Who will come to a man however well fitted to give the best of advice, who is nevertheless hard to approach?" [6]

During the period of Medieval Christianity the history of pastoral care is somewhat obscured by the extensive concern in the church with theological controversy. The development of clergy-laity distinctions during this period tended to inhibit face-to-face ministries with the notable exception of the institution of confession. However, the parish priest of the Middle Ages was the most learned person in the community, and men turned to him as lawyer, doctor, teacher, counselor, and friend. The sacrament of penance was a basic influence in this period and involved contrition, confession, and satisfaction. In the confessional the priest came into direct encounter with the individual and subjected him to a thorough spiritual examination. In order that the confession be made full and nothing withheld, the clergy were taught to probe the most secret places of a man's life. [7]

The practice in the early church of public confession had been gradually modified through permission and later the requirement of private confession to the priest. Since those who heard confessions needed instruction in dealing with offenders,

---

[5] *Three Books on the Duties of the Clergy*, bk. II, sec. 60, ed. Henry Wace and Philip Schaff ("A Select Library of Nicene and Post-Nicene Fathers of the Christian Church," Vol. X [New York: The Christian Literature Company, 1890]), p. 52.

[6] *Ibid.*, sec. 61, p. 53.

[7] Roland H. Bainton, "The Ministry in the Middle Ages," in Niebuhr and Williams, *op. cit.*, p. 97.

in the sixth century there appeared manuals for priests to use in assigning penance. The "Penitentials," as these handbooks are called, have been criticized as promoting casuistry. In spite of this and other weaknesses, they had as their main purpose the reconstruction of personality.[8]

As a matter of fact, it was the abuse of the confessional which was the chief point of attack in the Protestant Reformation. Luther's career of reform began in a pastoral concern over his people's belief that purchasing letters of indulgence assured them of salvation. The reformers apparently did not intend to eliminate the confessional; they only sought to remove from the priest any automatic power to forgive sin on behalf of God.[9]

Luther himself wrote, "Of private confession I am heartily in favor. . . . It is a cure without an equal for distressed consciences. But when we have laid bare our conscience to our brother and privately made known to him the evil that lurked within, we receive from our brother's lips the word of comfort spoken by God himself; if we accept it in faith, we find peace in the mercy of God speaking to us through our brother." [10] Luther regarded the binding and loosing passage of Matthew 18:15–20 as an authorization for all Christians to hear confessions and absolve.

The pastoral concern of Luther is prominent in his sermons, commentaries, and letters of spiritual counsel. He felt that the pastor's visits were as important as the visits of the physician, and he was convinced that many bodily diseases were the result of a morbid spiritual condition.[11]

The abandonment of the monasteries produced a large proportion of the problems which Luther faced as a counselor. Monks and nuns, widows, orphans, and needy students were attracted to Wittenberg, bringing with them a host of needs

[8] McNeill, op. cit., p. 135.
[9] Seward Hiltner, Religion and Health (New York: The Macmillan Company, 1943), p. 171.
[10] Cited by McNeill, op. cit., p. 167.
[11] Kemp, op. cit., p. 40.

both material and spiritual. With a genuine compassion born of his own spiritual battles, Luther took pains not to lose sight of these individuals. His counseling, while largely directive, was the first step away from priestly authority.[12] He emphasized the scriptural approach to the problem. The Bible is thought by many to have been his most important tool in counseling.

The best way for the student to appreciate Luther's counseling ministry is to read his *Letters of Spiritual Counsel,* which catch the spirit of this great pastor.[13] Issues related to marriage and a reinterpretation of sex are frequent in these letters. For example, one monk consulted Luther about his reluctance to set aside his vow of celibacy. Luther wrote that since by women "we were conceived, developed, born, suckled, and nourished, . . . it is quite impossible to keep entirely from them." As a further word of assurance he added, "This is the Word of God, through whose power procreative seed is planted in man's body and the natural ardor of his desire for a woman is kindled and kept alive." [14]

For a further example of the pastor as a counselor in the time of the Reformation, the student should study the life and work of Martin Bucer. In his book *On the True Care of Souls,* Bucer pointed out that Christian teaching from the pulpit and in classes is not sufficient. It is necessary to give the people individual Christian guidance. More than any other of the reformers, Bucer attempted to shape the church into a community of love.[15]

In summary, the chief result of the Protestant Reformation for pastoral counseling was the abandonment of the confessional as a sacrament and the emergence of the pastor, a figure

[12] C. Charles Bachmann, "Luther as Pastoral Counselor," *Pastoral Psychology* (November, 1952), pp. 35–42.

[13] Theodore G. Tappert, ed. and trans., *Luther: Letters of Spiritual Counsel* ("Library of Christian Classics," Vol. XVIII [Philadelphia: Westminster Press, 1955]).

[14] *Ibid.,* p. 273.

[15] Wilhelm Pauck, "The Ministry in the Time of the Continental Reformation," in Niebuhr and Williams, *op. cit.,* p. 137.

unique to evangelical bodies. The church was rediscovered as a congregation of saints, and the doctrine of the priesthood of believers gave every Christian a duty and a right to exercise special care not only for his own spiritual welfare but for that of his brother as well.

During the Puritan Age in England the pattern of society changed again in a radical sense. Many new situations were created, and people felt acutely the need of guidance in making moral decisions. It is not surprising that in the atmosphere of moral earnestness characteristic of this time pastoral counseling came to be regarded as one of the most important as well as one of the most difficult of all pastoral duties. Much of this counseling centered on what was described as "cases of conscience." From manuals or directories which were prepared during this time to give guidance to the counselor, we gain a picture of the variety of problems brought to the minister. "Cases of conscience" involved questions in such areas as family life, economic activities, military service, and the right use of recreation.

An impetus to counseling during this time was the attention which the ministry gave to "catechizing." Public teaching periods were often followed by a systematic visitation in the home. Sometimes the minister extended the hospitality of his own home for this purpose.

Richard Baxter wrote *The Reformed Pastor* primarily to urge upon his fellow ministers a method of private instruction of families.[16] Baxter felt strongly about personal work. To any minister who objected that he did not have time to know all his flock, Baxter recommended hiring an assistant out of his own salary, for it was better for him to live on part of his salary than to have any member neglected.[17] In addition to arranging to spend at least an hour with each family in his parish each year, Baxter developed a kind of group therapy approach in a series

[16] Winthrop S. Hudson, "The Ministry in the Puritan Age," in Niebuhr and Williams, *op. cit.*, p. 193.
[17] Kemp, *op. cit.*, p. 42.

of Thursday evening meetings at his home. Here people shared with one another their cases of conscience. Baxter was able to lead many of these to seek private help in addition to the group meeting.

The Puritan pastors not only made use of groups for pre-counseling, but such men as Henry Scougal stressed preaching as important in arousing the desire for personal help. John Dod did pastoral counseling in the church building in order to be readily accessible. When those who came were unable to state their questions, he would gently help them "to find the sore" and then would demonstrate such compassion as to encourage them to return.[18]

Jeremy Taylor remarked that the art of counseling "is not every man's trade" and that there were many who did some hurt to people by their lack of skill. On the other hand, there were men whose marked ability in dealing with the troubled soon gave them a reputation as counselors. On their own or at the suggestion of their pastor, individuals often traveled great distances to consult the more famous pastoral counselors of this time.[19] In his autobiography, Richard Baxter says of a particular year, "I was troubled . . . with multitudes of melancholy persons from several parts of the land, some of high quality, some of low, some very exquisitely learned, some unlearned . . ."[20]

Mental depressions such as Baxter describes seem to have been very common in the transitional society of the Puritan period.[21] Out of his clinical experience Baxter suggested three things which depressed people should avoid: (1) blaming their depression on the Spirit of God, (2) contact with objects that tend to tempt to carnal lust, and (3) placing religion "in too much fears, tears, and scruples."[22] In addition to the use of

[18] Hudson, op. cit., p. 199.
[19] Ibid., p. 201.
[20] The Autobiography of Richard Baxter, ed. J. M. Lloyd Thomas (London: J. M. Dent & Sons, Ltd., 1931), p. 216.
[21] Hudson, op. cit., p. 197.
[22] Baxter, op. cit., p. 217.

catharsis and prayer, Baxter advised the counselor to choose two or three "comfortable promises" for the person to "roll over and over" in his mind.[23] Particularly significant is Baxter's observation that in dealing with a depressed person it is important to have the help of a physician, since "till the body be cured the mind will hardly ever be cured." [24]

From such illustrations it seems evident that the Puritan Age was a time of significant developments in the pastor's heritage as a counselor. Among many modern procedures in counseling which the pastor of this time employed were empathy, listening, keeping confidences, nonjudgmental acceptance, and quiet optimism.[25]

Nineteenth-century America was the scene of important new trends in the cure of souls. Outstanding pastoral counselors of this period were Horace Bushnell and Washington Gladden.

All of Bushnell's ministry was spent in one parish. Orthodox evangelicals directed much criticism against his thesis, presented in his book *Christian Nurture*, that the child should grow up a Christian and "never know himself as being otherwise." This book represented a new departure of an order not seen since Jonathan Edwards and others had fixed the accepted character of the conversion experience in America as taking place with much storm and stress.

Bushnell knew from bitter personal experience the meaning of sorrow, doubt, sickness, and unfair opposition. His understanding of personality formation seems uncanny when he comments on the importance of infancy, "the age of impressions": "There is great importance . . . in the handling of infancy. If it is unchristian, it will beget unchristian states or impressions. If it is gentle, even patient and loving, it prepares a mood and temper like its own." [26] And again he commented, "Let every

[23] Hudson, *op. cit.*, p. 198.
[24] *Ibid.*, p. 197.
[25] *Ibid.*, p. 198.
[26] Horace Bushnell, *Christian Nurture* (New York: Charles Scribner's Sons, 1923), p. 205.

Christian father and mother understand, when their child is three years old, that they have done more than half of all they will ever do for his character." [27] Bushnell's custom was to spend one evening every week in the church office, at which time many came to seek his counsel.[28]

The name of Washington Gladden is usually associated with the social gospel movement and with the familiar hymn "O Master, Let Me Walk with Thee." Gladden was also a great pastor, and in his book *The Christian Pastor* he describes the pastor as, above all, "a friend." The minister, said Gladden, should be the one person in the community to whom the heart of anyone in need of a friend should instinctively turn.

Gladden recommended co-operation with the medical profession. He seems to have understood to a remarkable degree the close relationship between mental and physical health. In this connection he observed that there are some things "the doctor with his drugs can never cure, but that would be quickly put to flight if the load of shame and remorse that are resting upon the heart could be removed." In some instances the pastor may by gentle questioning draw forth the rankling secret and convince the troubled soul, by his own forgiveness, that the Infinite Love is able to save to the uttermost all who trust in him.[29] To do this is to be the bringer of health and peace.

Men like Bushnell and Gladden laid a good foundation for a more scientific approach to counseling. In the twentieth century the pastor's heritage as a counselor has been greatly enriched by the rise of the psychology of religion and the development of clinical pastoral training.

Psychologists of the latter part of the nineteenth century became interested in studying religious experience. Actually Jonathan Edwards was the American pioneer in the psychological approach to theology and wrote the first outstanding modern

[27] *Ibid.*, p. 212.
[28] Kemp, *op. cit.*, p. 57.
[29] Washington Gladden, *The Christian Pastor* (New York: Charles Scribner's Sons, 1899), p. 186.

work on this subject, *A Treatise Concerning the Religious Affections*. Schleiermacher in Europe had a similar role. In 1881 G. Stanley Hall studied religious conversion as a part of his famous work on adolescence.[30] His work encouraged many other men. The first great wave of publications in this area came at the turn of the century with the appearance of E. D. Starbuck's *The Psychology of Religion* (1899); G. A. Coe's *The Spiritual Life* (1900); and William James' *The Varieties of Religious Experience* (1902).

At this same time isolated courses were introduced into the curricula of seminaries. In 1899–1900 a course called "Psychology of Religion" was offered in the School of Religious Pedagogy of Hartford Theological Seminary.[31] Within a decade similar courses were being offered at the University of Chicago, Boston University School of Theology, and Newton Theological Institution. These courses were usually related to religious education, as was true at Union Theological Seminary in New York, where George A. Coe taught the psychology of religion and religious education.

A second wave of more systematic and critical surveys of the subject appeared between 1910 and 1920 and were written by E. S. Ames, G. M. Stratton, J. H. Leuba, G. A. Coe, and J. B. Pratt.[32] It was during the thirties that the literature of the psychology of religion began to give special attention to counseling as such. Karl Ruf Stolz made special reference to the religious counselor in *Pastoral Psychology* (1932). Dr. Henry Nelson Wieman and his wife Regina included a chapter on "Counseling Procedures" in their *Normative Psychology of Religion* (1935).

[30] Paul E. Johnson, *The Psychology of Religion* (New York: Abingdon-Cokesbury Press, 1945), p. 19.

[31] Francis L. Strickland, "Pastoral Psychology—A Retrospect," *Pastoral Psychology* (October, 1953), p. 9.

[32] For a resumé of the development of literature in the psychology of religion, the student may refer to standard textbooks on the subject. One of the best concise summaries is in the appendix to L. W. Grensted, *The Psychology of Religion* (New York: Oxford University Press, 1952). *See also* Kemp, *op. cit.*, pp. 100–107.

Mrs. Wieman had taught psychology and had been active in clinical psychology.

In 1938 John Sutherland Bonnell published *Pastoral Psychiatry,* one of the first books giving exclusive attention to the work of the pastor as a counselor. Rollo May's *The Art of Counseling* (1939), lectures given to Methodist student workers, was based on the new understanding of personality resulting from the work of Freud, Jung, Rank, Adler, and Kunkel. This book was the first systematic study of counseling. It was followed by the well-known works of Dicks (1944), Hiltner (1949), and Wise (1951).[33]

Hiltner, Wise, and May were all students at one time or another of Anton T. Boisen, who is generally acknowledged to be the father of clinical pastoral training. Because of this connection, it is important to trace briefly the unfolding of this second line of influence on the modern concept of pastoral counseling.

In 1893 Henry Drummond read a paper entitled "Spiritual Diagnosis" in which he advocated some form of clinical training for theological students: "The study of the soul in health and disease ought to be as much an object of scientific study and training as the health and diseases of the body." [34]

Drummond's conviction had come from his own "clinical" experience while he was in charge of the inquiry rooms in the Moody revival campaigns. There he had faced thousands of men and women in critical moments and had confronted every form of suffering imaginable. The accuracy of Drummond's insights into human nature at its best and its worst and his consequent popularity as a speaker and counselor can be attributed to his experience with Moody.

The first specific attempts to do what Drummond and others

[33] Russell L. Dicks, *Pastoral Work and Personal Counseling* (New York: The Macmillan Company, 1945); Seward Hiltner, *Pastoral Counseling* (New York: Abingdon-Cokesbury Press, 1949); Carroll A. Wise, *Pastoral Counseling—Its Theory and Practice* (New York: Harper & Brothers, 1951).

[34] Quoted in Kemp, *op. cit.,* p. 50.

began to see was needed took place in the nineteen-twenties. A physician, Dr. William Keller of Cincinnati, offered to provide some clinical experience for a limited group of seminary students during summer months. In 1923 this program was launched and later became known as the Graduate School for Applied Religion. It has since become absorbed into the curriculum of the Episcopal Theological Seminary in Cambridge, Massachusetts.[35]

Another physician, Dr. Richard C. Cabot of Cambridge, had an important part in the genesis of clinical training. A man of broad talents, Dr. Cabot was on the faculty of the Harvard Medical School; he later taught social ethics at Harvard College and natural theology at Andover-Newton Theological School. In the early twenties he became interested in Anton T. Boisen, a Congregational minister who as a result of his own experience as a patient in a mental hospital was convinced that the church was not adequately ministering to those "in the wilderness of the lost." [36] With the encouragement and financial assistance of Dr. Cabot and others, Dr. Boisen embarked on a chaplaincy program at Worcester State Hospital in Massachusetts which was to include clinical training. There were four students in his first summer class in 1925.[37]

Russell L. Dicks made a significant contribution to the movement by providing its first real literature. Dr. Cabot paid for the clinical program at Massachusetts General Hospital where Dicks became chaplain in 1933 and collaborated with him in writing *The Art of Ministering to the Sick*.[38] In many ways Dicks gave the same impetus to clinical training in the general hospital that Boisen did to similar work in the mental hospital. Boisen's *Exploration of the Inner World* (1936) ap-

[35] Rollin J. Fairbanks, "The Origins of Clinical Pastoral Training," *Pastoral Psychology* (October, 1953), pp. 13–16.
[36] *Ibid.*, p. 14.
[37] *Ibid.*, p. 15.
[38] For Dicks' own account of his work with Dr. Cabot, see his article, "The Art of Ministering to the Sick," *Pastoral Psychology* (November, 1952), pp. 9–13.

peared the same year as did the work by Cabot and Dicks.

From such beginnings the clinical pastoral training movement has grown until it is now an integral part of the theological curriculum.[39] There is little question but that clinical pastoral training has been the most valuable single influence in enabling the present-day pastor to function effectively as a counselor.[40] It has done so by insisting that the pastoral counselor accept the same disciplines required of those in other counseling professions. The essence of clinical training is supervised, first-hand experience in ministering to people in some condition of need. Obviously pastoral counseling cannot be adequately taught in a classroom where theory, as excellent and essential as it is, is not experienced in concrete interpersonal situations.

Changing emphases within clinical pastoral training point to the pastor's ultimate and abiding heritage as a counselor. From student's original concern with "What must I *do* to be of help to the person?" the question has changed to "What must I *know?*" to "What must I *say?*" and finally to "What must I *be* to be of real help to the person?"[41] This last question reminds the religious counselor that in the face of all the help which he may receive today from the sciences of man, he must never lose sight of his distinctive role as a minister of religion. He is first and foremost a religious counselor. In the eyes of his counselee he represents God and the church, and this fact is responsible for his being a counselor in the first place.

It is conceivable that the pastor may succeed in helping a counselee psychologically while at the same time he will be a failure as a pastoral counselor. In a real sense his success or

[39] Robert S. Michaelsen, "The Protestant Ministry in America: 1850 to the Present," in Niebuhr and Williams, *op. cit.*, p. 286.

[40] For more detailed history of clinical training, see Kemp, *op. cit.*, pp. 243–61; Carl J. Scherzer, *The Church and Healing* (Philadelphia: Westminster Press, 1945), pp. 229–48; and *Pastoral Psychology* (October, 1953), p. 37. See also the *Encyclopedia of Southern Baptists* (Nashville: Broadman Press, 1957), II, 1073 ff.

[41] Frederick C. Kuether, "The Council for Clinical Training," *Pastoral Psychology* (October, 1953), p. 20.

failure as a counselor will depend on the extent to which he can bring the skills and insights gained from related fields under the control of his basic identity as a man of God.

As he looks back over the "long past" and the "short history" of pastoral counseling, the minister senses something of his kinship with all those who, moved by the Spirit of Jesus, have sought to be a "near neighbor" to those in distress. And as he confronts his task today "under the aspect of eternity," the pastor can agree with Gregory the Great: "The government of souls is the art of arts!"

2. The Pastoral Director as Counselor

James Lyn Elder

Our forefathers were less nimble tongued than the Greeks. Therefore, the English language contains the word "bishop." Originally this word was *episcopos* and meant "overseer." Its nearest Latin-derived equivalent is superintendent, literally one who intends or plans on a comprehensive scale. The first letter of *episcopos* was dropped, the "c" was slurred into an "h," and the word bishop became respectable and took its place in our daily speech.

Both words—bishop and superintendent—point to an undeniable aspect of the Christian ministry—that of administration. The pastor is required both to think comprehensively or oversee and to guide his people effectively in the corporate realization of the plans which he and they have made together. His role is like that of the captain who, standing on the bridge of his ship, has primary authority and responsibility for her course and conduct.

To say all of this, however, is not to accept the Catholic concept of the bishopric as an office of centralized authority. Protestants criticize this idea as a perversion of a simple New Testament institution. And the essence of the error is that what was originally an informal congregational function has been hardened into an ecclesiastical office.

The term "bishop" in Scripture is roughly equivalent to another term, "elder," from the Greek word for which, *presbuteros,* the Presbyterians take their name. The latter term simply designates a member of the fellowship of advanced maturity, not

19

necessarily an older person (Timothy, for example, found his youth a handicap), but one who to some advanced degree has grown up into Christ.

The important thing to note, at least for our present purpose, is that the pastor, in earlier times and in the present, has an episcopal, or administrative, function. The church fellowship, like any other complex organism, needs intelligent direction of its growth. It also needs a developmental stimulus and requires spiritual maintenance and repair. The provision of all these things depends for the most part upon the "undershepherd," the minister.

It is quite apparent that in the New Testament there was a warmth and informality of relation between the bishop and the people such as is not evident in the more extreme forms of episcopal government today. The touching scene of Paul's farewell to the leaders of the Ephesian church and his tender admonitions to them give no hint of ecclesiastical pomposity. No distinction between "clergy" and "laity" existed in the early church; leaders simply rose like cream from out of the fellowship itself. They first demonstrated in practice their qualifications for leadership and on that basis were chosen for the task. But once appointed, these men continued to have a warm, reciprocal relationship with the church. A bond of sensitive sympathy like that enjoyed by Christ and his church existed between the fellowship and its ministers.

It is significant, therefore, that in a recent book about the ministry the suggestion was made that the leader of the congregation be thought of as a "pastoral director." [1] This word has both the connotation of administrative responsibility and the suggestion of shepherd-like tenderness and affection. Perhaps it does as well as any term to set forth the truth being stressed at this point.

[1] H. Richard Niebuhr, Daniel Day Williams, and James A. Gustafson, *The Purpose of the Church and Its Ministry* (New York: Harper & Brothers, 1956), pp. 79 ff.

Counseling and Administration Inseparable

One of the functions of this undershepherd of Christ is administration. That function is not simply clerical bookkeeping or ecclesiastical juggling or any such impersonal activity. Administration is always richly interpersonal, involving as it does the total person—heart, head, and hand—with whom the pastoral director works.

An analogy from one of the sciences may make the nature of administration plain. In all living things a twofold process is observed. First, various cells develop specialized functions, some becoming eyes, others feet, and others internal organs. Thus a process of differentiation is carried out. Then the parts so developed are related to each other in a vital harmony; they are integrated. Organic life would be impossible without the effective function of both differentiation and integration.

The church is itself a living thing; it grows, maintains, and reproduces itself. Paul indicates in Ephesians 4:11 that some members of the ecclesia develop certain capacities while others grow in yet other directions. A diversity and richness of abilities are thus to be seen in the fellowship. But there is also the most complete kind of integration of the various parts, for all "are members of the same body."

The administrative task of the pastor is suggested by the biological figure used by Paul. It is, first, to encourage in the membership the development of diverse ministries and then to guide these various ministries into a co-operating, productive relationship to each other.

Pastoral leadership is thus seen to be as "spiritual" as preaching, worship, or Christian education. It is not simply the spinning of ecclesiastical wheels, nor is it the laborious, uninspired job of keeping an organizational structure from falling to pieces. It is, rather, from edge to edge, a never-ending continuity of giving vital form to the spiritual forces at work in the fellowship.

Administration, of course, has the same goal as every other program in which the pastor engages: the advancing of the kingdom of God within and through the congregation. It is thus related to other ministering methods as one facet of a jewel is related to its other planes. And it goes without saying that the individuals and the personal growth needs with which the pastor is concerned are the same regardless of the direction from which he approaches his people. The chairman of an administrative committee and a troubled father seeking help for his son may frequently be one and the same person.

There is an overarching purpose in everything the pastor does. It is this which gives to his ministry strength and stability. And it is this which ties his counseling and his administrative actvities into an indivisible bundle.

Counseling an Effective Administrative Tool

On one occasion it was brought to the attention of Mr. Bronson, pastor of the Calvary Church, that Mrs. Swan, chairman of the housekeeping committee, had become very hostile toward the church and the pastor. Mr. Bronson kept this in mind and one afternoon called on Mrs. Swan at her home. Their conversation was as follows:

MRS. SWAN: Brother Bronson, I'm glad you called. There's something I want to talk to you about.

PASTOR: Oh? What is that?

MRS. SWAN: It's about the housekeeping committee you put me on.

PASTOR: I see.

MRS. SWAN: I hardly know how to put it, but I have the feeling that the church is asking more of me than they should, that I am just being used to do something nobody else will do.

PASTOR: I understand. You feel that a great deal is being asked of you and not much being given you in return.

MRS. SWAN: Well, yes, I guess you could put it that way. Now, take what happened Saturday night. Those young people left the recreation hall a complete mess after their party, and everyone said the next day that my committee was at fault.

PASTOR: I see. It wasn't your fault that the recreation hall wasn't clean for Sunday, but everyone said it was.

MRS. SWAN: Well—perhaps not everyone, but two or three made comments about it.

PASTOR: And this makes you feel that the church is asking too much of you.

MRS. SWAN: Well—as I look back on it now, perhaps it isn't the whole church but just one or two in the church who made me feel this way.

PASTOR: I understand.

MRS. SWAN: Maybe I just shouldn't let such little things get under my skin.

Counseling can be understood as helping people to help themselves by giving them opportunity and encouragement to clarify their thoughts and feelings through putting them into words. The foregoing example is typical of the way such a method may be effectively used in administration. Unexpressed, Mrs. Swan's emotional molehill had grown into the proverbial mountain. In talking it over in a relaxed, friendly way, she saw that it was much less of a problem than she had thought.

Church administration, as has been said, consists of helping members to develop their distinctive ministries on the one hand and of relating them to each other in a harmonious, productive way on the other. In both processes the organization of dynamic forces in the personality of the member is of fundamental importance. Human behavior grows out of attitudes, and attitudes are at any given moment but the cross section of the inner, emotional world of the person.

Counseling is the tool par excellence for getting at and altering emotional settings in the direction of the ideal. It is to be used largely as the pastor employed it in the case of Mrs. Swan. First, there was the appearance of a symptom: Mrs. Swan was expressing hostile emotions toward the church and its minister. This was the danger signal that indicated the need for counseling.

Second, the pastor called on Mrs. Swan. He exercised what

has been called the "strategic initiative." At this point he is giving the person with the problem both the opportunity and the encouragement to talk about her difficulty.

In the third place, when Mrs. Swan, with some hesitation, brought out her problem, the pastor was capable of accepting her statement and encouraging discussion of it. He did not feel it necessary to challenge her interpretation of the event or to give her quick (and probably superficial) reassurance concerning the appreciation of her which the church had. It was only as she was given complete freedom to express her feelings that she saw her problem shrink to its true proportions.

Counseling thus used may do for administration what no amount of clever organizational manipulation may accomplish. Instead of shuttling persons into and out of organizational slots in the attempt to find some place where they might fit, the counseling pastor aims at helping people to grow up, if possible, to the responsibilities they already have. In this way, beyond question, counseling is a valuable ally to administration.

Administration: A Doorway to Counseling

The foregoing principle may be stated also in reverse. Administration assists counseling fully as much as counseling helps achieve administrative effectiveness.

In the case of Mrs. Swan, for example, the pastor furthered the cause of housekeeping in the church by counseling with a disgruntled committee member. But his interest in Mrs. Swan, after all, was not simply in her ability to preside over a committee. He wanted, ultimately, Mrs. Swan to become the person she was capable of becoming. And to the extent that her experience with housekeeping responsibilities makes either her or her pastor aware of growth needs on her part—to this extent administrative processes may lead to counseling. Let us return to Mrs. Swan and see how this works.

Keeping in mind the incident given above, the pastor returned after some weeks for another visit to Mrs. Swan. In the course of their conversation, he referred to her service on the housekeeping committee, expressing appreciation for it. Mrs. Swan accepted his remarks with evident pleasure. Then he tactfully said:

PASTOR: You have had no further feeling, I hope, that you were not appreciated for your work at the church.

MRS. SWAN (*somewhat embarrasssed*): Oh, no. I think it was just a silly misunderstanding.

PASTOR: I see. As you look back on the experience, you feel it appears in a different light than it did then.

MRS. SWAN: Yes. I can see now that I got all upset about nothing at all. Even those few people who made critical remarks probably didn't mean them.

PASTOR: You think that you took their comments more seriously than they meant them.

MRS. SWAN: Yes, and do you know, Brother Bronson, this isn't the first time that has happened to me.

PASTOR: Oh?

MRS. SWAN: Last year at my club I was in charge of one program and worked very hard to make it a success. But one woman—a well-known crank—said right to my face that she felt the whole afternoon was wasted. I came home and was blue for days.

PASTOR; I see. The one critical remark made by this woman upset you, though there were others who probably thought your program was very good.

MRS. SWAN: Yes. After a while I saw how foolish I was, but just at the time I couldn't get over it. I suppose I just have to learn how to take criticism.

PASTOR: The problem as you see it is learning how to face such criticism and not let it upset you too much.

MRS. SWAN: Yes, I do.

At this point the interview could go in any number of directions. Mrs. Swan could go back into her past, discussing her childhood and the upsets that came about through hurt feelings. She might have, on the other hand, turned her mind to some current relationships involving family or friends. Or, she could go possibly in yet a third direction. In any case, she is thinking healthily and helpfully about her own growth needs. She is seeing herself with an increased degree of objectivity, and this is always an ingredient of maturity.

Now there are two things that administrative processes contributed to counseling in this case. And the same contributions may be looked for in others. In the first place, administration provided the setting and the incident which brought about the interview. In the second place, this particular administrative incident, in acid-test fashion, revealed the exact nature of Mrs. Swan's growth need. As surely as, or perhaps more surely than, an elaborate psychological test, it disclosed the counselee's habit of wearing her heart on her sleeve. It marked the location, as Cabot puts it, of the "growing edge of the soul." [2] Thus administration repaid to counseling the debt incurred earlier when counseling had contributed to administration.

Summary

The role of the Christian minister includes the responsibility for administration or oversight of the flock. This is as evident a scriptural function as preaching or teaching. Since it involves methods also encountered in nonreligious organizations, administration is not to be thought of as a necessary evil in the pastorate, an "unspiritual" chore to be done. On the contrary, inasmuch as the pastor deals in administration with the same person and the same problems he confronts in the pulpit, administration may be seen to be in every sense a spiritual opportunity.

This is particularly evident at the point of administration's relationship with counseling. Both of these ministries are tied together in the indivisible bundle that is the total pastoral program. Both are guided by a single concern, namely, the advancing of the kingdom of God. And both have the spirit of Christlike concern for individuals as their vesture.

[2] Richard C. Cabot and Russell L. Dicks, *The Art of Ministering to the Sick* (New York: The Macmillan Company, 1936), p. 14.

Counseling and administration are further alike in that both of them deal with people on an individual basis rather than at a congregational level. Good administration erects a sturdy organization as a stonemason does a cathedral, cementing one "living stone" at a time into the structure.

Often in the course of the procedure of getting the right member into the right place in the fellowship, however, or even after he has been settled in place, certain growth needs may appear under stress and in turn may lead to counseling. If the counseling is effective, the administrative process will be strengthened by having a stronger member in that position. But more will be accomplished than merely the improvement of the church's organization. A child of God will have been helped to become more like his Father, and this is a value which transcends all administrative concern.

Both counseling and administration are seen to be means, then, whereby the pastor performs his total task. They are the twin oars of a boat which, if it is to make progress, must be used simultaneously and with equal power. Together they make a matchless contribution to the over-all goal of the minister of Christ.

3. The Purpose of the Church and Its Counseling Ministry

Samuel Southard

Professor Elder has discussed the relationship between church administration and pastoral counseling. He has urgently stressed the importance of the over-all purposes of the church as the shaping force of the pastor's counseling as a representative of the church. This chapter, therefore, deals with the purpose of the church and its counseling ministry.

The purposes of the church are related to counseling in several ways. First, the church as a redemptive fellowship provides standards for personal growth and opportunities for spiritual maturity which direct and enrich the counseling process. Second, the pastor's identification with the church adds powerful symbols to his counseling ministry. Third, the American principle of voluntary church support has produced a unique personal relationship between pastor and people.

The Redemptive Fellowship of the Church

One of the characteristics of the Christian church is its ability to demonstrate God's love through human relationships. In the Christian fellowship a believer may find tangible expression of the supernatural grace that endows his life. The body of Christ is a partnership where people share a common devotion to Christ and have opportunity to connect their inward lives with outward conduct through the transforming power of the Spirit. The church is a school where men learn to live a new life.

This purpose of the church often throws new light upon the counseling relationship. A parishioner may protest to his pastor that he is filled with love for God and men. In his own eyes he is the most humble and unassuming of men. But the pastor has observed that in the church this man ceaselessly strives for glory. He is comfortable only with those whom he can dominate. His outward conduct gives little evidence of inner transformation.

Another person may speak of this same love of God within and yet present quite a different picture in the church. The individual may have experienced so many rejections by family and associates in the past that he believes the church rejects him if he but shows his face. He seeks to avoid danger by sitting passively in the corner while others lead. Yet this trembling soul may have deep spiritual strivings which would enrich the Christian fellowship and transform his own life if they could find expression. The pastor may hear the same words from both men, but his knowledge of their conduct in the church provides clues to a deeper understanding of their psychological and spiritual condition.

If the pastor's knowledge of the Christian community helps these men to measure their feelings more accurately, progress has been achieved. But the counseling cannot stop there. There is always the question, "Knowledge for what?" New-found insight must be related to goals of life. Here again the church's purpose helps the counseling process, for Christians are taught to see themselves as they are in order that they may become what they ought to be. The quality of their relationships can be changed for the better.

The standard for the Christian's life among men is the relationship which exists between Christ and his disciples. This should prevail also, in some sense, between one disciple and another.[1] Fellowship between man and man is to be upon the same

[1] L. S. Thornton, *The Common Life in the Body of Christ* (London: Dacre Press, 1950), p. 40.

basis as fellowship between man and God. In the parable of the
unmerciful servant, Jesus taught that the forgiving spirit of God
is to be shown in the forgiving spirit of his servants upon earth.[2]
The apostle Paul taught that God makes his appeal to men
through the attitudes and examples of his ambassadors, men
who have become a new creation in Christ Jesus.[3] When Christians love one another, they are imitating God.[4] To walk worthy
of God's calling is to forbear one another in love and walk honor-
ably among all men.[5] When unbelievers see clear and humble
communication between Christians in the church, they see evidence of the presence of God.[6] When they do not see this, the
gospel is hidden. This earthly fellowship among believers draws
its whole character and significance from the relationship of believers to God in and through Christ. The church is not to be
defined in terms of relationships among men but in terms of
the quality of the relationship that exists among men because
they have become sons of God.

In counseling, people can measure this understanding of the
church against their own misunderstanding of its purpose. One
middle-aged woman went through this painful process after she
saw the results of her own teaching upon her teen-age children's
lives. She came to her pastor with this story: Since childhood
she had been taught that her family was better than others in
the community. Her mother used the external standards of the
church to prove their superiority. The woman had adopted the
mother's method with her own children. "But now," she told
the pastor, "I know something is wrong. My son won't associate
with anyone his age. My daughter can't find anyone good
enough to date her more than once."

In the course of several interviews, the lady began to realize
that her attitudes had colored the conduct of her children. She
also admitted that the negative morality of her mother had in-

[2] Matt. 18:21–35.
[3] 2 Cor. 5:16 to 6:10.
[4] Eph. 5:1–2.
[5] Eph. 4:1 to 6:9.
[6] 1 Cor. 14:1–25.

terfered with her happiness and effectiveness as a wife: "I have gotten my husband into some terrible scrapes by my hyper-critical remarks to his associates." In these and other ways the woman showed her disenchantment with the way of life she had been taught and which she in turn had communicated to her children.

Then she began to talk about love as a better way. Her long-ings for affection were deep but had never been expressed. She had been taught that forgiveness was a weakness, but now she ached to be forgiven by friends for her pride and conceit. With her pastor's encouragement, this woman was able to share her discouragements and hopes with her husband. By seeking his support she let him know that he was important to her. To-gether they created a life which attracted warmth from their children. The pastor also guided the counseling conversations to specific ways in which love could be shown to friends and fellow church members. After much fear and trembling, the woman began to admit mistakes openly and identify with the misfortunes of others. Although she was not even yet entirely comfortable with anyone, she nevertheless was headed in the right direction. Some deep satisfaction now came through her personal relations. Before, her pride and narrow-mindedness had constricted these channels through which love must flow.

The Pastor's Identification with the Church

The church provides a purpose for living and the fellowship through which love may be made real. These goals and oppor-tunities are a part of any pastoral counseling. The church also invests the pastor himself with certain symbols which aid his counseling ministry. Certain expectations cluster about his role as a religious leader. His position in the church organization is a focus for some attitudes which might otherwise be missed in an interview.

Sometimes a counselee's feelings toward the church come out in his remarks about the pastor. A young man may come to his

pastor with the complaint that the church no longer fulfils his
expectations. He believes that the pastor is a scholar and thinker,
but he finds no such qualities among other members of the congregation. If the minister is as contemptuous of the church as
his young parishioner is, he will feed his own ego rather than
the soul of his counselee. But if he has accepted his responsibility as the leader of this flock, he may inquire into the amount of
responsibility which this parishioner will take in the Christian
fellowship.

Has this young man sought to grow in his Christian life since
his conversion many years ago? Is he familiar enough with the
organization of the church to know those men and women who
do inspire others by their conduct and thinking? Of course,
the young man may have sought after this and been rebuffed
by rigid and unfeeling leaders. But what is he going to do about
his situation? Sooner or later he must move from the idealism of
early adolescence to the mature realization that men of wisdom
and purity of heart are hard to find in any organization. Furthermore, the young man's contempt for those who do not meet
his standards must be challenged. Does he love only those who
love him? In what way is he then better than the Pharisees
whom he criticizes? By virtue of his well-thought-out position in
the church, the pastor may challenge such a man to seek a
deeper spiritual maturity.[7]

In addition to his specific position in the organization, there
are powerful religious symbols in the pastor's role. Professor
Oates has described the minister as a representative of God,
Jesus, the Holy Spirit, and a specific church.[8] To some people,
the pastor represents God as a visible embodiment of con-

[7] Other influences of the pastor's role upon counseling are discussed in
Wayne Oates, "The Findings of the Commission in the Ministry," *Annals of
the New York Academy of Sciences*, 63:3, pp. 415–17.
[8] Wayne Oates, *The Christian Pastor* (Philadelphia: Westminster Press,
1951), pp. 26–42.

science. For this reason, they approach him with the idea that he will condemn them. It is essential that he help such persons to see the difference between the parental training on right and wrong and the living precepts of God himself. An individual may also think that he can depend on the minister as he should upon God. He calls the pastor day and night for all types of service. Although the pastor represents God as a dependable ambassador, this does not mean that he can do for an overdependent parishioner everything that an indulgent parent once attempted. Instead, the counselee should have the assurance that this is a godly man who symbolizes the reality of God.

The pastor is also a reminder of Jesus. If God's love is incarnate in the heart of this man, others will be attracted by this image of Christ. The powerful psychological process of identification will lead men through him to God. The minister who has taken into himself the characteristics of Christ will find that others will seek to be as he is. They will love the Saviour because this servant has been Christlike. This is evangelism incarnate in the counseling process.

As an instrument of the Holy Spirit, the pastor is a teacher and comforter. People come to him because he may be the only person to whom they can talk in confidence. His pastoral role provides a feeling of trust which opens the door to spiritual confidences. The pastor's intimate knowledge of eternal truths also prepares the hearts of confused people to receive his suggestions during counseling.

Through his specific position and his symbolic role, the minister is identified with the church. But this does not mean that his complete guidance or full power comes through a visible company of believers. The pastor is also a representative of the Christ who died for the church. The minister's own personal relationship to Christ provides an immediate source of authority which must be considered along with his authority as a trained person and the man called to lead this congregation. Just as

Christ is the center of the church, so his personality is at the heart of the shepherd's calling.[9]

This means that the identification of the pastor with the church is never complete. There must always be a creative tension between the requirements of God which come directly to the pastor's soul and the demands of a congregation. A man who had recently lost his wife after a lingering illness asked his pastor if it were wise for him, a deacon, to begin the public courting of an attractive widow. During the course of several conversations, the pastor saw that the man had worked through much grief over his loss and was psychologically prepared for courtship. He also found that the man's children were beginning to demand a mother. Yet, at the same time, he knew that a hasty marriage would cloud the deacon's witness in the church.

The minister therefore assured the widower that his God-given need for marriage was reasserting itself after his first grief has passed away. He commended him for considering his church responsibilities at the same time, for this position meant much to him and to the people. With individual and community responsibilities in view, both pastor and parishioner could think creatively and realistically. If the pastor had immediately told the man to "do as you want to," he would have denied the im-

---

[9] A different point of view is taken by Professor Richard Niebuhr in *The Purpose of the Church and Its Ministry* (New York: Harper & Brothers, 1956). He urges the pastor to lay aside his authority as "man of God" and "ambassador for Christ" (pp. 68 ff). According to biblical standards, Professor Niebuhr is wrong, for the call of God is personal as well as social (Ex. 3; 1 Sam. 3:2–18; Isa. 6; John 1:35–51; Gal. 1:11–24). To know Christ and proclaim him as Lord is the essential purpose of every believer (1 Cor. 2:2; 2 Cor. 4 and 5; Phil. 2:5–12; Gal. 1:12; Col. 1). Professor Niebuhr would deprive the minister of this personal authority.

Further, he obscures the distinctly christological character of God by asserting that Jesus did not bear witness to himself (p. 31). Niebuhr seems to relate the church to God without reference to the uniqueness of Christ as God (p. 21). His de-emphasis of Christianity as the "true" (p. 46) religion obscures the real challenge of the Christian church. The Christian minister is the minister of Jesus Christ; the church is the body of Christ; the sinner is transformed by the Spirit of Christ. The clarity of the purpose of the church and the confidence of the ministry reside in the explicit and definite uniqueness of Christ as the full revelation of God.

portance of community support which came through approval
of his diaconate. If he had warned him of what "they" would
say, he would have provided no encouragement for a man struggling toward a renewal of personal fulfilment.

The Influence of the American Scene

The pastor's role and position identify him with Christ and
his church. But these identifications will have specific meanings
in each period of history and in each regional location. An understanding of the purposes of the church must include a consideration of the influences of time and place. In America
counseling has been influenced by the voluntary principle of
church participation, by the expectation of a persuasive ministerial personality, and by the activity of laymen in the church
organization.

The subtle magic of this new land overthrew the convenient
"church and sect" categories of Troeltsch and Weber. Instead,
American churches developed as denominations with societies
—foreign mission, home mission, and Sunday school—as an
extension of the local churches that were concerned for the
world.[10] In countries with state-supported churches it might be
true that "the minister is nothing apart from the church." [11] But
in America, with voluntary contributions and lay leadership,
the pastor was forced to rely upon an authority which came
directly from God. Without state sanction, the American clergy
relied upon spiritual depth, moral suasion, and on occasion
threats of divine vengeance. The result has been a sense of
dedication and courage among American ministers which
causes admiration among European visitors.[12]

[10] Sidney Mead, "The Rise of the Evangelical Conception of the Ministry
in America, 1607–1815," *The Ministry in Historical Perspectives*, ed. H. Richard Niebuhr and Daniel Day Williams (New York: Harper & Brothers, 1956),
p. 208.
[11] Robert S. Michaelsen, "The Protestant Ministry in America: 1850 to the
Present," *ibid.*, p. 287.
[12] *Ibid.*, pp. 212–18.

This spiritual manhood is directly applicable to pastoral counseling today. For one thing, any advice which a minister gives in the United States may be accepted or rejected. He can issue no directives which carry governmental authority. He is a "brother" in Christ more than he is a "father." He may be the first among equals who is heard because of personal respect. He is not a patriarch who is to be feared or placated because he can withhold financial favors or pronounce economic and social excommunication.

A second result of the voluntary principle in the American churches may be seen in the realm of clerical judgments. Forthright responsible opinions based on moral and spiritual judgments are expected and valued when they come from a minister. The minister who moves in the Reformation tradition does not consult an ecclesiastical handbook. Nor does the American minister consult any statute of government for the majority of opinions which he gives. Authoritative judgments have been especially well received in the South, where the clergy embody the best of the traditions of the Old South. The ministry was one of the few intact professions after the Civil War and, in the judgment of Professor Robert Michaelsen, did much to perpetuate the vision of an idyllic ante bellum culture.[13] Because his judgments are an integral part of the culture, the Southern clergyman can speak with an assurance and with a hearing that is not possible in sections of the United States where culture and profession are not historically allied. However, he runs a greater hazard of being merely a reflection of his culture rather than a participant in social growth. His counseling may be thought of as a reinforcement of time-worn clichés.

The lack of government support in America has forced the minister to rely heavily upon his personal persuasiveness. Individual winsomeness is often the charm which draws people to a pastor for counsel. During the counseling hour, his ability to be warm and affectionate may strengthen and stimulate the

[13] *Ibid.*, p. 254.

counselee toward new personal growth. Furthermore, the minister may put himself across to his people in preaching and teaching so that they arrive in his office with a problem to present and confidence that he can help them. As one counselee said, "I listened for six months as you told us your philosophy of life in sermons. Then I knew I could talk to you about my trouble."

There is one warning, however, about the formation of a "ministerial personality." Personal attractiveness may be substituted for real spiritual authority. Unless the pastor feels a sense of direct leading by God and a commission to serve him in this particular church, he may succumb to the temptation of manipulating individuals by contrived mannerisms or persuasive speech.

The pastor must rely upon both God and men for the effectiveness of his counseling ministry. Unfortunately, both pastoral and psychiatric practice has been highly individualistic. Little attention has been given to the able and consecrated lay people who could perform many pastoral functions. Yet, in the American tradition, churches are run by laymen.

The increasing demands for pastoral care and counseling will stimulate the training of lay men and women for visitation of the sick and counsel for those in trouble. This is a new frontier in counseling but one that is necessary and rewarding. It will give laymen concrete evidence of their priesthood to each other and provide care for the entire flock of God. To meet this growing need, this volume contains specific chapters on the training of group leaders and the counseling of counselors. In this way the purposes of the church may be fulfilled in an expanded ministry of counseling from both pastor and people.

Part II

The Personhood of the Pastoral Counselor

Thoreau once said that we counsel with "the whole being." The pastoral counselor cannot separate his work from his total personhood. Therefore, his own emotional health and "attitudinal orientation" must be considered seriously as providing the spiritual atmosphere and direction of counseling. Samuel Southard and James Lyn Elder discuss these two vital subjects.

4. The Emotional Health of the Pastoral Counselor

Samuel Southard

Pastoral counseling involves personal relationships. The interplay of personalities—pastor and parishioner—may be described in various ways. To Dr. Paul Johnson it is an experience in which the pastor "empathizes" with his parishioner; he feels the deep burden of his counselee without trying to carry the load himself. For a contributor to this book, Dr. Richard Young, the key word would be "sharing." Counselor and counselee strengthen each other by relating similar experiences. When one reads the works of Dr. Wayne Oates, he finds yet a third descriptive term, "confrontation." The counseling hour requires that two people be themselves, that they speak to each other as person to person. They are to confront each other as persons. Each of these emphases enriches a basic presupposition: pastoral counseling is a personal relationship.

The personal involvement of counseling lays heavy requirements upon the emotional life of both pastor and parishioner. The minister may meet some situations with serenity and understanding. But on other occasions his emotional reaction may be inappropriate. He may overidentify with his parishioner, absorbing all the emotional heat of the parishioner's problem and adding his own. The result is an excess of heat with little light. At other times he may give rapid-fire "answers" to an issue before it has completely emerged. For some reason the particular subject makes him anxious. Again, he may retreat emotionally from the counselee. He tells himself that he is being "nondirective," when a more objective examination would reveal that he is noncommittal and withdrawn. From these and many other observations the pastor feels his own personhood pulsating through his counseling experiences.

Does this mean that the counselor's personality is the most important ingredient in counseling? No. The emotional health of the minister is an essential factor, but it is not always determinative.[1] Although there has been no research on this question which is known to this author, several other factors seem to be crucial in the counseling situation.

First, the pastor's technical counseling skills, his knowledge of people, and his grasp of theological truth are important. A theological student had been thoroughly drilled in classroom knowledge of the grief process and had observed the work of an experienced chaplain with bereaved persons. A few days after this observation he was called to the emergency room of a hospital where he skilfully dealt with a difficult grief experience. Nurses, doctors, and relatives were complimentary. Yet this same student was usually preoccupied with the resolution of deep conflicts within his own soul. His inner turmoil rendered him ineffective in some types of counseling, but he was quite adequate for others. In clinical training he developed enough poise to help people with the common crises of life.

Second, the counselee's emotional life vitally affects the outcome of counseling. If the parishioner is eager for help, works hard on his problems, and has many psychological talents upon which to draw, these will be the major factors in his recovery. The "client-centered" therapy of Dr. Carl Rogers has demonstrated the decisive influence of the counselee upon the out-

---

[1] In the related fields of clinical psychology and psychiatry a debate rages around the question: Must a therapist undergo psychoanalysis himself? Freudian analysts insist this is necessary to handle delicate problems of transference when the counselee projects feelings about parents upon the therapist. Followers of Dr. Carl Rogers deny the presence of transference and the necessity of psychoanalysis for the therapist.

come of counseling. His work is a needed corrective to earlier psychological presuppositions. At one time it was assumed that the counselor was *the* key to health. A more modest approach is now indicated.

Third, it must be admitted that the ultimate criteria of successful counseling eludes the grasp of man. Only the arrogant and inexperienced have conclusive answers at this point. Mature and experienced therapists, such as Dr. Karl Menninger, admit that the client's turn from "regression" to "progression" in therapy remains a mystery.[2] Christians affirm that counselor and counselee must face a third unseen Person. The Spirit of God operates in moments of extremity and perplexity. Those who confess their limitations and daily wait upon God will find light rising up in the midst of darkness.

The conclusion is that the minister's emotional maturity is essential, but it is not the only measure of adequate pastoral counseling. A large number of counselors have experienced some emotional stress in their own lives and have found a satisfactory resolution of that crisis. Some stress seems to be essential to give sensitivity to human suffering. But counselors also need the personal assurance that problems can be solved.[3]

In the discussion which follows, attention will first be given to the counselor's personal background, which usually provides awareness and assurance for the counselor. Then his present relationships with family and other significant persons will be considered. These are the day-to-day satisfactions of life which provide an emotional tone of well-being for the pastor. Finally, there must be some recognition of the emotional responses evoked by particular counselees. No pastor is ever so perfect

[2] *The Theory of Psychoanalytic Technique* (New York: Robert Brunner, Inc., 1958).

[3] The research reported in the May, 1958, issue of *Pastoral Psychology* indicates that ministers seem to enjoy as good emotional health as other professional people and the population at large. The emotional problems which are prevalent among ministers appear to be (1) sensitivity to failure, (2) blame turned upon themselves rather than upon others, (3) conflict about inner expectations which they have of themselves.

that he is immune to those whose troubles reactivate quiescent problems in his own life.

The Shepherd's Personal Development

A pastor's awareness of personal need and assurance of adequate help will be conditioned by his childhood and adolescent experiences. The process by which a shepherd of God learns to feed the sheep of his fold satisfactorily involves a balance of feeding and frustration. "Feeding" means adequate love in childhood from significant parental figures. "Frustration" means creative insecurity. The child must learn that some things are expected of him, that he can give as well as receive.[4]

When the cycle of feeding and frustration is interrupted, the later counseling ministry of the pastor will be handicapped. The man who has not been fed, who has not received love and acceptance, will be chronically hungry. He cannot give of himself to people in need because he does not have enough of himself to spare. His lamp of life has never been filled to overflowing. The interviews of such men are pinched and narrow, sparse and bare. They look brusquely for the facts about a problem and then move quickly to announce a solution. There is no hostility, only the sharpness of a bone without flesh. No time is wasted on pleasantries, the savoring of a quiet saying, or reflective appreciation for some new insight. Time is saved, but the full body of personal relations is lost. People may appreciate such pastors as counselors but know little about them as individuals. They can do a job, but they cannot fill a heart. Why? Because no one ever filled theirs with joy, satisfaction, and approval. Their family had no time to "waste" on them, and they do not know how to "make" time with their people.

On the other hand, there are pastors who were fed too much in childhood and adolescence. Shielded from the world by indulgent parents, they accept adulation and dependency as a

[4] Peter A. Bertocci, *Religion as Creative Insecurity* (New York: Association Press, 1958), pp. 54–56.

natural way of life. Like fat cattle, they trample down grain and muddy the waters. If a counselee struggles to bring forth a new thought, an overfed pastor will snatch it from him and claim it as his own. When people pour out their anguish, he puts forth sleek and superficial answers: "Buck up, it will be all right tomorrow"; "The Lord always cares for his own"; "You're making too much of this"; "Think of the other people who hurt more than you do." Many times this pastor does not even hear the deeper tones of a distressing cry, for his ears are fat with the unstinting praise of parents. His eyes are heavy from the ceaseless contemplation of his untried, idealized self. He does not anticipate and seek out the unspoken despair of those who know they have failed.

The shepherd who can best feed the flock has received love and discipline as a child. His parents have strengthened him with confidence that he can do good, but they have also faced with him the realistic temptations to do evil. As an adult he can manifest confidence in a counselee at the same time that he names the failure for which this parishioner suffers. A young wife asked her pastor to call because she was desperate and on the verge of suicide. When the pastor arrived, she confessed with great agitation that she did not know if her child belonged to her husband or to a neighbor. "My sister keeps telling me that it wasn't adultery," she said, "but it is, it is!" "Yes," said the pastor quietly, "it is adultery. Now let us talk about how you came to such a place in your life as this." The woman grew calmer and began to speak of her disappointments in marriage. She felt the unspoken support of a man of God who would see her real condition and believe in her as a person in spite of it.

The Power of Present Relationships

Many pastors will recognize that the security of this counselor was dependent upon more than his previous personal development. His present relationships to his wife, children, and others would stabilize or shake his ability to handle an involved marital maladjustment. A pastor whose marriage was unstable might have been quick to condemn this woman, for her adultery might remind him dramatically of his own unfulfilled desires. His swift denunciation of her visible conduct would repress his hidden fantasies. Or he might show great sympathy for the woman's troubles because he would feel them akin to his own.

With a satisfying home life, a pastor would be protected from both these dangers. On the one hand, he would consider adultery distasteful because his memory would be filled with satisfying affection from his wife and children. He can rightly assume that a deep rift exists in the marriage before a person drifts into the swirling waters of sexual license. Therefore, his attention would center upon the relationship of husband and wife up to and including this open break of faith. He would not seek to satisfy his own latent desires by probing for details about the adultery.

On the other hand, overidentification with the woman would be measured against the realism of his own home life. He might discuss this woman with his wife and seek her counsel. In fact, the wife might introduce the subject. This could easily happen if the pastor failed to bring the time and place factors under control and stayed for several hours with the woman. "Why are you so late tonight?" his wife would ask. As his excuse would unfold, an alert helpmate would sense the personal involvement and remark, "Well, why are you so anxious to make excuses for her?" Pastors who have received this merciless but helpful barrage can fill in the rest of the details for themselves.

Obviously, a wife will not notice her husband's predicament if he is habitually late for supper. Unless the pastor leads a regulated, disciplined life with his family, neither he nor his wife will see danger signals at once. They may pass each other in the house all day and fall exhausted into the same bed at night, but they do not know each other. Quiet, reflective hours with the family are necessary for the restoration of a mature perspective.

Guilt comes like a gray ghost to enervate the counselor who neglects his children. With a straight face he tells a business-man, "If the doctor says that you must slow down, do so. Take time for your children. Enjoy them again. They need you at home." But the pastor's eye is not bright with the accumulated memories of happy days with his children. His secret self whispers, "What about you?" His counsel is not strong because his home life is weak.

Sometimes the pastor's preoccupation with family troubles is rooted in chronic disorder. But at other times his concern may be natural and understandable. There are personal crises which demand attention, even though they modify or disrupt a coun-seling ministry. A pastor lost his only daughter in a traffic ac-cident. He was two hundred miles away at the time. No one would tell him about the true condition of his daughter over the phone. He drove for four hours in agony, saying, "Is she dead or alive?" Among the many sympathizers there was only one who drew him aside so that he could express his grief.

For a time this pastor was dazed. He went through the mo-tions of his work, but he was inwardly struggling to accept this sudden tragedy. Those who came to him for counsel sensed the burden upon his heart. Many offered sympathy even when they came to ask for his help with their own trouble. This man needed time to think out his own grief; for a little while he did not have the outgoing concern for others which had been char-acteristic of his ministry. After several months, life began to re-turn to his soul. In the days which followed, his ministry to those in sorrow was even more meaningful than before. But for a season he had to draw into himself. This he should do without guilt or sense of failure.

The pastor's family relationships will influence his counsel-ing, but a stable professional person will not be blown off course by every gust that ripples the ocean of love. The previous ex-amples have been of chronic neglect or sudden disaster. Other problems in the home may be resolved while the pastor continues to meet the emotional needs of his people. A chaplain observed a striking example of this in a pastor whose wife had just given birth to her third child. The infant was critically ill in the hospital. After visiting his wife and child, the pastor received word from the chaplain that the infant of a parishioner had just been brought to the hospital. The pastor went to another ward where he stayed with the parents until their child died. He then went by the chaplain's office to call a funeral home. The chaplain remarked that it was hard for the pastor to minister to one child when his own was sick in the hospital. The pastor thought a minute and replied, "Well, I hadn't thought about that. I guess I've just gotten used to helping people in trouble without connecting it up with my own." Ten years of disciplined pastoral experience and a satisfying home life gave this minister stability in a crisis that might have been linked to his own.

The pastor's counseling ministry will also be affected by significant people outside the family. He will probably be most sensitive to their acceptance and hostility. Both of these feelings will find some expression in his emotions during counseling.

When a pastor knows he is accepted as a competent preacher and counselor by most of his people, he can tolerate a good deal of anxiety about certain problems. This can be illustrated from counseling with engaged couples and depressed persons who may commit suicide. With engaged couples, community acceptance enters counseling in several ways. One of the most common questions is: "Shall the minister talk about sex?" If a pastor has heard from several prominent laymen that *Sex Without Fear* is too "raw" or "lewd" a book for him to distribute, he may hesitate to give a copy to the next engaged couple who desire him to marry them. When unfavorable comments persist, a young minister in his first pastorate may be discouraged from an honest approach to marriage problems.

The pastoral counselor's reactions depend also upon his own

stability. Sometimes he links present opposition to deception by his parents in the past. The pastor revives a long-standing suspiciousness of people and begins to see himself as a persecuted saint. He would like to help people, he muses to himself, but they will not let him. His defenses mount up against a hostile world of his own devising. He can no longer counsel, for he must guard himself against everyone, even those who come for help. This regression does not occur just because there is some criticism of one aspect of counseling. Chronic suspiciousness is piled like dry leaves in the hollowness of his soul. It takes but a spark to consume him utterly.

When a pastor has built up solid layers of confidence in his ministry, he is less likely to be emotionally devastated by some threatening experience. This will be true of suicide threats. A new minister who has not the security of tried and tested acceptance may lie awake at night wondering what people will say if a counselee attempts suicide. He is as worried about the consequences for his own ministry as he is for the life of his parishioner. After a time professional people, prominent businessmen, leading society women, faithful church workers, and many others will express in manifold ways the love and acceptance they have for him. He then will face the possibilities of suicide with more concern for his parishioner. His future ministry will not be dependent upon the impulses of one man.

The other major community influence upon counseling is hostility. A pastor who is in conflict with important members of his church or community will see residual emotion seeping into his counseling hours from many directions. At times he may talk openly with a counselee about church conflicts. Why? Because this is his major concern, and he must relate everything to it. People in trouble can be quite distressed by this. They look to the pastor as a source of strength and to the church as a visible rock upon which they may stand. But now all they hear is the beating of the waves of hostility that echo from within him.

Another pastoral reaction to hostility is depression. This may help or hinder the counseling ministry. One pastor may be so bitter that he hears little of the intimate feelings which a person is sharing with him. But another may be searching his own soul for a deeper understanding of God and man. The stories which his people relate about despair, loneliness, and fatigue take on new significance, for he stands in the same dark valley with them. He may say little, but his quiet appreciation leads one parishioner to tell another, "That man has suffered a great deal. He knows what I've been through."

The resolution of hostile feelings is often most difficult when a pastor's enemy is in trouble. If the parishioner distrusts the pastor, he will avoid him and seek guidance elsewhere. But some crises demand a ministry from one's own pastor. A pastor may call on a hostile father when he hears that the man's son has been seriously injured in a motorcycle collision while drunk. Simple honesty may clear the air. The pastor can admit that there are differences between them but that he is here to be of what service he can as a pastor in a time of need. On one such occasion a man burst out, "Yes, I've been rough on you, but if you knew what I go through at home, you'd be jumpy too! My boy drinks, but what am I to do?"

The Addition of Two Personal Equations

The family and the community are significant determinants of the emotional atmosphere of counseling. But there is another intimate force in operation—the personality of the counselee. In this delicate area the pastor's personal reaction pattern may be an accurate barometer of stormy sessions to come.

It is bad enough for a pastor to accept the inevitable conclusion that some people do not seek his help because they don't like him as a person. But it is even more humiliating for a minister to recognize that he is rejecting a counselee for reasons over which he himself has very little control. Yet each man has his limitations. If a counselee reminds him unconsciously but unmistakably of a domineering father, new emotion will flow through the old stream of memory. The pastor may find himself fighting this man without conscious cause. Why is he so quick to condemn this parishioner? What makes him so impatient, so eager to tell this man exactly what is wrong with him?

At times the voices from the past may be less strident. Instead of clamoring for revenge, a seared memory may counsel escape. Then the pastor finds his heart closed to one who has just begun to knock. Why? Because this sounds like the extractive pleading of a former friend. The question, "What is he trying to get out of me?" looms up.

These dim murmurings may whisper clues for more effective counseling. One pastor found that he had to brace himself whenever one lady came for a weekly conference. He had to look hard for an opportunity to insert his own questions and comments in the chinks of her chatter. She reminded him so much of the women in his childhood household! And yet, he told himself, she was a different person. Why be vindictive to her? She is fighting someone else—a father, husband, or brother. The pastor is her helper, not her competitor. With these thoughts, the pastor formed the conviction that an honest appraisal, shorn of his animosity and defensiveness from bygone days, must be made. So in the midst of their fifth interview, he said, "Mrs. —, I observe that you talk so rapidly and forcibly that I can hardly get a word in edgewise. Perhaps you have observed this too. Can you tell me why it is so?"

The woman sighed deeply, looked at the floor, and then said in a small voice, "I had a nervous breakdown four years ago. My husband has always told me that I would have to go back to the hospital. I have been so afraid I would with all these problems. So I talk to convince people that I'm sane. I guess I'm just trying to convince myself." The connection of past with present irritation over female verbiage had brought this important symptom to the pastor's consciousness. His courage to face this woman was a testimony to his ability to resolve similar emotional reactions which were fashioned in childhood.

On other occasions a pastor must admit that he cannot help a particular parishioner. The two cannot stand each other. The pastor is bored, frustrated, or angry, or he feels these emotions successively. Once he knows himself, he may resolve the problem by referring the parishioner to another professional person. Or he may offer him a book, an impersonal object that may give help without activating personal relationships.

Whatever the reaction may be, the pastor is listening to all of himself. He is not bowing before his idealized image, vowing that he will be everybody's counselor. Instead, he is growing in grace as he accepts the relationship between his previous attitudes and his present emotional reaction. His sensitivity to the Christian fellowship is enlarged as he recognizes the influence of friends and enemies upon his personal ministry.

5. The Attitudes of the Pastoral Counselor

James Lyn Elder

The telephone rang at the pastor's elbow. He laid aside the church committee report he had been reading, picked up the phone, and said hello. The voice at the other end of the line, shaky with emotion, said, "Brother Baird, this is Helen Jacks. May I see you this afternoon?" Quickly the minister looked at his schedule for the day and as quickly evaluated the meaning of the tremor in the girl's voice. Then he said, "Why, certainly, Helen. Can you drop by on your way home from work?" "Yes," answered the girl, "I'll see you then." Goodbys were said, and both phones were hung up. A counseling interview had been initiated.

Let us freeze the action at this point as if this were a motion picture which we were seeing. In the scene are a busy pastor and a distraught young woman. They are linked to each other by an electrical current flowing through a telephone wire. From what we have heard them say, we know that the conversation is more than casual. The tremor in Helen's voice and the sympathetic tone in the pastor's, as well as his concerned facial expression, tell us that here we are seeing drama of the strongest kind.

The next act will occur when a tap comes at the pastor's door. He will open it to find Helen there and invite her in, and they will begin their conversation. At this point the counseling interview will begin in earnest. This covers the "long section"

53

of the events leading up to the drama. What now of the cross section, of the factors at work simultaneously in the drama?

Attitudes in Counseling

We are not concerned at the moment with the broader dimensions of Helen's thought and feeling, but we are concerned with those of her pastor. Beneath the surface actions which we observe we may detect and measure impulses in motion. We may inquire into their sources, forms, and intensities. To raise these questions is to ask in what areas attitudes in counseling are particularly important. It is also to inquire what the ideal attitudes in these areas are, what some of the harmful ones may be, and how the pastoral counselor may improve what Carl Rogers calls his "attitudinal orientation." [1] To help us to answer these questions, let us start the "projector" again and go on with the interview.

The time is late afternoon, the scene is again the pastor's study. As he sits scanning his pastoral records, a light knock comes at his door. He walks quickly to open it and on seeing the girl says:

PASTOR: Hello, Helen. Come in.
HELEN: Thank you, Brother Baird. (*She enters and sits tensely on the edge of a chair.*)
PASTOR: You are right on time.
HELEN: Yes. (*She smiles nervously.*)
PASTOR: And how is everything with you?
HELEN: Oh, all right, I suppose, in some ways, but in others not so good. (*She smiles again, but tears appear suddenly in her eyes.*)
PASTOR (*quietly*): I see.
HELEN: I mean, I'm well, and things at home have been a little quieter than usual, but in other ways I'm pretty upset.
PASTOR: You are troubled about something other than your health or your family.
HELEN: Yes, although I suppose it includes both of them—or will

[1] Carl R. Rogers, *Client-Centered Therapy* (Boston: Houghton Mifflin Co., 1951), pp. 19 ff.

eventually. I don't know how long I can go on without breaking down, and I know that when my family learns what I'm going to tell you—well, it will just be awful.

PASTOR: I see.

HELEN: Brother Baird, what would you say if I told you I was mixed up with a married man?

PASTOR: Mixed up with a married man?

HELEN: Yes, someone who lives near my home.

PASTOR: I see. This man lives near you.

HELEN: Oh, Brother Baird, I don't know what to do. I've thought about it so much and haven't been able to talk with anybody. Everywhere I look there's a blind alley.

PASTOR: You see no way out of the situation.

HELEN: No, I don't. It all started innocently enough with just riding to work together. Then he started to tell me how unhappy he was at home, and I guess I was flattered by his confiding in me, and before I knew it things had come to be serious.

PASTOR: You found yourself involved with him before you realized it.

HELEN: Yes, and I didn't know what to do about it. I know it can't go on, and yet I don't know how to stop it. When you said in your sermon last Sunday that no problem was too big for God—well, right then I decided to come and talk with you.

PASTOR: I see. That statement in my sermon helped you decide to come to see me.

HELEN: Yes.

Again, let us stop the action but this time turn off the projector completely. More, much more, is on the film, but for our present purposes what we have seen is sufficient. Let us ask, with reference to what we have witnessed, what attitudes Mr. Baird displays and how they are related to his counseling ministry.

Perhaps the best place to begin would be at the moment the study telephone rings. Mr. Baird's nearness to a phone indicates that he keeps himself, for at least part of the time, where people can reach him. He feels it important, probably, not only to be present in the pulpit on Sunday but in some accessible spot during the week.

Another revealing bit of action takes place when the pastor hears Helen Jacks' voice. The committee report he was reading with interest is quickly laid aside. He does not divide his attention by continuing to look at it while he listens to her. Evidently he is a pastor to whom the care of the "one" is, for the moment at least, more important than administering the "ninety and nine."

It is further indicative of Mr. Baird's attitudes that he has at hand a schedule of his day's activities. This tells us something about his stewardship of time as a pastor. And the fact that he quickly decides, from Helen's voice, that her problem is a serious one and should be dealt with immediately reflects also the way he feels about his members and their concerns.

Additional evidence of his counseling attitudes is to be seen in the way he conducts the interview. His attention to what Miss Jacks is saying, his skilful assistance in helping her to put her feelings into words, and his refusal to be quickly moved either to condemnation or pity—all these tell us something of his feeling about what he is doing.

What Attitudes Are

The way ministers feel about certain things, Carroll Wise points out, is determinative of their effectiveness as counselors.[2] The reason for this is that by "attitude" is meant readiness to act. It is almost as though a spring were coiled to move in a certain direction and, at the release of a lever, were propelled into action. In her excellent discussion of attitudes involved in counseling, Karen Horney points out that attitudes are basically relationships between the counselor's self and all that is involved in interviewing. They are inner positions which, when activated, determine behavior. As we have seen, both the counselor's motives and his values are bound up with his "attitudinal orientation" and are involved in what he does. His skill and power in

---

[2] Carroll A. Wise, *Pastoral Counseling: Its Theory and Practice* (New York: Harper & Brothers, 1951), pp. 8 ff.

the interview are products of his attitudes; the latter are like
artesian springs out of which all other things flow.

In the light of all this, we feel compelled to ask in what areas
these important attitudes lie, how they are related to counseling, and how they may be improved for a more effective ministry.

Areas of Attitudinal Importance

What we have said so far concerning Mr. Baird's meeting of
Helen Jacks' problem suggests the areas in which the counselor's
attitudes are of great importance. Perhaps, though, it would be
of help to us to do a bit of verbalizing ourselves at this point. Let
us define as precisely as possible what these areas are.

First, of course, comes the pastor's attitudes toward himself as
a minister and toward the ministry in general. And behind these
lie his comprehension of the gospel and his understanding of the
nature of God. If, as someone has put it, "A man's religion is the
most important thing about him," it is certainly true that for the
pastoral counselor the most important thing is the understanding which he has of the ultimate reality which he represents. All
that the minister does is inevitably bound up with his theology.
The axiom, "Like priest, like people," could be taken a step
higher: "Like God, like minister." The "man of God" will inevitably demonstrate a functional resemblance to Him whom he
represents.

If, for example, a pastor thinks of God as austere and aloof, he
will tend to do little or no counseling. He simply will not have
any meaningful communicative relationship with his people. Or
if his concept of God is that of a moralistic tyrant, it is a judge
and not a helpful counselor whom the church members will find
in the study. Or again, if the minister has a kind of "marshmal-
low deity," counseling will be pushed to one side by a morbid
indulgence and a cheap brand of reassurance.

Only when the pastor's God is one who is at home in the counseling situation will anything resembling an effective interview

take place. Those attitudes essential to good counseling must be derived from the concept of personality associated with the pastor's image of God.

Closely related to his theology and inseparable from it is the minister's understanding of the pastoral role. What kind of counseling he does, if any, will be determined by this understanding. In the case of Mr. Baird there was evident a comprehension of the ministry as one devoted to serving the needs of people. There was a quality of warmth and tenderness about it. But it could easily have been otherwise had the pastor considered his function to be different. If he had thought of himself as an ecclesiastical functionary, for example, he would have had little time for or interest in Helen Jacks and her problem. But the fact that he did give her both his time and his attention makes clear his attitude toward and comprehension of his ministry.

A second area of attitudinal importance in counseling is that regarding the people with whom the pastor counsels and the problems they bring to him. This attitude, of course, will be linked to those concerning God and the counselor's ministry. For purposes of this discussion, however, it may be treated separately. What we think of people will inevitably be expressed in how we act toward them. If we are not sociable, we will pull away from people, resenting them as interruptions into our little worlds. If, on the other hand, we are interested in them and have compassion for their difficulties, we will go out to them in warmth and helpfulness.

How important it is, then, that the pastoral counselor have the kind of attitude that will attract persons with problems to him and then make possible his giving them the kinds of help they need. It is safe to say with reference to the attitude toward people, as was said in regard to the pastor's concept of God and his ministry, that it will either be a base upon which counseling can stand or a boulder by which it is crushed.

The third area of importance insofar as pastoral attitudes are concerned is that in which lies the counseling method itself. Whether this tool is used at all or how effectively it is employed, even by the minister with adequate attitudes toward his ministry and those whom he serves, will depend mainly on how he feels about it.

Counseling is the newest technique in the pastoral ministry, just as it is a fresh addition to the psychological, medical, and educational disciplines. It must shoulder its way into the church between teaching, preaching, and administration. Its essential character and ultimate value are still subjects of debate among theologians. And it is only in recent years that it has been taught at all in seminaries. These factors combine to make it difficult for the pastor to have the same knowledge of and reliance upon counseling as he has toward his other tools. But if he is to be an effective interviewer, his attitude toward the right procedure is required to be as mature and as strong as those suggested above.

Ideal Attitudes for Pastoral Counseling

It is all very well to stress the importance of attitudes for counseling and to indicate the areas of particular significance, but by what standard may we measure our attitudes to determine their adequacy? In the years that pastoral counseling has been employed, what criteria have been evolved? Perhaps the answer to this question may be seen best by beginning our film again to see how Mr. Baird, who is presented here as a good example, proceeds in his interview with Miss Jacks:

PASTOR: You have thought about your situation and looked at it from every angle, and there seems to be no way out, so you've come to me.

HELEN: Yes. As I listened to your sermon on "God's Grace and Man's Need," I decided to come. And this may sound funny to you, but I feel better already.

PASTOR: You feel better about your problem?

HELEN: Yes. Just reaching the point where I'm able to talk about it, not feeling I'm alone with it—you just can't imagine what a relief this is.

PASTOR: I see.

HELEN: Oh, Brother Baird, I know how wrong all this is. I've tried to fool myself and say it's just kindness on my part, since his wife is so hard to live with and all. But I know deep down that I haven't the right to come between them, to say nothing of what I'm doing to the children.

PASTOR: To the children?

HELEN: Yes. Don't you think my encouraging this man to pay attention to me takes some of his interest away from his children?

PASTOR: And you feel this is hurtful to them.

HELEN: Yes. Oh, what am I going to do? Wrong as I know this is, it's the first happiness I've ever really known, at least since my father died. I just don't see how I can go back to having no one again.

PASTOR: Wrong though you know it is, this relationship has still given you a great deal of satisfaction, more than you have had at any time since your father died.

HELEN: Yes. And, you know, it all started—my being with him, I mean—not long after father's death. As a matter of fact, I was still in a state of half shock when we started seeing each other.

PASTOR: I see. You were still grieving for your father when this man began paying attention to you.

HELEN: Yes. I hadn't thought of it before. But do you think there could be any kind of relation between the two things—my father's death and my attachment to this man?

PASTOR: Do you feel there is?

HELEN: Well, perhaps there is. I don't know.

Again the projector is turned off and the lights come on. Helen is still far from having solved her problem. Perhaps she never will completely settle it. On the other hand, she may go on to a profound and growing spiritual development. In any case, we have witnessed a fairly good example of some ideal attitudes as they relate to pastoral counseling.

In the first place, Mr. Baird evidently sees his ministry as more than ceremonial, moralistic, rationalistic, or coercive. He sees himself truly as a shepherd of the sheep. Like his Master, he lays aside everything else to go after the one who is lost. When Helen Jacks called him to make the appointment, he laid aside an administrative report to give her his full attention. Furthermore, as we have seen, he had made himself available for just such service as this. He sees himself not simply as a preacher but as one who has a far more profound and comprehensive service to render.

He feels, evidently, that he is there to be used; he is, in a sense, expendable. His relation to his people is a kind of boulevard over which at times he takes the initiative, and over which, going in the opposite direction, at times his people take the lead. And when his people "call the play," he follows their lead and tries to meet the need they reveal to him.

Further, this pastor conceives his ministry as being essentially an interpersonal encounter. He does not, like the Old Testament prophet, simply send a staff to confront the people's needs. He gives himself in understanding and acceptance; he makes of himself a bridge over which they may go to God. In his attitude toward himself and his ministry, then, he reveals the ideal: a ministry devoted to serving human needs, a ministry centered on individuals, and a ministry operating on the basis of interpersonal encounter.

In Mr. Baird's attitude toward Helen Jacks and her problem we see again something of the ideal. As has been indicated above, this pastor's brightest focus of attention was on persons rather than administrative details. In his scale of values, human beings count far more than organizations.

But this is not an abstract attitude; there goes with it a capacity for the kind of relaxed, warm interpersonality (by which is meant the reciprocal understanding between persons) we see between Miss Jacks and her pastor. Our surmise is that in their relationship previous to this interview there has been laid down a basis of friendship, respect, and acceptance making possible such rapport.

And when Helen reveals her problem, the minister's attitude is subjected to its severest test. Here is one of the church members confessing, to an incipient degree at least, to adultery. Will Mr. Baird be shocked, or angered, or depressed? Or does he have sufficient emotional strength to remain stable, objective, and helpful? We have seen the answer in his response to Helen's communication. He accepts her statement with no visible sign of shock or alarm, thus expressing his basic respect for and trust in her. By this attitude he is saying, "There is more to you than this relationship, no matter how wrong in itself you may feel it to be." And Helen, experiencing this reaction, accepts the pastor's evaluation and begins to regain her own sense of perspective with regard to herself.

Mr. Baird is showing that he expects people to have problems, that to him being a person, in fact, means having difficulties of one kind or another. He demonstrates, at the same time, his optimistic feeling that problems can be dealt with helpfully. This he does by encouraging Helen to talk about her difficulty and by discussing some aspects of it himself.

Although the idea is not put into words, Mr. Baird's serious response to Helen's problem suggests that in her difficulty he sees the growing edge of her soul. He is undoubtedly aware that the Christian faith aims at a certain high quality of interpersonality. He is also certain that this standard can only be achieved by giving individuals the opportunity to work out, through a "feeling-thinking-talking" technique of counseling, some understanding of their relationships to others. As he aids her to clear up her interpersonality with regard to her lover, his wife and family, her own parents, and her fellow church members, he is helping her to strengthen and enrich her relationship to God, which is greater than but inclusive of all human interpersonality.

The third attitudinal area in which this pastoral counselor manifests his ideal is in the interviewing method itself. This is by no means the least significant of his attitudes, for it is the means whereby his previously discussed emotional-ideational positions are made effective.

The principal element of this attitude is one of confidence in the counseling procedure. Preacher and teacher though he may be, and largely directive as those ministries are, Mr. Baird shifted with no discernible effort to a less aggressive technique of counseling. His easy use of the method reveals not only mastery of it but acceptance of it as well. Throughout the conversation with Helen he employs the procedure consistently.

At least two-thirds of the interview consists of statements made by the counselee. And when Mr. Baird does talk, it is primarily to help Helen to continue. He limits his response to expressions of understanding and acceptance, generally. In some less frequent instances he abbreviates and simplifies material previously communicated by Miss Jacks and recommunicates it to her for further amplifying.

Implicit in this attitude is a belief in the capacity of individuals to arrive at solutions to their own problems. This in turn rests upon confidence that within every individual are drives tending in the direction of wholeness. The counseling procedures work co-operatively with these dynamic forces to bring about healing of the whole person.

In spite of what has been said about Mr. Baird's belief in a certain approach to counseling, it is evident that he does not employ it in a mechanical, slavish manner. He does not interrupt with his responses in any compulsive, rote-like way. Nor does he merely parrot what Helen has said. Rather, there is a flexible, creative use of the less directive procedure which shows that the minister, while trusting the method, sees it as a tool to be used, not a tyrant to be served.

Developing Right Attitudes for Counseling

The discussion above indicates that in all pastoral counseling attitudes are determinative. They either make possible or impossible an effective—that is to say, helpful—interview. The three areas in which attitudes are of particular importance are those regarding the ministry in general, people and their problems, and the counseling method. Ideal attitudes in each of these areas have been suggested. The question of how we may improve our attitudes for the purpose of increasing counseling effectiveness now arises.

The first answer to this question lies in becoming aware of the importance of attitudes. We shall understand the ministry to be more than simply a collection of techniques; it is a spiritual enterprise emerging from the depths of the counselor himself. His attitudes will leave their mark upon everything that he does.

In the second place, the minister may honestly acknowledge the extent to which his own attitudes fall short of the ideal. Such frankness with regard to his limitations may form a large part of any improvement program.

Third, let the pastor continue to study those areas in which attitudes are of such importance. Theology, for example, should be interpretive of the nature of the ministry; it should issue in increasingly effective attitudes. If it does not, perhaps the doctrine itself should be critically reviewed.

The study of human nature and experience is one in which the minister should be continuously engaged. If a sense of estrangement from people or a fear of them has kept the counselor from developing right attitudes, let a closer contact with them, a fuller knowledge of their problems, difficulties, and potentialities help to produce the right attitudes. With regard to counseling, both study and practice should result in an increase of confidence. Added books and articles on this ministry are appearing continuously. They are available to anyone who will make use of them.

In a number of ways, then, the pastoral counselor may strengthen, deepen, and enlarge his attitudes. He may, by faithful efforts to grow, become within himself that kind of shepherd who can ably guide his sheep into the life abundant.

Summary

Attitudes are of basic importance to pastoral counseling. They will determine objectives, methods, and motives. Beneath all the counselor does, for better or worse, will be his attitudes.

The areas of particular importance are those regarding himself and his ministry, his people and their problems, and the counseling method. The ideal in each of these areas is to have those attitudes which will result in an increased effectiveness in counseling.

The pastoral counselor who wishes to do so may improve his attitudes by examination, honesty, and continuing effort to improve them. He will have the satisfaction of seeing his work in this direction bear rich fruit in an augmented ministry.

Part III

Pastoral Counseling:
Its Process and Procedures

The specific details of the process of counseling are set forth in this section. The pastor makes his contacts with prospective counselees in informal situations and through his visitation. The telephone is a formidable factor to be dealt with in the modern pastor's work as a counselor. The counselees whom he has genuinely helped become referral persons who send other needy individuals to him.

Time must be budgeted wisely, for this is one of the pastor's most important means of interpreting and cutting through the blockages that hinder people's spiritual growth. The disciplines of time must be assumed and understood by the pastor. For instance, the pastor must learn how to use the short-term interview situation wisely. At the same time, he must not fail to give himself unstintingly to longer-term, multiple interview counseling.

As he does these things, he encounters recurring problems in the counseling situation which he must appreciate in all their complexity. He must continuously study published literature concerning counseling and develop increasing skill by doing so. Furthermore, he must understand his own limitations and know when and how to call upon other counselors for their assistance. Even when he does call in the help of other counselors, however, the Christian minister retains his unique relationship of durable spiritual concern for the counselee.

6. Making the Contact: Informal Pastoral Relationships

Wayne E. Oates

The pastoral counselor must have the capacity to sense the eternal in the commonplace. His work often begins in some seemingly insignificant, everyday event, far removed from a formal request for help on the part of the person who needs it. In this respect the work of the pastor falls into the royal tradition of the Lord Jesus Christ's pastoral ministry. For most of his contacts with people were of a very informal nature. He asked a woman who had a severe marital difficulty for a drink of water, and the giving of that drink of water memorialized her as the "woman at the well." As he walked along, he saw a small man in a tree and literally invited himself to dinner at the publican Zaccheus' house. On his way to visit in the home of a bereaved family, a suffering woman touched the hem of his garment. The only thing he ever wrote, apparently, was written in the sands of the market place as he dealt with the sins of an adulterous woman suffering at the hands of her condemners.

The pastor and other religious workers, therefore, can never become so professional in their pictures of themselves that they underestimate the importance of informal relationships both as powerful ministries in and of themselves and as points of vital contact for beginning more formal counseling relationships.

An informal pastoral contact is one in which the pastor's role is either unknown, quiescent, or incidental to the relationship at hand. The two people meet as ordinary human beings in the everyday simplicity of living, not *as* pastor and *as* parishioner. Their basic identity in relationship to each other makes little of either of their social positions. Next Thursday evening at the Parent-Teachers' Association meeting at the local public school I may sit down beside a prominent executive or a garage mechanic. But we are not related to each other *as* executive, *as* seminary professor, and *as* garage mechanic. We are related to each other apart from our various social roles vocationally and on the basis of our common identity as parents and members of the P.T.A. This is an informal relationship. Many different kinds of such informal contacts provide the pastor with opportunities for being lastingly helpful in the moment and for starting more formal counseling relationships.

Anonymous relationships.—Many times a minister is thrown into contact with people in dire need who do not know him as pastor. Casual contacts on busses, trains, and planes are examples of this. Much vital service can be rendered to people under such circumstances because it seems easier for some people to talk with a stranger than with someone whom they know and to whom they feel responsible. A certain amount of anonymity helps a person to feel free and to communicate more easily. The work of the average pastor has very little anonymity in it. As a result, the forces of superficial respectability keep many people from availing themselves of the help of their pastors. Chaplains in hospitals and military service remark that people will "open up" to them in ways that the people themselves say they could never do with their pastors. A pastor may also notice that many people from outside his own congregation come to him for help that they could get from their own pastors. Their reasons for doing so often are that they know their pastor too well and value his personal friendship too much.

The average pastor has two kinds of difficulty in anonymous relationships. One is that he may smash through the person's privacy and compulsively thrust his role as a Christian worker upon him. The other is that he will be reluctant to reveal his identity as a pastor. Either extreme reflects insecurity and anxiety to the stranger. But in the event these extremes are avoided and the person does unfold some personal problems, need, or concern to the pastor, then several things need to be borne in mind.

First, the pastor should be very careful not to try to "solve" the person's problem for him in such a short, superficial contact. On a rare occasion the timing of an "answer" may be such as to be permanently helpful to the person. But more often than not the person is confused by final answers given by a total stranger. A much more effective method would be to let the person talk to the limit of his intention and the time available. Then the best procedure would be to explore the person's life situation, searching for some more permanently related counselor near him. A referral would be unusually meaningful. Also, helpful literature could be recommended. A direct sharing of one's own experience as a Christian in solving a similar problem would be one way of bearing one's witness.

Friends and relatives.—Another informal relationship is fellowship with friends and relatives. We do violence to our friends and close relatives when we push them into a counselee role. The pastor can best serve his wife by being a good husband, not by becoming a counselor to her. He responds to his close friends as a totally committed fellow sufferer, not as a formal counselor. Relationships become confused, tense, and strained when the counselor tries to practice on those nearest him. This reflects immaturity and inexperience on his part and ministers to them only in that it provides an amusing topic of conversation when he is not around. The surgeon does not operate on those nearest him, and often great pastoral ministries to our own loved ones are best rendered by someone else. This does not always follow, but a word to the wise at this point is sufficient and should never be forgotten.

"Market place" ministry.—The pastor should not sit in his office and wait for people to come to see him for counseling.

My own practice, for instance, has been not to observe office hours until I had enough demand for counseling to justify it. The informal contacts of a pastor in the market place, if sensitively responded to and appreciated, will provide the beginning of an abundance of openings for starting office counseling relationships. As Professor Drakeford will point out in a succeeding chapter, wise use of a careful appointment system will capture the advantage of the initiative a person takes in a market place encounter to reveal a need for personal counseling. The following case record given by a student pastor will reflect many of the ways in which casual contacts can be extremely significant, even though they happen quite unexpectedly. This case also shows how completely frustrating to a tense and anxious person can be a pastor's failing to bring the relationship under the control and order of time and place.

THE FIRST CONTACT

Mr. Angle is a man in middle life. He is married to a woman who is sensitive and highly emotional; she tends to be a tyrant in her home. There are two daughters, one married and living away, the other attending a university. Mr. Angle is a good man, always ready to do a kindness, but he is without confidence in his own opinions. He allows his wife to run over him not only in family life but also in business. This man has lived a very active life. He has owned a farm, carried on a business as a cattle buyer, and has been a butcher and grocery store proprietor. This has necessitated long hours of work.

The major part of his time has been taken up with the store. Both he and his wife have worked hard at it, and as a result their home life has been sadly neglected, their social life has been nil, and their church life has been limited to writing a check. Their married life has been on the verge of a breakdown for a number of years, but for the sake of the girls and their sense of the wrongness of divorce they have held on.

They have spent all their energies on the store, opening on

Sundays as well as weekdays. By their attitude they have forced other stores to keep open as well. Money seems to be the controlling force in their lives, and they will do anything for an extra dollar. This attitude has cursed their lives because they think they can buy their way through life.

The student began his record with this entry: "Mr. Angle came to me one evening just as I was leaving the church and said, 'I've got to talk to someone. I'm going crazy.'"

MINISTER: I'm very glad you came. I hope I can help. What seems to be the trouble?

MR. ANGLE: My wife is driving me crazy. She is constantly nagging me from morning until night.

MINISTER: For what reason?

MR. ANGLE: I don't know. She is continually underrating me before our children and other people, as though I were without feelings or respect.

MINISTER: Why does she do this?

MR. ANGLE: She wants me to be like the doctor and other community leaders and dress like them. She wants me to take an active part in the community like the others—attend social functions and run for the council.

MINISTER: How do you feel about it?

MR. ANGLE: Since I sold the store, we have no other income except the farm and stock buying and selling. I love my farm and stock, but my wife hates it. Yet she likes the money from it. I come home at night after spending all day in the open, and I'm very tired. It's hard to keep my eyes open, even to read the evening paper.

MINISTER: What is your wife's reaction?

MR. ANGLE: She wants me to sell the farm and give up butchering. She's always nagging me about the house, too.

MINISTER: You have one of the best houses in the city.

MR. ANGLE: Yes, I know. But she wants a new one—like other people in our own age group.

MINISTER: Does she give any reason for her dissatisfaction?

MR. ANGLE: She says she wants a modern house, with all modern conveniences.

MINISTER: But she already has those.

MR. ANGLE: Yes, but she is not satisfied. The biggest mistake of my life was not building her a new house long ago. Last year I had the chance to sell the house for eight thousand dollars, but she wouldn't let me.

MINISTER: How long has this nagging been going on?

MR. ANGLE: For a great many years. It has been a hell on earth. No one knows what I have been through during these years. I go to bed night after night and pray I may never awake. Yet people think she is a wonderful woman. She plays the piano at the Eastern Star, is welcomed by her friends, and has a prominent place. When she comes home, she is a devil gone mad. All the money we have accumulated has not brought us happiness. I would trade it with anyone for happiness.

MINISTER: What do you think is the underlying cause?

MR. ANGLE: Her mother told me she had had a shock while pregnant with my wife. Her small son was scalded to death. So when my wife was born, she was highly nervous and hysterical.

MINISTER: Do you think prenatal influence can affect a child?

MR. ANGLE: I am sure of it. You can't tell me that prenatal development is not affected by such a shock. Her mother is like her, hysterical and nervous.

MINISTER: It may be that your wife is in need of medical treatment.

MR. ANGLE: She is not in good health. She has a weak heart and is liable to drop dead at any minute.

MINISTER: Do you think her physical health is responsible for her mental quirks, moods, and depression?

MR. ANGLE: I don't know. (*Looks at watch.*) Well, I must go.

MINISTER: Maybe the only thing to do is to humor her and be kind, sympathetic, and understanding. She is sick and needs help.

MR. ANGLE: I don't know. I dread going home.

COMMENTS

We can readily observe that the pastor has an excellent informal relationship to this man. As is so often the case, the man stopped the pastor while the pastor was on his way somewhere else. He was on his way home, apparently tired and eager to end the day's work. The man poured out a burden of personal difficulty upon the pastor's already tired mind. The pastor, in turn, pitched right into the difficulties and sought to "solve" them right then and there. He wound up with the cold comfort of "humoring, being kind, being sympathetic" with the wife. The man might have felt guilty about the time because he looked at his watch. Or, on the other hand, he might have been too busy to take time to deal seriously with his own marriage problem.

The pastor would have been much more realistic and honestly helpful if he had listened understandingly to the man for a few minutes and then frankly admitted that he needed some time to think about the problem in order to be of the most possible assistance. Likewise, he would have been much more effective had he scheduled an appointment when both of them could have spent some unhurried time in a controlled counseling situation. Here they could explore the many facets that the problem might reveal.

Four factors must be brought into clear focus before the counselor actually has a secure counseling relationship established. First, the counselor's role must be explicit, clearly defined, and mutually understood by both counselor and counselee in a help-giving, help-receiving relationship. Second, the time factor must be clearly understood so that hurry, imposition, and fatigue are ruled out as far as possible. Third, a place of discreet privacy in the home or, preferably, in an office must be arranged. And, finally, the counselee and counselor must share responsibly the initiative for setting all this in order.

Instead of arranging an ordered situation, Mr. Angle's pastor attempted to deal with him in the awkward and fatigued circumstances just described. The pastor's part in the interview amounts to little more than "getting the man off his hands" for the time being. He left the man's personal distress to chance. The pressure of Mr. Angle's difficulties again came to the surface in his appeal for pastoral help in a post office contact.

THE SECOND CONTACT

This is the next entry in the report: "The next time I saw Mr. Angle was in an informal visit in the post office. When I saw him I said, 'Hello! How are you coming along?' "

MR. ANGLE: Oh, you have no idea what I am going through. It's hell on earth. I wish I were dead. It's getting worse. Things haven't changed a bit. I'm going crazy. I've tried to humor her, be kind and sympathetic, but it doesn't make any difference. She's a tyrant and a bear. I got up this morning and got my own breakfast so as not to disturb her. I love bacon, and as soon as I put it on to cook, she got up and told me to take it off because it smells up the house. So I had to go without.

MINISTER: You mean she wouldn't let you have bacon for breakfast?

MR. ANGLE: Yes.

MINISTER: I am afraid you are far too lenient. Why don't you assert yourself. There is no need for you to be treated like that. Have you no rights of your own?

MR. ANGLE: That was the beginning of the day. I've done my best to give her all she wants. I've worked hard, provided money, and she is comfortably well off. I bought a car for her, and anything she wanted. She has a good bank account, and I've signed over everything. She wants more and more and is never satisfied. I've provided my daughter with five thousand dollars for school expenses, but she keeps drawing on my account.

MINISTER: Why don't you put your foot down?

MR. ANGLE: I told her she must stop it, but her mother sided with her and said she must have the benefits of an education and social life to the full. My wife has done the same with our eldest daughter.

MINISTER: In what way?

MR. ANGLE: By sending her money and buying her things.

MINISTER: Why should she do that when your daughter is married and has a wealthy husband?

MR. ANGLE: Because she wants to make up for what we couldn't do when she was at college. She only had a couple of years' education and then had poor standings.

MINISTER: You find it rather expensive, don't you?

MR. ANGLE: Yes, it's crippling our finances and makes me work harder to make up. Sometimes I think they only want me for the money I provide.

MINISTER: Do you really mean that?

MR. ANGLE: Well, it seems that way.

MINISTER: Haven't you spent too much time on business and acquiring wealth at the expense of your faith in God and service to the church?

MR. ANGLE: Yes. I know I haven't lived right. I've put material things before God, and I have been wrong.

MINISTER: Why not start life afresh, with the help of God?

MR. ANGLE: There is no hope of that. I've let this go too long. I'm too set in my ways.

MINISTER: There is always hope when things have gone beyond man's help. It is found in Christ. Why not turn to him in repentance and ask his forgiveness?

MR. ANGLE: I shall try. (*Silence for a few minutes.*)

The student continued: "Just when I thought I was getting some place, he began to talk about more problems of his wife and family. This has happened every time I have gotten near the climax. I tried to bring him back, but his problems are greater than God in his mind."

COMMENTS

Notice again how tense, strained, and uneasy the whole relationship became when the minister tried to settle the problem in a casual, offhand way and did not make provision for the man to deal with his problems on a more ordered, private, and serious basis. He tried to push his religious guidance in lump fashion through the barrier of the man's concern over his marriage situation. He never created a sense of need on the part of the man for a distinctly religious solution to his problems. The relationship bogged down in a failure of communication between the pastor and Mr. Angle.

The pastor concluded the conversation in the post office with a real feeling of frustration. He seems to be contending with some hidden possessive force which he does not understand and which stalemates his every effort. If he had taken time to interview this man on an exploratory basis, as is suggested in succeeding chapters, he at least would have broken through the wall of anxiety and hostility which separated him from Mr. Angle. As it is, he more or less left Mr. Angle beaten down with one suggestion after another.

THE THIRD CONTACT

The next encounter with Mr. Angle runs true to form with the previous ones. He was to see the pastor in an informal way; he has had no leadership at all from the pastor in making of these informal contacts a formal counseling relationship. He is desperately pleading for help. But he is dealt with in a hit-or-miss fashion with the ungleaned corners of the minister's time and attention.

"The next time I saw Mr. Angle was after an official board meeting. I had at last gotten him to the place where he and his wife were coming to church—off and on. At least I had given him a chance to divert some of his interest to church service. He was on the board and had much to contribute. Following the board meeting he waited until the others had gone and then poured out his tale of woe."

MR. ANGLE: I simply must get this off my chest. My daughter has had a row with her mother over her going out with a Catholic boy friend. We had the worst commotion in our house tonight that we've ever had. My daughter has been going out with this boy for some time, and tonight she talked of getting married. We nearly lost all patience. I said, "Your mother and I have been very patient with you. We have reared you in a nice home. You have not wanted for anything, and now we're spending thousands of dollars a year on your education so that you might have a chance and a future. Now you want to throw it over and be married to a kid who has no means of support except the GI allowance. A cheap, common, farm boy, uneducated and a nobody. You will have to live in a trailer."

MINISTER: What? Leave school and live in that overcrowded section?

MR. ANGLE: Yes. She'll never take it. She's had too many home comforts.

MINISTER: You knew he was a Catholic and she a Methodist.

MR. ANGLE: Yes.

MINISTER: Did you try to squelch it before it became serious?

MR. ANGLE: I did, but my wife encouraged him to spite me. She allowed him indoors, to stay overnight, and made him welcome.

MINISTER: Did your wife know how you felt about this?

MR. ANGLE: Yes, but she has belittled me so much that my word did not amount to anything. It is two years since they started going together.

MINISTER: Has your wife's attitude changed?

MR. ANGLE: Yes, now that it is too late she sees her mistake but hates to admit I was right.

MINISTER: In what way has she changed?

MR. ANGLE: Well, she swears that if she marries this boy she will never speak to her. She will disown her and not give her any inheritance.

MINISTER: Is that wise?

MR. ANGLE: No.

MINISTER: How do you feel?

MR. ANGLE: She's my own flesh and blood, and I wouldn't disown her. As long as I have a nickel, it's hers. I'll stand by her.

MINISTER: Hmmm.

MR. ANGLE: They don't speak except to quarrel. The girl is hysterical and swoons, and her mother has a heart attack. The house is in a commotion. It's enough to drive a man crazy.

MINISTER: Uh, huh!

MR. ANGLE: I have told her it is not fair to throw her life away and thousands of dollars and see nothing for it. She is so sex crazy. Always phoning up next day, writing to him every day.

MINISTER: When did she begin thinking of marrying?

MR. ANGLE: This summer, since coming home from the university.

MINISTER: Does Laura do anything during the summer to support herself? Does she have a job?

MR. ANGLE: Why, no. She just sleeps late and does what she wants. Goes to the movies with that boy.

MINISTER: Is it healthy to let her loll around subject to embraces and kisses, if nothing else?

MR. ANGLE: I suppose not.

MINISTER: It is reasonable to suppose that with overstimulation night after night by her boy friend that her appetite for sexual things relative to marriage might be increased.

MR. ANGLE: I can see that now. We've allowed her too much liberty, but it's too late now. We must suffer the consequences.

MINISTER: It is not too late to help her see the complications of marriage and sex life. I have here a book you may take along with you. [*Mastery of Sex*] You can remedy the situation. She is an intelligent girl. If you try to help her to see marriage from the Catholic point of view, she may change her mind. I will give you some materials on the matter.

MR. ANGLE: I'm afraid it's all our fault. We've made a mess of our lives and our children's. We have not lived right.

MINISTER: But you can start afresh, by the help of God. Why not try his way?

MR. ANGLE: I will try.

COMMENTS

In this final contact the pastor was moving through a third level of counseling with Mr. Angle without ever having clearly defined the relationship as one in which counseling was needed. He did not construct a time and place arrangement whereby Mr. Angle could, without any more tension than necessary, gradually explore and gain insight into his difficulties. The end result was that the pastor was thrust into the position of working out Mr. Angle's problems for him in the form of pat advice. This obscured the man's direct relationship to God in Christ and made him overly dependent upon the pastor instead. If, to the contrary, the pastor had taken the time to convert the informal market place, after-meeting conversations into a more ordered process of multiple-interview counseling, he would have gotten more to the root of the man's troubles, established a more enduring relationship to him in his times of need, and discovered a more satisfying growth with Mr. Angle. As it was, the pastor had to say, "I felt disappointed and frustrated, as I did not seem to be getting at the root of the trouble."

By way of summary, then, let us say that the pastor can make contacts for more intensive kinds of counseling through his informal pastoral ministries of market place, social gathering, and after-meeting visits. But he must skilfully shift appeals for more complicated problem help into a more formal interviewing situation. This calls for serious attention to the budgeting of time in pastoral counseling.

7. Making the Contact: Pastoral Visitation and Counseling

James Lyn Elder

Visiting in the home is at the heart of what Seward Hiltner calls the "shepherding perspective." [1] In the parable of the one lost sheep (the emphasis is not on the ninety and nine) Christ drew a picture of the seeking shepherd. This drama is reproduced, no matter how faint the resemblance, whenever the pastor makes a call.

The members of most churches expect and want their minister to visit them. And the pastor himself, in most instances, assumes from the outset that this will be part of his program. But until now too little attention has been given to the function of pastoral visitation and to the way in which it is related to the rest of the minister's work, particularly to his counseling.

In his book *Pastoral Counseling*, Dr. Hiltner speaks of the "precounseling ministry." [2] By this phrase he means all that takes place between the pastor and his people before they come to him for help. Hiltner has in mind, of course, particularly those things that will draw people to the pastor and those that will prepare the way for a helpful interview. The minister's sermons, his administrative procedures, his conduct of worship—all these are part of this precounseling service, but visiting is at the forefront in a special way.

---

[1] Seward Hiltner, *Preface to Pastoral Theology* (New York: Abingdon Press, 1958).

[2] New York: Abingdon Press, 1949, p. 128.

Pastoral ministry may be conceived as a kind of "stimulus and response" between pastor and people, with the minister providing the initial "push" and the people responding in terms of understanding, acceptance, and growth. Thus visiting may be seen as the beginning of the process. It is the point at which is begun the program that will continue to the advancement of the kingdom in terms of congregational maturity.

A Pastoral Visit

A number of significant results are achieved by pastoral visitation. Perhaps the following incident will help us to see some of them.

Pastor Seller steps up on the porch of a small cottage and rings the doorbell. He has come to call on the Olsens, who united with his church the previous Sunday. While waiting for the door to be answered he notices that the yard is untended, the house itself is somewhat run-down, and the entire neighborhood is shabby.

The door opens and Mrs. Olsen stands there. She is wearing an apron and has flour on her hands. On her face are mingled expressions of pleasure, surprise, and embarrassment.

MRS. OLSEN: Oh, hello, Brother Seller. Come in. And please excuse my appearance. I'm baking.

PASTOR: Oh, that's quite all right, Mrs. Olsen. Am I interrupting you? If so, I can come back.

MRS. OLSEN: No, sit down. I'm glad of an excuse to rest a minute. (*She wipes her hands on her apron.*)

PASTOR: Since you folks joined our church last week, I've wanted to come by and say hello. On Sunday at church it's pretty hard to find time to visit.

MRS. OLSEN: I know it is. And I certainly appreciate your coming by. With all you have to do I don't see how you have time to do much visiting.

PASTOR: Well, at our church we feel that getting to know each other is as important as anything we can do—and more important than some things.

MRS. OLSEN: I certainly appreciate that. I've always felt that churches should be that way. (*At this point she gets up to close a door leading into another room.*) I'd better close this, I guess. My husband sleeps during the day, you know.

PASTOR: Oh, Mr. Olsen works at night?

MRS. OLSEN: Yes, and it's been pretty hard on him. For years he had a regular daytime shift, but when the plant laid off so many men last month, John had to take night hours.

PASTOR: I see.

MRS. OLSEN (*looking around with embarrassment*): I'm ashamed for you to see things the way they are, with the house and yard such a mess. With my husband working nights and his mother here for me to look after, neither of us seems to have time to do anything.

PASTOR: Oh, Mr. Olsen's mother is here?

MRS. OLSEN: Yes, she's been with us since John's father died two years ago. She's getting up in years, and you know how much care old people need. (*There is a little note of sharpness in her voice. She stands.*) Let me see if she's awake and dressed, and I'll bring her out to see you. She always loves to see the preacher, and if she finds out one was here and she didn't see him, we'll never hear the last of it.

(*She leaves the room, closing the door behind her. As the pastor sits waiting, he hears the murmur of voices, with Mrs. Olsen saying something in an exasperated, impatient tone. With a flushed face she returns to the room in which the pastor sits.*)

It's no use. She's in one of her moods today. She just can't—or won't—understand what I'm saying to her. (*She remains standing.*)

PASTOR (*standing also*): Well, I'll come back to see her another time, Mrs. Olsen. And I'll see you folks again, too. Please tell John I'm sorry to have missed him. I'll have to call at a time when he's awake. Is there anything I could do for you today?

MRS. OLSEN: Yes. Please have a prayer for us.

PASTOR: I surely will. Let me do that now. (*He prays.*) Our Father God, in whose image we are made and by whom we are redeemed, grant us always the sense of thy presence. Strengthen us to do thy will and to that end give us love and wisdom. Bless this home and these thy children. Supply their every need through thy riches in grace in Jesus Christ, in whose name we pray. Amen. (*The pastor remains silent for a moment, and then looks up to find Mrs. Olsen wiping tears from her eyes.*)

MRS. OLSEN: Thank you so much for coming today, Brother Seller. I can't tell you how much it has helped to talk with you. And please come back again soon.

What This Visit Teaches

The pastor has returned to his study; he has left the run-down and tension-filled home of the Olsens. As he and we think back on the visit, what does it suggest concerning the relationship of visiting to counseling?

In the first place, we see in Mr. Seller's call an interpretation of the Christian community. Presenting himself at the door of the Olsen's home, especially so soon after they had joined the church, was in itself an interpretive act. It said, "See, the church is primarily individuals in a face-to-face relationship. It is individuals who are concerned about each other, who are communicative with reference to each other."

In the interview that followed, this exposition continued; it was implicit in every attitude expressed and every word spoken. The pastor's awareness of even Mrs. Olsen's befloured hands expressed his acceptance of and respect for her and her activities. This acceptance-respect theme continued throughout the entire visit. Mrs. Olsen's comments concerning her husband and his mother were heard with interest and accepted by the minister. And all of this combined to say to Mrs. Olsen not only in a general way that the church was a community of concerned persons but also that she herself was accepted as one of them. The visit provided an opportunity for the pastor to give this interpretation of the fellowship and for the member to receive it.

In the second place, as this visit demonstrates, pastoral calling is informative. And it is informative in a two-way manner. From the viewpoint of either Mr. Seller or Mrs. Olsen, the visit was educational. Mr. Seller, for example, learned significant things about his new church members. Their economic status, Mr. Olsen's vocational problems, their intrafamily tensions—all these bits of vital data he added to his fund of knowledge concerning this part of his flock.

On Mrs. Olsen's part, this visit taught her much about the kind of pastor and church to which she and her family had become related and what her pastor's philosophy and practice of the ministry were. By his attitude of attentive listening to her complaints regarding her mother-in-law and by his noncondemning attitude toward those complaints she learned that he was someone to whom she might express her true feelings without fear of condemnation and judgment.

In the third place, visiting provides an opportunity for people to do the very thing that Mrs. Olsen did: she aired her feelings. We may imagine that with a husband who slept most of the day and an aged, semi-invalid mother-in-law to care for, Mrs. Olsen was apt to feel isolated. There was the dangerous probability that she frequently shut her feelings up inside herself until they reached the exploding point. Then the emotion was apt to be expressed in a destructive way toward the husband, the mother-in-law, or anyone else unfortunate enough to "trigger the bomb." Part of the ensuing damage invariably involved Mrs. Olsen, of course, and left behind, no doubt, a considerable debris of guilt.

Now perhaps such "ventilation" as occurred in this visit is not part of counseling in the strictest sense of the word, but it is certainly related to it. In nearly every interview, no matter how deep the process of insight-attaining goes, there is also an element of "getting-it-off-one's-chest" for the counselee and a consequent gaining of relief.

At the same time, Mrs. Olsen was unconsciously perhaps, but none the less certainly, testing her minister. She was trying to see, in her expression to Mr. Seller of her hostility toward her husband's mother, if the pastor would react defensively or maintain that attitude of steadfast attention and acceptance needed for her healing. Such testing is familiar to every counselor; it is the counselee's way of determining whether he may with confidence proceed with the interview. In the case of Mrs. Olsen we may assume that she was satisfied with the result of her testing.

Finally, pastoral visiting helps establish that relationship of rapport, of confidence and affection, between counselor and client without which the entire procedure is impossible. We have already seen how this relates to the client's understanding of the nature of the church and to their personal acquaintance with each other as individuals (Mrs. Olsen as a person with problems, Mr. Seller a person with resources). We have further seen how this was strengthened by the testing procedure Mrs. Olsen engaged in. Whatever rapport and empathy may mean, they stand for interpersonal relations of a warm, strong kind.

If in the future a need for more thoroughgoing counseling arises, there will be already established a basis of interpersonal relationships upon which it may be set. Mr. Seller's precounseling visit has effectively paved the way.

Summary

Pastoral visitation is as much a part of the ministry as any other activity. It is inherent in the shepherding tradition. Furthermore, it is integrally related in a number of ways to the ministry of counseling.

First, there is the larger precounseling ministry of which the visit is an important part. It is often the first step toward the kind of interview in which pastor and member may progress together toward insight.

Second, and more specifically, the pastoral visit interprets the nature of the Christian community as one of interpersonal concern, one in which warmth and understanding sufficient for healing purposes may be found.

In the third place, there is in the ministry of visiting an important informational aspect, whether viewed from the perspective of the pastor or of the person visited.

Finally, there is established a basis of an interpersonal kind upon which counseling may later take place. These and possibly other values attach to pastoral visitation as it relates to counseling. And all of them combine to throw vivid light upon the importance that visiting should be understood to have, especially as it relates to pastoral counseling.

8. Keeping Confidences in Pastoral Counseling

Wayne E. Oates

The combined public and private character of a pastor's work creates some real problems in his work as a pastoral counselor. He is usually, in his own community at least, a well-known person. He mingles in all sorts of social functions, informal gatherings, and family occasions. He hears much idle conversation and is tempted to contribute his share to loose talk in the community. He may be so eager for social acceptance as a "hail-fellow-well-met" that he will fail to keep his tongue in gear with his judgment. In doing so, he loses the power of discriminating between the time to speak and the time to be silent. Being called upon for continual public addresses of one kind and another, often with little or no opportunity for careful preparation, he may let the pressure of the situation cause him to fall back upon his most recent private conversations for ideas if not for illustrations. Furthermore, people in his community who want to hurt other individuals may tell him things without being responsible for having told him and at the same time expect him to do something about the situation. Or they may be like pointer dogs, with their eyes trained on the pastor for the slightest gesture that will reflect an interpretation of another person's troubles.

All of this stresses the powerfully "radioactive" character of the pastor's work as a counselor. The "fall-out" can be extremely serious for the whole community, because the pastor does not counsel in a vacuum nor even in the neatly controlled setting of the professional counselor in a clinic. In this fact rests both the challenge and the despair of the pastoral counselor. Inasmuch as he cannot give the kinds of anonymity to his people in the pastoral situation which they need, how then can he create a controlled, noncontaminated, antiseptic environment in which their needs can nevertheless be met? Several suggestions can be made.

The Pastor's Preaching and Public Speaking

The pastor as a counselor usually uses the information he receives from counselees in public addresses and sermons because of a lack of careful preparation of these messages. He simply uses free association with an idea, and his most recent experiences collect to it. Therefore, one of the best ways he can avoid harming people by making inadvertent references to those with whom he has privately counseled is to prepare his messages more carefully and not to agree to give more messages than he can prepare for adequately.

However, even the pastor who does this will occasionally plan to use illustrations from his counseling. Several "ground rules" should be observed if he does so. First, he should use illustrations that point to positive, inspiring, and heroic traits in the counselee and not to derogatory, sneering, or cynically humorous attitudes the pastor may have toward the counselee. Holding a person up to ridicule as a horrible example is always humiliating and harmful. For a pastor to do it is reprehensible.

Second, the pastor should, inasmuch as in him lieth, get the permission of the person or persons involved before he uses information or ideas they have given him. He should be as careful about this as he is about publishing material from other people's books or manuscripts. He should always get permission to quote. The only books that most people write is the "flesh-and-blood tablets" of their own lives. Therefore, they are the author's and should be consulted before being quoted.

Third, the pastor would do much better to get his illustrations from literature such as novels, plays, poetry, and biography than to use the personal problems of his counselees as illustrations. Especially should he master the dramatic story of the Bible and use biblical biography, parable, and dramatic happening for illustration. This is an enchanting way to teach the Bible and at the same time to achieve a persuasive homiletical purpose.

Fourth, the pastor should very carefully avoid the temptation to try to turn his preaching into a counseling session. Many of the same attitudes of warmth, acceptance, empathic understanding, and dramatic silence characteristic of counseling are inherent to effective preaching. But the situations are different in that counseling is two-way communication, and the accent is on the counselee's doing the talking. Preaching is one-way communication, and the accent is on the preacher's doing the talking. The real art of preaching, it seems, lies in the capacity of the preacher to create the silent, nonverbal responsiveness in the audience which makes a measure of two-way communication possible in preaching. The misuse of counseling illustrations creates a feeling of having been misrepresented without consultation. It not only keeps people from coming for counseling in time of need; it also keeps them from coming back to hear sermons! This is the only way they have of answering the preacher.

Finally, the pastor can and should do something in his preaching to encourage people to have confidence in him as a personal counselor. The preacher who lashes and whips people about divorce will have self-righteous people applaud him for his stand, but the alienated, guilt-ridden, and self-condemning person contemplating divorce will avoid him. In other words, his attitude of understanding, wisdom, and appreciation of people—which neither condones nor condemns—has a powerful stimulus on the confidence of a person who needs counseling.

Furthermore, the pastor can interpret the ministry of counseling from the pulpit. One pastor did so in a sermon entitled "Help Wanted." He began with the sovereign power of God: only God is self-sufficient, and even he invites our comradeship in his work. He continued with man's false sense of self-sufficiency and challenged the current conception that to ask for help is a sign of weak faith. He moved, in the fourth place, to discuss the Christian fellowship as a burden-bearing community of people who help each other. He concluded with a discussion of the role of the pastor as a representative of God, as a fellow sufferer who often leans on others himself and as a counselor who comforts others by means of the comfort wherewith God has comforted him. He assured them of three things as a counselor if they came to him for help: He would listen to them with a whole heart and an understanding mind. He would not try to run their lives for them or override their own powers of decision. He would not repeat what they told him without their permission!

The Nature of Information Received in Counseling

A promise not to repeat information received in counseling raises some real questions as to the nature of this information. We usually receive three kinds of information in pastoral counseling.

Community knowledge.—Our counselees often give us information about themselves which is community knowledge. Many people know these things. The fact that the counselee strictly enjoined us not to tell this may lure us into naïvely assuming they have not said this to anyone else. The fact is that they may have spoken "confidentially" with many people. In routine first interviews, the pastor should always ask to whom else the counselee has talked about the matter. This will reveal, if carefully and patiently done, the extent of spread of the communication.

The experienced pastor has also learned that when he gives a vow of confidence to a person he should require one in return. He should strictly charge him to go and tell no one. Otherwise, this person may be spreading the story all over the community and at the same time holding the pastor to vows of confidence. He may even accuse the pastor of having divulged that which he himself told. Also, exacting a vow of confidence from the pastor may be the way one marital partner has of seeing to it that only one side of the story gets told or of establishing a secret and clandestine relationship to the pastor. This is particularly risky in the case of the wife's conferring secretly with the pastor.

Privileged communication.—Another kind of information received in counseling is what has come to be called "privileged communication." This is information given to the counselor on the agreement that it will not be communicated to anyone else without the specific permission of the counselee or, more generally, to anyone except other professional people with whom the pastor is working. For instance, the pastor as a marriage counselor routinely assures the marital partners that he will not quote them to each other. However, with specific permission for a certain purpose, the counselee may grant the counselor the privilege of talking over a certain matter with the other spouse. More commonly, the pastor needs to confer, for instance, with an adoption agency about the desire of a sterile couple for a child. He is given the privilege of communicating their needs to an agency. Or a specific confession, such as of a premarital pregnancy, will be communicated to an obstetrician to whom the pastor refers the person for examination and medical care. Or, less commonly, people who are seen in a teaching center for counselor-training are discussed without reference to their personal identity by the counselor with his supervising professor. These are instances of "privileged communication."

Pastors need to be extremely cautious about making parlor conversation with their fellow pastors about people with whom they have worked. To the experienced and seasoned counselor there is no more boring conversation. But beginning students and counselors who have very few people come to them for help talk in a nonpastoral and professionally unethical way too often. A part of *being* a pastor is to consider communication with a suffering person a *privilege* and not a pastime, work and not recreation!

Confidential or "confessional" information.—Some highly personal information comes to the pastor which should never be told to anyone *except* by the person himself. No one who has not gone through the spiritual disciplines of time, attention, and understanding which would enable that person to tell them himself has a right to this information. A pastoral counselor has a right to know only those things about a person which his relationship to that person can justify. He does not *need* to know more than this, because knowledge about people is not the heart of pastoral counseling. A durable and secure relationship to people is the heart of pastoral counseling.

Therefore, the pastor needs both a good memory to remember many things the counselee tells him and a good "forgetter" to forget certain things as far as telling them to anyone else is concerned. These are usually things which people literally tell to God in our presence as helpers and encouragers. Therefore, they are not things that really are ours to tell except as we talk with God in prayer in behalf of that person. Then we are not giving information to someone who did not already know it before we ourselves did! This is actually confessional material in the Protestant sense of a voluntarily given and not ecclesiastically required confession.

The Pastor's Family and His Counseling Ministry

Inevitably ministers ask the question about telling members of their family, especially their wives, about the counseling work. Should we share information with our wives? Do you talk all these matters over with your wife and let her know to whom you have talked that day? Several things need to be said about the relationship of a minister's wife to his counseling.

First, the wife usually answers the telephone at the minister's home. Many times church people and nonchurch people alike will tell her before they tell the pastor about their troubles. She serves as an intake supervisor for much of his counseling. Therefore, just as in the case of the doctor, it is important that the pastor's wife know where and when he may be reached. This is not a sign of her dominating him; it is a part of his work. In addition to that, especially if there are little children in the home and an emergency arises, the wife is a more serene and secure person if she has the sustained awareness that she can reach her husband when she needs him personally. This is a part of his pastoral care of those in his own household. For the pastor's wife is the only woman in the community whose pastor is also her husband!

On the other hand, the wife can be exceptionally helpful in several ways at the home telephone. First, she can give out information which often is all that people who call want. If her husband is out of the city, she can guide the person to additional sources of help in an emergency if her husband and she work this out in advance. If the need expressed can best be met by someone else, she can help the caller to find that person. Second, she can, after having explained her limitations of time, be a good listener on the telephone and point out to the prospective counselee what can be expected of counseling— that it takes time and willingness to work at it and that it can be helpful. Third, she can protect her husband from some of the demands that come his way by explaining his schedule and previous commitments. "Can the pastor see Mr. X *this* afternoon?" she may be asked. If it is a foregone certainty that the pastor has the afternoon filled with a funeral, a wedding, and an equally desperate counseling situation, then she may help to arrange another time.

All of this calls for exceptionally good communication between the pastor and his wife. The pastor who leaves his wife to guess and wonder about his responsibilities often forces her to have to say, "I haven't seen him today." In a time of real exasperation she may say, "Only the Lord knows where he is! He never lets me know anything!" Pretty soon that pastor will need a counselor himself!

Second, the pastor's wife can be his counselor to a limited degree. He, in turn, can be her counselor to a limited degree. Instead of saying "counselor," it might be better to say "teacher." Marriage is a learning relationship. Many of the skills of tenderness, patience, and warmth a pastor has to learn from his wife. Therefore, instead of telling his wife about the particularly personal details of the lives of the people with whom he counsels, the pastor does better to let her get acquainted with *him!* People's problems in general can be discussed, especially if they involve community knowledge. But the pastor does much better to concentrate the precious time he has with his family on inquiring into *their* needs and letting them inquire into his than on sharing a great majority of the personal secrets of other lives in which he has participated as counselor.

Third, the pastor does well to share with his wife and children the privileged communication which they need to know. Many times members of his family are also involved in the lives of those with whom he counsels. With the privilege granted him by the person so involved, he can, according to the rules of all privileged communication, share information with the members of his family *for a purpose.* That purpose should be specific, well thought out, and planned. For instance, a pastor's wife may teach a certain young matron in her Sunday school class. The younger woman may have confided in him some of her feelings about her mother, who is long since dead. She now needs a motherly woman with whom she can talk informally. She would like to talk with the pastor's wife but admires her so much and stands in such awe of her that she is timid about visiting in her home. The pastor can ask the privilege of making it a little easier by talking with his wife himself. With permission and privilege, then, the pastor tells his wife about this person's needs because the wife herself can be genuinely helpful.

But unnecessary, indiscriminate, and garrulous talking with members of one's family can mutilate their relationships to the members of the church. Furthermore, the fact that the pastor does *not* share all this information with his wife often strengthens his people's confidence both in him and his wife. It comes as something of a surprise to some church members to realize that a particularly personal bit of information, however important or unimportant, was held inviolate in the confidence of the pastor, even from his wife. His wife, in turn, can say, "Well, no, John did not tell me that. I am sure that he felt that if you wanted me to know it, you yourself would tell me."

The Protestant Witness Through the Pastor's Home

All of this discussion serves to point up the distinctly Protestant understanding of the pastor as a counselor. He bears his witness to the whole counsel of God, not alone but through having become "one flesh" with his wife. His identity as a husband, a father, and a good manager of a household are a vital necessity, not an unwelcome interference with or a sideline to the pastoral calling. Catholic ideas of the priesthood have seeped underground into the unconscious feelings of many Protestant pastors, however, to cause them to think of their roles as husband and father as being separate and apart from their calling as pastor. As a result their home life is often ridden with furtive feelings of guilt, anxiety, and neglect. But nowhere does the unity of the pastor's role come more vividly into focus than in the work he does as pastoral counselor.

9. The Budgeting of Time in Pastoral Counseling

John W. Drakeford

Recent articles in national magazines have helped to emphasize the problems which ministers face in finding time to fulfil all their pastoral obligations. Some of this has been overstated and the mistaken impression given that preachers across the country are suffering from nervous breakdowns. Nevertheless, the minister does face difficulties in wisely using his time. He is constantly faced with what one writer has called "the problem of busyness." [1] The pastor is not a specialist in the strict sense of the word. He has to be a preacher, an administrator, a teacher, an organizer, a promoter, and sundry other things. It sometimes seems as if, like the apostles in the early church, he needs to stop and request the church to help him so that he can give himself "to prayer, and to the ministry of the word" (Acts 6:4).

Apart from the many differing demands on his time the minister will soon discover that his pastoral ministry itself can become a time-consuming matter. Russell Dicks says:

A physically ill person needs to be seen every week, a dying person every day, a shut-in every two weeks, an older person at least that often. Every person should be called upon twice a year whether he has special spiritual needs or not, while six to twelve hours of listening time is needed by grief-stricken persons. Two to four hours

[1] William E. Hulme, *How to Start Counseling* (New York: Abingdon Press, 1955), p. 136.

are needed for pre-marital counseling with each couple the minister marries; while if he is to work effectively with persons suffering from marital difficulties, from twelve to twenty hours and often far more are needed; and now the final blow: if one is to be helpful with an alcoholic, from one to two hundred hours are needed.[2]

This pastoral side of things in general and counseling in particular can easily result in the minister's spending a disproportionate amount of time in this phase of his work. He can reach the place where he gets a desperate feeling that there is not a moment that he can call his own. Suppertime, when the preacher might reasonably expect to get a few moments with his family, seems to be the favorite target, and the telephone is constantly ringing with calls from people who are reasonably sure that this is the best time to catch him.

Nevertheless, it is well for us to strike a balance of debits and credits in this counseling ministry and try to decide just how important it is in our work. One of the great problems we face in our present-day church life is our craze for statistics and good figures in connection with our own particular churches. Such an emphasis tends to minimize the importance of the individual. Counseling is a valuable antidote to this trend and helps to put the individual back in the center of the picture.

Moreover, we sometimes need to stop and ask ourselves what, precisely, we are busy about. Hulme says, "Busyness is one of the most acceptable escape mechanisms of our day." [3] It is possible that we might be merely running on the spot, like the character in *Alice in Wonderland* who had to keep running to stay in the same place. A minister is always tempted to make his work appear in its best light, and, conscious of our activist concepts, he is anxious to be known as a hard worker, even if he really isn't. Tead, in speaking of the leader, says that it is important that he "dramatize" his energy. "It will help if he *looks*

[2] Russell L. Dicks, "Finding Time for Counseling," *The Minister's Consultation Clinic,* ed. Simon Doniger (New York: Channel Press, Inc., 1955), p. 33.
[3] Hulme, *op. cit.*

forceful, vigorous, and energetic." [4] Ministers are often past masters of this art.

Having persuaded his people that he is so busy, the minister who wishes to do serious counseling work may discover that this very factor works against him. People who have problems with which the minister could be of so much help are reluctant to come and see him because it might take up his valuable time when he is so busy. To counteract this feeling will be necessary for the minister to let it be known just how important he considers counseling and his willingness to be of help. One minister, in making such an announcement, said, "I am not really as busy as I seem to be; I am only trying to impress my deacons. I always have time to see someone who needs my help in some personal matter." The congregation smiled, but it got the point that the minister was willing to help.

Regular Hours and Appointments

The setting up of regular hours in which the minister will be available in his office can be of great value. It is of help particularly to the young minister who is most anxious to commence counseling and does not know how to get started. The announcement in the church bulletin, or some other place, that the minister is available for conferences about anything that is of concern to the members each afternoon from three till five tells the whole congregation that the minister can be reached at a certain time other than at his mealtime. It also helps to give the impression that there is method in the arrangement and helps to channel the prospective counselee into the correct setting such as the office.

Another value in this setting up of regular hours and announcing them is that it gives the person who is troubled the idea that he is not alone. This person sees, perhaps for the first time, that there are others who need this help and that if they

---

[4] Ordway Tead, *The Art of Leadership* (New York: McGraw-Hill Book Co., Inc., 1935), p. 90.

can be helped, so can he. A woman who was having trouble in her marriage relationship came to a minister and said, "I didn't know that this kind of help was available. I imagined that church people shouldn't need outside help in their home life."

Setting up the hours will not be easy. A number of factors will enter into deciding when they will be. Probably they will mostly be during the day, but the minister will have to consider the nature of the church membership. It is often advisable to have at least one evening or a Saturday morning or a similar time which will be convenient for the prospective counselees. The pastor will need to remember to provide himself with a way of escape. There are certain people with whom time will be wasted and from whom he will need protection.

There are some disadvantages involved in the setting up of arbitrary hours. Such a procedure will sometimes hinder the counseling process. A person may be hesitant to come lest he will be one among many who are waiting. There is also the possibility of the pastor's becoming the target of those who resentfully announce, "I came at the time stated as your office hours, and you were not here." So the announcement of office hours should add, "Please call the church office to make an appointment" or, "Conferences by appointment."

There are in fact some authorities in the field who see the appointment system as an essential ingredient in a successful counseling situation. Such a system saves the minister from trying to deal with situations in inappropriate places. He meets one of his church members in the supermarket and the following conversation ensues:

PASTOR: Hello, Mrs. Jones, and how are you today?
MRS. J.: Fancy seeing you here, Pastor. You know, I have been thinking about coming around to see you about a little matter I have on my mind.
PASTOR: Why don't you come around to the church office and let us have a visit? When would suit you best?

It is possible that some sort of informal counseling might have been done on the spot. If this problem was some very elementary matter, it could be successful; but if it was anything of vital importance, there is very little hope of a successful counseling relationship's being set up. This is a precounseling situation, and the very fact that the pastor suggests setting up an appointment shows that he thinks that the church member's problem is important.

Another value in the appointment system is that it is a very personal arrangement. The counselee gets the feeling that this is something that belongs to him. The minister is going to set off a period of time that will be his. Such a feeling helps to form a good relationship and can get counseling off to a good start.

Yet another value of the appointment idea is that the counselee is provided with the opportunity of taking the initiative. In his list of "Characteristic Steps in the Therapeutic Process" Rogers places at the very first, "The individual comes for help," and then proceeds, "Rightly recognized this is one of the most significant steps in therapy. The individual has, as it were, taken himself in hand and taken a responsible action of the first importance." [5]

In this perspective we can see the appointment itself as being a therapeutic tool. Confirmation of this fact comes from a study made by Dr. Robert L. Faucett of the section on psychiatry at Mayo Clinic. A study was made of people who had telephoned for appointments regarding personal and marital problems. The clinic was unable to work with these people, but a questionnaire sent out to them six months later showed that more than 50 per cent of them were getting along satisfactorily and no longer had need for help. Dr. Faucett concluded that the process of making up one's mind to get help and actually getting in touch with a person or agency serves as a dynamic in it-

[5] Carl Rogers, *Counseling and Psychotherapy* (Boston: Houghton Mifflin Co., 1942), p. 31.

self in problem solving. So the appointment may serve a useful purpose apart from the skill of the counselor.[6]

Sometimes a pastor thinks that setting up the appointment system may deter people from coming to him. He sees some people as being prepared to drop in when they have a spare moment and feels that setting appointments may place an unnecessary burden upon them. However, from another point of view this very burden may in itself be an advantage. If these people went to a physician, they would have to pay a fee, and practitioners of psychoanalysis insist that the payment of a fee is an essential part of therapy. Here, then, the minister asks his parishioner to pay a fee, as it were, by investing his time, thus inconveniencing himself. Having made an investment in the process, the counselee is more likely to be helped.

From a practical point of view the procedure of appointments will have much to commend it in that it will help to save the pastor from the dilemma of having people come to see him at the wrong time. It has been announced that the pastor will be in his office at certain hours, so a parishioner comes in to see him. The pastor has to leave for an engagement in a few minutes but does not want to turn the prospective counselee away. So the interview is carried on with the pastor uneasily stealing furtive glances at his watch and feeling the tension rising within him. In such a frame of mind he is wasting his time trying to counsel. The setting up of an appointment can help to save such a situation.

Making Appointments

When we see the appointment itself as a counseling tool, we will come to be very judicious in its usage. Not only does the counseling process take time but there also needs to be a spacing of interviews to allow time for growth. Rogers remarks about this: "Not only is the client able to communicate only a small

[6] Rex A. Skidmore, Hulda Van Streeter Garrett, and C. Jay Skidmore *Marriage Consulting* (New York: Harper & Brothers, 1956), p. 280.

fraction of the attitudes and feelings he is experiencing, but it is also true that what he thinks through in the interview is but a small fraction of what he works out in between interviews." [7] This idea of the persistence with which the counselee continues to grapple with an insight should be constantly before us. All too frequently we have magnified the dramatic concept of counseling. We see it in the imagery of the prisoner in the cell feeling his way along the darkened wall and suddenly touching a hidden spring which causes a hitherto unknown door to fly open and let the light stream in. So the cause of the neurosis is suddenly revealed, insight comes, and the counselee goes out a new creature. Even in recordings of counseling interviews time limitations frequently cause the makers to leave out the long hours of repetition and regression, and we get the impression that it is all straight ahead from insight to insight.

In actual fact, dramatic insight is a product of the novelist's imagination. Insight comes slowly. There are often only small increments; old habits of thought are reluctantly surrendered. All this takes time, and the individual needs periods in which he can consolidate his gains. Rogers helps us again: "This deep conflict and confusion, the facing of fearful attitudes within oneself, calls for little further comment, except perhaps to point out again that often the most crucial struggles occur outside of the interview itself." [8]

Having this in mind will save us from some of the pitfalls that beset the pathways of the unwary pastoral counselor. A pastor will sometimes proudly relate an experience in which he talked with a person "into the early hours of the morning." When a pastor does this, he may be unwittingly denying the person the opportunity to make his greatest gains. It is highly improbable that much will be accomplished beyond the first forty-five minutes of an interview. There is always the possibility that

[7] Carl R. Rogers, *Client-Centered Therapy* (Boston: Houghton Mifflin Co., 1951), p. 74.
[8] *Ibid.*, p. 121.

the pastor will spend a lot of time telling his counselee things which he could have discovered for himself had there been a series of shorter interviews.

Another important consideration in setting up appointments is that of sticking closely to the predetermined time. There are some people who will endeavor to stretch out the period of the counseling session. There are reasons for this that need not bother us now, but it is important that the pastoral counselor be prepared for such situations. Just as the period is coming to a conclusion, the subject will begin to produce, and the temptation will be to prolong the session. There may be exceptions, but as a general rule it is best to stay with the predetermined time. Ericson states: "The establishment of time arrangements tends to encourage both participants to spend the time more wisely." [9]

Even Rogers, in his nondirective technique, is very definite about the setting up of limits. One of the most important of these is the limit on time. "The client is free to keep an appointment or to break it, to come on time or to come late, to use the hour in idle talk in order to avoid his real problems, or to use it constructively. There is a limitation, however, that he is not free to control the counselor and gain more time, no matter what the subterfuge." [10] So in the structuring of the counseling relationship it is well for the pastor to say at the outset, "I will be very happy to counsel with you once a week for forty-five minutes each period. This forty-five minutes will be yours to utilize in seeking the answers to the things that are troubling you." Another effective technique for concluding an interview is for the counselor to rise to his feet and make an appropriate concluding statement.

Using appointments will also help to space conferences further apart. Although some of the depth therapists indicate the

[9] Clifford E. Ericson, *The Counseling Interview* (New York: Prentice-Hall, Inc., 1950), p. 91.
[10] Rogers, *Counseling and Psychotherapy*, p. 89.

importance of daily contacts, such is not necessary with the people whom the pastor will seek to help. Rollin Fairbanks has suggested conferences which are spaced two weeks apart.

Similarly a pastor can often use conferences of a shorter duration. There is nothing sacred about an hour or forty-five minutes. A lot will depend on the counselee and the experience and the skill of the counselor, but for many pastors thirty minutes will suffice and facilitate the setting up of more appointments. However, it is at this point that a warning should be given about two types of people. One is the person who wants to have a "therapeutic flirtation" and can never stay for more than ten minutes at any one time and consequently never shows any improvement. The second is the chronic neurotic who has no intention of abandoning his neurosis but wants to use the counselor as a crutch to lean upon. A firm hand and the judicious use of the appointment system can save the pastor from both of these.

Counseling Techniques and the Time Factor

In the consideration of the use of time in counseling one of the questions that immediately comes to mind is that of which particular technique of counseling requires the minimum of time. With such a limited amount of time at his disposal the method to be used will be very important to the pastoral counselor.

On the face of it, it seems as if the more directive methods of counseling are the least time consuming. So the obvious thing to do seems to be to ask the counselee the nature of his problem, formulate a plan of action, and send him on his way. Like so many other issues in counseling, this is an oversimplification. It is a well-known fact that the first issue raised in counseling is very often not the real source of trouble for the counselee, and the enthusiastic problem solver may not be even touching the real issue.

The nondirective technique would not seem to commend itself as the best method for short-term contacts, but Rogers explicitly denies this. In this approach the all-important thing in a counseling relationship is for the counselee to be given the opportunity to talk out his attitudes. Rogers comments:

> The client leaves without, to be sure, any artificial "solution" to his problem, but with his situation more clearly defined in his own mind, with the possible choices clarified, and with the comforting reassurance that someone has understood him and, in spite of his problems and attitudes, has been able to accept him. He is more competent to meet his situation than the client who leaves the interview with much half-digested advice, resentful toward some of it, feeling that he has been wrong in many of his own actions, and less sure of himself than before.[11]

For the pastoral counselor there is much to ponder in this concept. We are so used to making authoritative statements that it requires special restraint for us to take the role of a listener. There is a special warning even in the phraseology which is used in the statement by Rogers: "If we can recognize this limit and refrain from playing a self-satisfying Jehovah role, we can offer a very definite type of clarifying help, even in a short space of time."[12]

Because the pastoral counselor represents a particular philosophy of life, there will be times when he will have to speak. It is hard to generalize, but it seems as if the interviewer should be as passive as ever he can in the early stages; but if there is little progress and time is pressing, a more directive approach should be used.

In connection with this the importance of brief counseling should be noted. In an effort to define this some writers have stated that any relationship which does not involve seeing a parishioner more than twelve times could be designated as brief counseling. Others name a limit of five or six interviews.

[11] *Ibid.*, p. 172.
[12] *Ibid.*, p. 247.

However we look at it, the fact remains that most pastoral counseling will be brief counseling. There are three reasons for this: The first is the limitations of a minister's time. We have already referred to the variety of other calls on the minister's time. Fairbanks has even gone to the trouble to point out ways in which the pastor can avoid spending too much time in counseling. Some successful pastors report that their contacts have seldom been more than four to six. Eight to twelve hours a week is probably the most the pastor of a medium-sized church will be able to devote to counseling.

The second reason that most pastoral counseling will be brief counseling is the limitation of the pastor's training. Many pastors will have had some sort of training in counseling and some will have read in this area, but not many will have had the extended work which is necessary for the competent psychotherapist. The training that the pastor has had will probably be adequate for the brief encounter, but extended sessions may lead him into deep water. The third reason is the limitations of the pastor's nonprofessional setting. The professional therapist has a very special setting in which to do his work; he charges a fee, he sets up appointments, he breaks the relationship at will. With the pastor it is otherwise. He has another relationship and responsibility to his parishioners; he must continue to meet them in a church and at social activities. This nonprofessional setting of his counseling precludes long contacts.

Hiltner suggests that brief counseling can perform at least three functions. First, it can help the parishioner to "turn the corner" with reference to his situation. By talking the matter over with the pastor the counselee has been able to clarify the situation and make a decision. It is still the parishioner's decision, but he was helped out of a stalemate. Secondly, it can constitute "supportive counseling." A person may be in some crisis which has shattered his world. Insight is not involved, but the counselee needs to feel that there is someone who is concerned and to whom he can pour out the whole story. The pastor in this situation often merely stands by and supports the parishioner through the crisis. In the third place, Hiltner indicates that "it can do no harm." As long as the counselor works in the light of certain simple counseling principles, there is a chance that the parishioner may be helped but not much possibility that he will be harmed by the process.[13]

It is well for the pastoral counselor to remember that in extended counseling the relationship always has a tendency to change. As rapport is gained the counselor is able to vary his technique and gauge how much the counselee can take. But it should also be remembered that the longer the process goes on the deeper will be the material which emerges. In this more extended relationship the attitudes of the counselee will become stronger. Feelings of hostility and love and alternations between the two will frequently manifest themselves. Ability to handle these is something that only comes with long experience in counseling relationships.

It is necessary, too, for the pastor to remember that in a small community extended counseling is likely to be misunderstood. Tensions and feelings of guilt may nullify all that has been accomplished. For most situations brief counseling will be the type which is most appropriate for the minister to use.

[13] Seward Hiltner, *Pastoral Counseling* (New York: Abingdon-Cokesbury Press, 1949), pp. 82–84.

10. The Exploratory or Short-Term Interview

Wayne E. Oates

Much of the help which a pastoral counselor renders to his people is given in a single interview. He should have the ability, the consecration, and the training to deal with people on a more intensive basis. However, the great number of people whom he serves and the many other ways he has of serving them make it important that he know how to use one-interview opportunities to the fullest possible advantage.

Many kinds of counseling done by a pastor actually require only one conversation. He confers with a college student about a summer work opportunity. He talks with a parent about children's spending as it is related to Christian stewardship. He talks with a man and his wife about the wisdom of her changing her denomination in order to unite with the church to which her husband belongs. He confers with a member of the choir about the various music schools supported by the denomination. He talks over the wisdom of a parent's transferring his child to a private school until the furor over integration in the public schools passes over.

Those who have done more intensive study in dealing with personality problems are likely to neglect such one-contact counseling. However, the student worker, the director of religious education, the pastor who is the only paid member of the church staff, and the pastor of a large church are all alike loaded down with this kind of conference interview. This can-

not by any stretch of the imagination be classified as therapeutic counseling, but to say that no real help comes to people
here is badly misleading. To the contrary, when such interviews are rightly timed, they may accomplish what dozens of
therapeutic interviews were aimed at but did not succeed in
accomplishing. Furthermore, a one-interview conference may
well open the way for more intensive counseling in that it provides a pastor with the opportunity to explain just what such
counseling is intended to accomplish in the way of growth and
insight.

Basic Assumptions of One-Interview Counseling

The one-interview situation has several basic assumptions
which usually hold true. If these do not hold true, the pastoral
counselor should angle for another interview or make a referral
to someone else who can give more time and attention.

First, the counselee should have taken the initiative and
asked for help. The all too brief time cannot be used in foisting
help on a person who has not asked for it. When the person has
enough awareness of his need to seek help, then the pastoral
counselor is more apt to be able to follow a one-interview
procedure such as will be suggested below.

Second, the problem presented usually is fairly objective
and clearly related to reality and is not a cover for some deeper
problem. Often it is one in which the person is making a decision
such as choosing a college, evaluating his responsibility for his
retiring parents, or discussing whether or not to drop out of
school. Such problems *may* reflect deeper, more unconscious
personality involvements, but only the inexperienced, freshly
trained, and eager counselor assumes that such problems are
always veils behind which personality disorder lies. In other
words, the pastoral counselor is assuming, often on the basis of
long acquaintance with the person, a dependable degree of
emotional stability and maturity.

Third, the one-interview situation is usually based upon

the assumption that the pastor has other avenues for being meaningful in addition to a formal counseling procedure. He may be related to the person as a neighbor, he may be a discussion leader in a group where the person is a member, or he may see the person regularly at a civic club luncheon or a YMCA health club. In other words, the pastor has a continuing relationship to the counselee. Vivid among such other relationships is his role as a preacher Sunday after Sunday in the person's life.

Limitations and Goals of One-Interview Counseling

We find two extremes among pastoral counselors today: those who try to accomplish everything in one-interview contacts and those who think nothing really constructive can be done unless an extensive series of therapeutic sessions can be arranged. Both of these approaches miss the real values of one-interview counseling because they do not perceive accurately the goals and the limitations of this kind of service to needy people. The goals of one-interview counseling must be set strictly within the limitations of such work.

The limitations.—One-interview counseling certainly, by reason of the time element itself, excludes the exploration of unconscious recesses of the personality. Free association, word association, dream exploration, and more extensive uses of nondirective counseling procedures are not available even to the person qualified to use these approaches when he has only one interview in which to work. Furthermore, the counselor is limited from using interpretation of either such psychological factors as the transference relationship or such theological and exegetical problems as would characterize therapeutic and/or educational approaches of longer duration.

The goals.—However, several specific goals can be accomplished by careful use of one interview. For instance, spiritual exploration of the issues at stake in a decision or a relationship can be initiated. Usually a person who is sufficiently motivated to seek the help of another can see only one way through or out of his problem. In one interview, additional alternatives may be discovered. In the second place, basic information can be imparted, and new light will thereby be shed upon the resources at hand for solving a difficult problem. In the third place, guidance of the person to other persons who can aid him can be given. For instance, a person struggling with the decision to become a missionary can be guided to the counseling services of his denomination's foreign mission agency. In the fourth place, spiritual support can be given, and the loneliness of suffering and decision can thereby be removed. And, finally, the purposes of God and the spiritual meaning of the issues at stake can be directly interpreted in a brief way. This is different, however, from giving moralistic advice, which usually squelches the relationship. The door of the relationship should always be left ajar so that the person can feel free to come back again if he chooses to do so. The main hazard of easy answers and pat solutions is that it breaks the continuing relationship between the pastoral counselor and his counselee.

The Process of One-Interview Counseling

The standard procedure which has proved most useful to many pastoral counselors for handling the one-interview situation is somewhat as follows:

Time limitations.—First, the counselee should be tactfully made aware of the time limitations in which he and his pastor are working. Usually the time factor is uppermost in the minds of those who come to pastors about a serious matter. It is the person who has nothing in particular in mind who tends to be oblivious to time. The person with the problem often wishes to get out as fast as possible when he starts the interview. Therefore, he may even mention the time and say, "I know you are busy, and I don't want to take up much of your time. But I would like about five minutes." He may, on the other hand, not say anything but merely perch on the edge of his chair.

In any event, the pastor should tactfully reinterpret or interpret for the first time the time situation. This should be done in the beginning and not at the end of a conversation. He may say in answer to the statement above, "Well, I have more than five minutes, if you yourself are not too rushed to relax for a half hour and tell me what concerns you." Or if no reference has been made by the visitor as to time, he can say, "Let us talk over together our time situation. Do you have anything pressing you at this time? . . . Let me explain my situation . . . If this is not enough time, we can arrange for more later."

The hearing-out phase.—Second, the pastor then should give two-thirds to three-fourths of the time that is available to hearing the person's story. He should put all other objects of attention out of his mind and listen with his whole person. He should give himself to that person's story with complete abandon. This abandon and dedication enables the person to talk more easily and clearly.

A young man twenty years of age came to his pastor to tell him of the recent sudden change in his father's behavior. The father had been a quiet man but had gradually become explosive, demanding, and domineering. He had formerly been a considerate and understanding person, but now he was critical, harsh, and judgmental. This change had been going on for the last two years, but it had come to a breaking point and something had to be done. The son had always had a lot of fun with his father—going fishing with him, riding with him on the rural mail route where his father was a carrier, and helping out with the chores around the small farm after they got home in the afternoon. But now the father only occasionally asked the boy to go with him. The real crisis had come, however, when for the first time the father had cursed the mother. Strangely enough, the father had begun to lose interest in the church; and the pastor, too, had noticed that he had not been to church regularly.

For all of this the father's own explanation was that he is

"nervous" and "does not feel well." He said he has "the shakes" and can't sit still. He brushed these feelings off and went on to work, saying that he can't let the heebie jeebies keep him from making a living. However, the son worried about these violent temper spells and particularly about his father's driving a car and "getting all nervous."

Now the son wondered, he told the pastor, if the thing for him to do was to drop out of the local university and help his father with earning a living for the younger children. His reason for thinking this was that his father said, "Nobody around the place can be counted on to earn any money but me." With this the young man broke down into tears and wept profusely, saying, "I love my daddy, but things are getting worse and worse. I really want to keep on in school, but he seems to want me to stop and go to work. I know he does not feel well, although mother thinks he is just 'putting on' and that it's just the devil that's got into him. What am I to do?"

Detailed inquiry.—The pastor took hold of the situation to inquire into details which have been left out, overlooked, and submerged in the pressure of the suffering person's stress. Several questions are routine:

How was it the person finally decided to come to see the pastor? In the situation described above, the boy just the night before had come between his mother and father when the father had struck the mother in a fit of anger. After this he decided he needed help.

What other measures have been tried to solve the problem? In the above instance, the young man had tried doing the mail route himself for two days a week to give his father some rest. He had talked with his older brother, who is married and away from home; the brother in turn had given the father a "good talking to about his meanness" to their mother.

What other counselors has the counselee conferred with? In the above instance, the pastor was the first person outside the family to whom they had talked. They had not suggested to the father that he see a doctor. No medical diagnosis of his condition had been made.

Other questions which will give the pastor a clearer picture of the total situation may need to be asked in individual instances. Rightly asked, they can fill in the gaps in his information and help him to be more intelligently understanding and not just sentimentally concerned. The detailed inquiry should be conducted with quiet certainty and wisdom mellowed by whatever experience the pastor has had up to this moment. But its main objective is to develop a total perspective of the situation confronting the counselee and to cause the counselee to feel that the counselor really sees it as it is.

Exploration of alternatives.—As has been said before, people under pressure tend to be able to see only one alternative for solving a personal problem. Yet, one of the reasons they come to a counselor is that they are not sure of this alternative. Therefore, one of the most important things a pastor can do is to search with the counselee for additional avenues of release. In the detailed inquiry with the above described young man the pastor discovered several very important facts. The father was a veteran. His own father had had similar troubles, had left home, and had finally killed himself; he had refused help himself, and no one had sought to get help for him.

The pastor began to put these facts together with the fact that the father had never been to a medical doctor for a thorough diagnosis. Therefore, he asked the young man if he had ever thought of getting his father to go for a thorough medical examination at a medical center. The boy had not considered this. Then the pastor pointed out that it might well be that much more was wrong with his father's health than any of the family had imagined. He noted also that the family income was modest, especially with children in school. He suggested that possibly the father could get medical assistance through a veterans' hospital. These things were new angles to the inexperienced college student.

Guidance.—The pastor at this stage of an interview moves into the guidance phase. He can institute such guidance as is indicated, such as summarizing the two alternatives now available to the young man in our present interview. He can appeal for a delay on any decision to drop out of college until the young man and his family know more about the total medical situation of the father. At the same time he can urge that they get the father to go for a thorough examination. This gives something tangible to work on, something to do about the problem.

The actual outcome of this problem will be of interest to the reader. The father was discovered to be in the first phases of a degenerative disease of the central nervous system called Huntington's chorea. A heavy hereditary component in the illness explained why earlier members of the family had had such problems. Highly skilled medical counseling of the family was needed. The pastor moved along with the guidance of the doctors, but most of his pastoral care was given on a visitation basis at later times.

Spiritual support, interpretation, and instruction.—Of course, the last phase of the interview becomes not so much an interview but a fellowship of suffering and an inquiry into the meaning of this suffering. Likewise, the vital experience of prayer for guidance and understanding became not just appropriate but inevitable. The increased knowledge upon this reflective process of exploration made prayer all the more meaningful. The words of the Scriptures and the power of prayer became something far more than just panaceas recommended for a boy who was having trouble getting along with his father.

Obviously the problems which the boy brought to this interview were not solved in the sense that they were erased. Huntington's chorea is not a problem that is solved in some easy, magical way. The problems were faced, and new courage was gained for dealing with them constructively rather than destructively. New strength was gained in the pastoral interview "for the living of these days." A hasty, precipitous decision was averted, and plans were later worked out for the young man to continue his schooling. In a very real way, the pastor became a parental figure to the young college student just at the moment that the total personality of the father began to collapse with a dread disease.

The processes of interviewing are, by reason of space, only briefly considered. Note needs to be made here that skill in interviewing depends heavily upon the backdrop of information, experience, and clinical insight which the pastor has accrued through whatever years of work he has done. This can be sharpened, increased, and made more effective by intensive clinical pastoral education under supervision.

11. The Process of Multiple-Interview Counseling

Richard K. Young

A perennial question with the pastor is, "How am I going to spend my time?" If we are to emulate the life of our Master, there is no question but that we will find some time to work intensively with people who are in trouble. A very practical approach to this problem is for the pastor to decide how many hours per week he can give to working with people who seek help on a formal basis. If emergencies arise, the counselee can be called and scheduled for another hour. It is to the pastor's advantage to set aside ten or fifteen hours per week and let his people know that he is available at these times in his study. Such an arrangement would tend to eliminate some of the odd-hour calling at his home.

Many times the pastor is approached by an individual in the corridor of the educational building, immediately after church service, or even in the grocery store or post office and presented with a problem. An individual rarely states the real nature of his problem in a brief encounter, and the pastor is handicapped by not having access to the factual background. Instead of trying to deal with these problems in a brief encounter, it would be wiser for the pastor to say, "Now look, this is important. It has to do with your life, and I do not think we ought to stand here and deal with the situation in a few minutes. What time do you leave work? How about coming by my study at three o'clock on Tuesday afternoon when we can sit down and talk without interruption?"

117

A specified number of hours for office counseling will also enable the pastor to avoid becoming involved to the point of spending two or three hours with one situation. Many pastors make a mistake when they attempt to deal with a marital problem at one sitting. When a pastor is confronted with a knotty marital problem, he should spend a reasonable length of time allowing the individual to blow off steam in the immediate situation. Then he can set up formal appointments to see the individuals separately. This will give them something to look forward to and also cause them to realize that the pastor understands something of the seriousness of the problem. One pastor who spent about three hours with a marital situation had the couple kiss and make up and had prayer with them. But he was amazed to find out later that the couple separated and did not spend that night together.

Insight into a problem comes gradually, and one tires easily while discussing an intense emotional problem. Much better results will be obtained through one-hour sessions at stated intervals. Or another way of stating the same idea is that it lets a person have the opportunity to try his wings for a while. Insight must be tested in actual life situations.

When the person comes for his first appointment, it is important to remember that most people are sensitive about having to ask for help. Many of them may have toyed with the idea for quite some time before gaining courage enough to ask for help. Therefore, an irrelevant remark may be appropriate in helping to put the individual at ease before the counselor says, "I believe you wanted to see me and talk over something that you are concerned about."

The following are suggestions on how to deal with the first hour in the counseling relationship.

First, let the individual state his problem in his own way without any interruptions. Any person having a problem serious enough to want a formal appointment to talk about it will be able to talk freely during his first hour with very little guidance on the part of the counselor. A common mistake made by the beginning counselor is to start discussing the problem with the individual the moment he has stated it.

For about thirty minutes of the first interview the counselee should be left completely free for any emotional outpouring of immediate apprehension and of his own confused impressions of the cause of this condition. In case of weeping, intense agitation, and acute anxiety, he should be allowed to pour out his feelings, and no attempt should be made by the counselor to control or stop such expression. Usually when the acute phase subsides, the individual is more receptive to emotional support and reassurance.

Second, the individual may talk freely for approximately thirty minutes with very little guidance from the counselor except signs of interest through his facial expressions or perhaps a nod of his head. During this time the counselor has had opportunity to observe the emotional blockage and something of the individual's grasp of his problem and ability to deal with it.

Third, except for the depressed person, the counselor will find that he may even have some difficulty in getting control of the situation again because the person is so engrossed in ventilating his emotions. The counselor should then watch for any pauses or opportunities to "take the ball" into his own hands and "call the plays" during the remainder of this hour. If it is appropriate, he can begin by saying, "I can certainly understand how, with all the pressures you have talked about, you have come to feel the need to do something specific about your problem." Or he might use this opportunity to reassure the individual concerning the confidential nature of the interview and his willingness to help in any way possible.

Fourth, for the next fifteen to twenty minutes the counselor should proceed with a question and answer method. The first hour is the only time a question and answer method is used extensively during the counseling process. This hour is actually an evaluation conference. It is imperative that the counselor know certain facts to determine whether or not there is a need for help from other professional people. Some facts that should be known at the end of the first interview are:

Did the individual come for counseling on his own initiative or at the insistence of someone else? If the individual came upon the insistence of someone else, the counselor has the problem of creating an atmosphere in which the counselee will experience a need on his own for counseling. The pastor will frequently have an adolescent brought in by his parents, or marital situations in which the husband or wife insists that the other seek counseling. When this is the case, it is usually better to get this problem out into the open immediately and attempt to establish the right kind of a relationship.

We must face the fact that it is impossible to help any person who does not really want help. A student nurse announced to her supervisor that she was going to drop out of nursing school. The supervisor insisted that she talk with a chaplain. The student nurse was expecting the chaplain to try to talk her into staying in nursing school, but the chaplain began by saying, "I am really not interested in whether or not you stay in nursing school, but I am very much interested in helping you find yourself. Maybe you are really not fitted for nursing, and you had to come into the school to find out. Do you have any specific plans when you drop out, such as going to college or business school?" Often the individual has not thought this far at all, and this will furnish a beginning point to learn something about the individual and to establish a counseling relationship.

Has this person sought help elsewhere? What help was given, if any? The pastor soon finds that there are individuals in a community who run from one professional person to another. They stay with one person just long enough for the situation to become painful and then "take off." Recently the writer gave an appointment to an individual. In the first interview he discovered that the person had not only talked with several ministers in the community but had actually had three hours of counseling with an associate and then had failed to show up for further appointments. Upon learning this fact he said to the individual, "It seems to me that you have not stayed with any one person long enough to really get help. We want to help you in any way possible, but I must insist that you go back to the same person you started with and work with him."

How long has it been since this individual has had a medical checkup? If physical complaints are mentioned, the individual should always be referred to his family physician.

Is the emotional difficulty deep-rooted and of long duration? When did the individual first become aware of the problem? In this connection the counselor will be trying to decide whether or not there is a great deal of immaturity in this individual. The longer any emotional problem exists, the more feelings are engendered and the more involved it becomes. Actually these questions have to do with protecting the pastor's own time. If he has only a given number of hours a week in which to work intensively with individuals, he should not take on many long-term situations that will require more time and help than he is able to give. Some pastors have become involved with too many alcoholics in their communities. It is not a question of sympathy or compassion but a matter of facing realistically that the minister has responsibilities to all groups in the church.

In the evaluation process the counselor should watch for any suicidal tendencies that might be present. Is the person mildly or severely depressed? Does he seem to be overwhelmed by his problem? Any individual either mildly or severely depressed is always potentially capable of committing suicide. If the counselor suspects suicidal tendencies, he may say to the counselee, "Have you ever felt like just simply giving up because of the pressures?" The counselor should remember that rapid loss of weight and the inability to return to sleep after waking in the early hours of the morning are prominent symptoms. Difficulty in going to sleep at night does not apply here nearly so much as awakening around two or three o'clock in the early morning and not being able to go back to sleep. Any time the pastor suspects suicidal tendencies he should refer the person immediately to his family physician.

The counselor should evaluate the person's religious resources in terms of his home background, conversion experience, and present church relationship. By all means this should be done in a noncondemnatory manner. The counselor may simply say, "Since I am a minister, you naturally would expect me to want to know whether or not you have a vital relationship to God. We will certainly need and want his help as we discuss what you are facing in life."

Examples of First Interviews

The pastor must decide during the first hour in every instance whether he is going to counsel with the individual himself or refer the person to some other source of help. The following examples are actual problems that were presented during a first interview and contain all the facts that were known before a disposition of the case was made.

A thirty-eight-year-old woman stated her problem as: "My mind is split. Part of the time I think I am one person, and part of the time I think I'm another." The counselee went on to say that she was terribly mixed up. She seemed to be very much divided. There were times when she felt like she was the devil and wanted to burn her husband and even her children. There were times when she felt that she was saved and times when she felt that she was lost. She would say to herself, "God loves me," and then she would say, "Oh, no, there is no God." This sort of conflict dominated her entire conversation. She also said she had terribly vulgar and evil thoughts so wicked that she couldn't even express them. She was afraid of something she might do and felt that something had to be done for her.

Other facts which the counselee related revealed that she is the youngest child in a family of four sisters and two brothers. Her family quarreled frequently, but she had done her best not to be the kind of person who is always fussing and quarreling. She did not come out of a religious background, but her husband's background was very religious. She felt that she was closer to her mother than to her father.

The counselee was converted about three and a half years ago in a revival meeting under an evangelist. She talked at great length about this experience. She said she had many doubts when she started to be baptized because she didn't have the same experience that some of the other girls had. After her conversion she became very much interested in the Bible and read it through almost completely. She said, "That's when my trouble started." In another revival meeting at a later time she felt that she should have gone up and given herself to the Lord again but did not. As a result, she felt that "the Spirit of the Lord just came out of me, and the Lord turned his back on me, and I have been in this terrible conflict ever since." She discussed at great length the fear that she might commit sin against the Holy Spirit. This person came on her own initiative and felt desperately that something must be done for her. When asked if she had sought help elsewhere, she said that she had seen a psychiatrist three months ago. The psychiatrist told her that she needed to be hospitalized, but she did not agree. She felt that her problem was "a religious one, but the psychiatrist felt like it wasn't."

The divided self, the intense feelings toward her husband and children, and the compulsive thinking about having committed the unpardonable sin all tell us that this individual is deeply disturbed. The pastor can render a signal service by catching these symptoms early and getting the person to specialized help before he or she breaks completely. You will note that this illness manifested itself in religious terminology. Many times a pastor, because of his religious role, can persuade these people to get help when they will not listen to a doctor. The counselor said to this individual, "All of us are subject to the pressures of living day by day, and an emotional disturbance is no respecter of persons. To get emotionally sick is no more reflection than to get physically ill. God understands that you are under tremendous tension. There are people who are trained to work with your difficulty just as there are doctors who are trained to set a broken leg. You would not hesitate to have your leg set if it were broken. I would like to make an appointment for you with a psychiatrist friend of mine."

A thirty-five-year-old man, a high school graduate, stated his problem this way: "I tire easily; I just seem to go down as the day goes down. Then there are times when my heart seems to beat faster than it ought to, and I have mild pains in my chest and back. Sometimes at the end of the day I have a headache, and I believe all of this is coming from tension. A friend of mine said something about counseling he had had and said I ought to come to see you."

This man had been married for ten years and had three children. He grew up in a family of five children, one of whom died in childhood. There are two boys and two girls living, and the patient is the younger boy, with one sister younger than he.

He grew up in a Moravian family but became a Baptist after his marriage. His wife had been a Baptist, although she did not go to church very much until after they were married. Now she is regular and very active. He, too, takes an active part.

The counselee stated further that when he was first married he lived for over two years with his in-laws. He seemed to make a real point out of the fact that he had never had any trouble with any of the in-laws. He now lives across the road from a brother-in-law and a sister-in-law in a house of his own. He said, "I feel hemmed in by them, but we do not have any trouble with each other. However, I feel that they are criticizing me at times. My wife and I don't get to visit *my* people as much as I'd like to, for she does not care about going."

The counselee said he was not too happy in his job and spoke of how hard he has to work. He said he felt that the company for which he works was not entirely fair with him and that he did not feel secure in his job, although he had been with them for seven years. He is afraid that they might get mad and fire him for the least little thing.

He said the only help he had had was from a preacher who "loaned me some books on psychology to read."

In this particular case physical symptoms are prominent in the problem. Many times the pastor may be tempted to go ahead and counsel with a person presenting physical complaints, especially when there are facts pointing in the direction of emotional tension. The pastor should never succumb to this temptation but should always refer the patient to his family physician. At the same time, a return appointment can be made for counseling.

This young man's physical examination was negative, and he was seen for nine hours of counseling. It is interesting that his stated problem had to do with tiredness and physical complaints when his real problem was related to his inability both to accept his hostile feelings and to stand up for his own rights. In the counseling process he relived many of his childhood experiences and was able to express a good deal of hostility toward his in-laws.

He came to see that his Christian faith demanded honesty and responsibility in his relationships more than it called for denying his real feelings. Getting some of his hoarded emotions out helped him to understand better why his in-laws reacted to him as they did. Thus he was able to establish a more mature relationship to God and his family and to become an individual in his own right.

A fifty-one-year-old farmer stated his problem as, "I've lost my salvation." He showed considerable anxiety, which was manifested by wringing his hands, running his hands through his hair, and burying his face in his hands as he talked. He accounted for the "loss of his salvation" by two actions: he had "signed" for his daughter to get married too young and he had "signed" for his son to join the army. The onset of his condition came about two months ago on a night when he was up because of inability to sleep. He stated that not only did he feel that he was unsaved but that it was impossible for him to be saved. The counselee continued to talk round and round like a broken record about his salvation and how it was connected to what he had done to his son and daughter.

When asked about his sleeping habits, the counselee said he had no difficulty in going to sleep but for the last few weeks he had continuously waked up after two or three hours and had had difficulty going back to sleep. He had not sought help elsewhere. In discussing his religious background, he said that he joined the church when he was nine years of age, grew up in a Christian home, and had been "an active churchgoer all of his life."

Some ministers have been known to try and deal with a problem of this nature by reading verses of Scripture in an attempt to convince the individual that he is saved. Any person who is depressed and anxious and who has one idea dominating his mind has an emotional difficulty that is deep-rooted. A few positive statements are certainly in order to reassure the individual. The counselor might say, "The very fact that you are upset over your salvation is evidence that you have a better self. But at the same time you are depressed and sick, and this type of thinking is only a symptom. God understands this much better than I do. You need specialized help for this difficulty." Remember also that the depressed person is potentially capable of suicide. This individual was referred to a psychiatrist.

A fourteen-year-old boy was brought to the counselor by his pastor and his father with a stated problem of delinquency. The boy had broken into a store in a small village, and the community was shocked when he was apprehended, because he had such a good reputation. He had a paper route in the village and was a regular attendant at Sunday school.

The story that finally came out in the first interview is as follows: "I had a fist fight with another boy who made slurring statements about my father because of his drinking. The next day I forgot to do something that my father told me to do, and he beat me more than he should have. I do not know why I broke in the store."

One can see from this brief record that a delinquent is not born a delinquent. This boy had obviously gotten into a state of rebellion in relation to his father. But the real reason for presenting this situation is to illustrate that the counselor often has to create an atmosphere or environment in which the individual will talk. The counselor talked to the pastor and the father for a few minutes and then took the boy into his office.

The boy sat down in the chair and looked at the counselor in a very sullen manner. The counselor then said, "Now look, Bob, I know you are not here because you want to be here. You're here because your father and your pastor brought you. You are humiliated, and you are scared. I got in trouble two or three times when I was growing up, and I know a little something about how you feel. Now if you do want to talk some, I will promise you one thing, and that is I will not tell your pastor or your father anything you do not give me permission to say."

Any time a person is "brought" for counseling, the counselor attempts to create an atmosphere whereby the individual will speak out on his own. This is not always possible, particularly with adolescents. Here the counselor attempted to establish direct relationship to the boy apart from his relationship to the pastor and the father.

Mrs. A., a thirty-four-year-old woman, stated her problem as a marriage difficulty. When she was seated in the office, it was obvious that she was extremely nervous, as evidenced by her facial expressions and the clasping and unclasping of her hands. Her first statement was, "I am anxious to do something about our marriage. We have separated three times in the past eleven years. My mother and family have told me that I cannot come home any more; so if we separate again, I have nowhere to go."

Mrs. A. is the mother of three children and is expecting another one in three months. In her parental home she is the youngest of four children with two boys and one girl older than she. All are married except one brother. She is nine years younger than the next youngest sister. Her mother is living at the present time in another city. She said that she does not have a very good relationship to her mother and never has had. "She was always strict on me, and everything had to be just right." She stated that she felt closer to her father than to any other member of the family. "He was more sympathetic and cared more about me than any other member of my family." Her father is not living now; he died about three years ago.

Mrs. A. said she was embarrassed to talk about the problems in her marriage but she knew something must be done. "We just can't seem to agree on anything any more. I even hate to pick up after him around the house any more. Isn't that silly?"

The counselee was referred by her local physician who, in

seeing her during her pregnancy, noted her nervous tension. When she told him of the unhappiness in her marriage, he suggested counseling.

Closing the Interview

A discussion on how to close the interview in the first hour of the counseling relationship is now in order. To summarize, the counselee has been allowed to state his problems in his own way without any interruption for approximately thirty minutes. The counselor showed his interest through facial expressions, a nod of the head, etc. The next ten to fifteen minutes were used to gain additional facts so that a conclusion might be reached concerning the disposition that should be made regarding the case in question. If there is ever any doubt, always work in co-operation with the family physician. The final ten to fifteen minutes of the first hour should be used for positive statements to the counselee regarding possibilities of help with his problem. In the case of the marital problem presented above, the pastor would plan to continue counseling with this person as well as to keep in touch with her physician.

If further counseling is indicated, the last part of the hour should be used to structure the relationship. The counseling process should be explained and illustrated with material that came out during the first thirty minutes.

The counselor might say, for example, in the case of Mrs. A., "Frankly, I think we need to spend several hours on this problem. You did not get this way in a day's time, and certainly it will take some time to gain insight and understanding into some of the reasons you respond as you do in your marriage. All of us have ways of responding to every life situation we get into. Something on the street that would upset me might not upset you at all. As you talk out your life experiences, the two of us will be going along together, looking and trying to gain understanding into the reasons for your actions.

"Do you remember saying a little while ago that when you

were growing up in your own family your mother was an excellent housekeeper and you were taught that everything should be in its proper place? Then a little later you said that there was a constant irritation in your marriage because of your husband's sloppy behavior around the house and that you are always having to pick up behind him. Now, when you put these two things together, although they are a long way apart in time, can you see how this type of thing would irritate you much more than it would some other person who came up in a home where things were not so orderly?

"This is the type of thing we will be doing as you talk out your life for several hours in the counseling relationship. We shall attempt to get as much understanding as we can as to why you respond in certain ways. As you do this, you will ventilate your emotions, and you will also come to see and understand yourself more clearly and more objectively. If you would like to come back for further interviews, I shall be happy to work with you."

An appointment can then be made for the same time a week later. The counselor needs to take a confident attitude, but he will not promise too much in the way of superficial reassurance as to what may be gained through the counseling process. The counselor may suggest, if the situation is appropriate, that the individual may experience a good bit of relief during the next two or three days because of having done something specific about his problems. This relief, however, is only temporary, and the counselee should be warned not to become discouraged if this feeling does not last until the next appointment.

The counselee who presented the marital problem described above returned for six additional interviews. At the same time, her husband was also seen by another counselor. In the following chapter the recurrent problems of longer-term counseling are described and illustrated with the remaining interviews between Mrs. A. and her counselor.

12. Recurrent Problems of Longer-Term Counseling

Richard K. Young

According to a study made in the out-patient pastoral counseling service at the North Carolina Baptist Hospital, more counselees are lost or fail to return at the end of the first hour than at any other time in the counseling process. This fact underscores the crucial importance of the first hour in counseling and accounts for the extended treatment of its management in chapter 11.

Space does not permit a presentation of seven recorded hours of counseling with one individual, which would be ideal. The interviews that are presented here contain the basic facts that came out during each hour. Even though this limits the value of the case material, one can observe from the facts alone something of the process of counseling as it takes place from one hour to the next through the nature of the material that comes out each hour. In other words, the facts will show some progression in terms of the depth of the material as well as the insights the counselee gains as she relates the facts to her present life situation.

The Second Hour

Mrs. A. was neatly dressed and on time for her appointment. Her first remark was, "I am feeling a little bit better and certainly hope that something can be done to help us with our problems." Still, she was quite nervous during the interview as evidenced by the movements of her hands and her facial expressions. She said that she believed that she talked to her husband a little more during the past week—not that she was doing it purposely—but she thought she was able to talk with him a little more freely. The counselee did not continue to talk voluntarily at this point. After a slight pause the counselor said, "Well, where would you like to start today?" Mrs. A. replied, "What would you like for me to tell you?" The counselor said, "You can either talk further about your marriage, or you may go back and tell me something about your home background when you were a child."

The counselee then started talking about her relationships in her family during the time she was growing up. She said she was the "baby" in the family and was nine years younger than her next oldest sister. She had the feeling that her mother had hoped the family was complete by the time she came along, and she has always felt she was somewhat of a burden. She said the older brothers and sisters were either already married when she was born or were married soon thereafter. The only one in the family she felt close to was her father. The sister just older than she made life miserable for her. This sister married a wealthy man and has everything she wants from a financial standpoint.

Mrs. A. spent a good deal of time telling how this sister had always been the boss of the family. She was extremely good looking when she was growing up, and everyone said she had inherited all the looks of the family. Mrs. A. expressed considerable feelings toward her sister and her mother during the hour. "I always wore clothes that had belonged to her when I was growing up. She still looks upon me as an object of charity and sends me clothes that she is tired of wearing. Her gifts to my children on birthdays are never toys but always clothes. She never brings the gifts directly to my house but leaves them with a brother of mine and has him call me to pick up the gifts."

The counselee said that her father was the only one that had ever shown any love toward her, and after her mother forbade her to come home, her father used to come by and see her. "He was crazy about my children, and I felt he came to see the children more than he did to see me." She wept profusely as she told how "he kept these visits a secret—never told the other members of the family that he was visiting me."

Mrs. A. expressed emotion from time to time and talked freely during this hour. An appointment was made for the same hour the following week.

The counselee asked at the beginning of the above interview for some direction as to where to start. It takes several hours for an individual to understand what is expected in counseling. Therefore, the counselor will be explaining or structuring the relationship from time to time but should do so only as the need arises.

The second hour should be a continued catharsis and experience of being understood. Very few individuals will have difficulty talking during the second hour. The counselor should be as intent on following the feelings of the individual as he is on remembering the facts. He should keep the conversation moving through showing an interest and through nondirective responses. Using such expressions as "I see," "Uh-huh," and "Is that right?"; repeating the last phrase of a sentence; or even saying, "In other words, if I understand you correctly, this is what you are saying . . . " will aid the counselee to continue talking. Actually the counselor is not contributing anything to the conversation. Such expressions do not interrupt the associational process that is taking place in the mind of the person. By all means, the counselor should be cautioned not to get into the habit of using one of these phrases continuously. It can be very frustrating to have someone grunt every time you finish a sentence.

The individual should be kept talking during the second hour. The only time the counselor should get into the situation in a positive manner is when the counselee dips into an important area and glosses over it. When someone sticks a nail in his foot, it must be disinfected from the bottom of the hole outward. There is no easy way to do this. A painful spot in the emotions must be taken out and looked at from all sides, and a philosophy must be formed concerning the experience. Then, when it is put back in, it will not fester and cause trouble. To do this requires that the counselor follow the counselee's feelings very closely. He may want to interrupt with something like, "You said a minute ago that you felt your mother did not understand you. Could you explain that a little more?" This serves to keep a person in the area of importance and helps clean out the emotionally painful areas. It may also help the counselee to see some of the things which may be more important than he realizes.

The most important thing in the whole counseling process is the relationship between the counselor and the counselee. The counselor can be too nondirective or too directive and strain this relationship. Of course, if the counselor loses the relationship completely, he has lost his opportunity to help the person. If it becomes necessary to let the counselee struggle with the telling process for his own good, this may threaten the relationship. Nevertheless, the counselor can consciously rebuild the relationship toward the end of the hour.

The second most important element in counseling is the catharsis or cleansing process that takes place as the individual pours out his story and feelings to another. Hence the counselor does not use a question and answer method, nor does he attempt to pull information out of the individual until he is ready to tell it. Real catharsis takes place only as the individual shares his feelings in a voluntary relationship. The pastor's role as a representative of the Christian community lends depth to his relationship as a counselor when the catharsis is prompted by an awareness of sin. Likewise, his courage of acceptance and forgiveness is used by the Holy Spirit to give the courage of confession to the counselee.

Therefore, the second hour should be used to keep the individual talking as much as possible without placing a strain upon the relationship. The counselee should see the counselor as going alongside him in this spiritual journey.

Thus far we have seen Mrs. A. as a person who has felt rejected by her mother since early childhood and who at the same time is carrying hostility toward a pretty sister who bossed her around. She felt close to her father in growing up but has no satisfactory relationship with any other member of the family.

The counselor cannot help drawing some conclusions even in the early hours of counseling, but he should always have an open end to his thinking. He should never get his mind fixed on his conclusions to the point of getting blind. It takes many facts pointing in one general direction before a pattern in a personality can be established.

The Third Hour

The counselee was on time for her appointment. As she took her seat, the nervous mannerisms noted in the two previous interviews were still present. Mrs. A began by saying, "I think I feel a little better, but things at home are about the same." The counselee then spent about fifteen minutes telling how she had never been able to talk with anyone about her marital problem. The counselor was the first person she had ever really tried to confide in. She shared her concern over the fact that she had never been open and honest in expressing her feelings to her husband and ended up by saying, "He doesn't understand." She also said that she didn't feel any members of her family had any real interest in her problem.

At this point in the interview there was a long pause and then Mrs. A. said, "I just don't know what else to talk about. I was thinking on the way over here today that I have told you all I know. You just ask me some questions, and I will be glad to answer them about anything you ask." The counselor then proceeded to restructure the counseling relationship by saying that he would be glad to ask questions, but actually this would hinder Mrs. A. from remembering many small details. The counselor then spent about five minutes summarizing all that he knew about the counselee thus far and suggested that she might describe in more detail some of her relationships to her husband and her family. This allowed her to go in any direction that she chose.

Mrs. A. then brought up again some of the times that she had separated from her husband and described her feelings in living with her family while they were separated. "They feel that I have taken advantage of them. They said my daddy had done more for me than he should have." She then described with much feeling how her mother declared she could never come back again if she and her husband separated. For four or five years she didn't go home again, and when she did it was because of her father's death. Since her father's death, she has been with members of the family on one or two occasions but has not felt wholly at ease with them.

Toward the end of the interview she again became emotional as she complained that all her life was a drudgery. She and her husband had hardly any friends and never went out or participated in any social life at all. Putting her head down on her knees, she sobbed as she said she wanted more than anything in the world the love and affection of her husband.

The counselor gave support at the end of the interview by praising the counselee for the good job she was doing in expressing herself and making herself understood. An appointment was made for the next week at the same time.

The main thing to notice in the above interview is what this writer chooses to call the "bogged-down" stage in counseling. Some people naturally tend to be more talkative than others, but in every counseling situation this problem will arise. Usually in the third, fourth, or fifth hour the counseling process will need a definite restructure. What actually happens is that the individual has talked off the surface material and is getting closer to the defensive mechanisms within his personality. The counselee realizes consciously or unconsciously that he must go more deeply into his feelings, or he will continue to repeat himself. It is always painful for him to drop his defenses so that he sees himself realistically. To do so means to take responsibility for his actions.

The counselor will be tempted to get into a question and answer method during this "bogged-down" stage. In the above interview the counselee was sincere when she said, "You go ahead and ask me some questions," because the relationship was good. She probably would have answered anything that the counselor could have asked. If the counselor allows himself to get into a question and answer method at this point, he will defeat the counseling process.

Again, the counselor will be tempted to start interpreting and giving advice. He does not have a wise enough perspective in the third hour to start interpretation, and counseling is not giving advice. The over-all objective of the counselor is to help the individual find himself, to discover his inner potentialities, and to be able to make his life decisions more adequately.

Furthermore, the counselor who is acquainted with the non-directive school of thought may tend to keep silent too much during the "bogged-down" stage and cause a strained relationship. It is true that the counselee has talked freely for nearly three hours. Some counselees may even speak up and say, "I am talking too much. After all, I came to you for help; I am going to let you talk some." This is no place for the counselor to remain silent or to repeat, "So then you feel like I should talk some." If the counselor conceives of counseling as a spiritual pilgrimage, now is the time to let the counselee know the counselor's role in the relationship. There are several ways to get through this "bogged-down" stage.

First, the counselor can summarize all the facts that have come out in past interviews. He might begin by saying, "Well, let's see what we have been talking about since you have been coming." After summing up in detail all the facts known thus far, the counselor may conclude by saying, "You have talked out all these facts, but I know hardly anything about your mother, or your school adjustment, or your social adjustment as you were growing up." He might say, "I wonder why you have not talked in this particular area." If the counselor does a good job of re-membering the facts in details, he will find that the summarizing will help to deepen his relationship to the counselee. Some counselees may speak up and ask, "How could you remember all that? I know you are seeing other people." The fact that the counselor remembers helps the counselee to feel like a person who is worth something in the eyes of the counselor.

Second, the counselor can give new direction to the counseling process through association. The use of word-association has been found helpful in situations where the individual had more than average difficulty in continuing to talk. A standard list of words for the counselee to respond to is not necessary. The counselor simply says to the counselee, "How about dropping your head back on the chair, closing your eyes, and start-ing to say words for me." Since the person has already asked the counselor to ask questions, he will usually be co-operative. The counselor warns the counselee that after he says a good number of words he will tend to stop or block. The counselor explains further that the first fifteen to twenty-five words will not be sig-nificant, and if he stops and opens his eyes when he blocks, the whole process will be defeated.

A further requirement is that the words be said with the same speed or rhythm with which the counselee begins. The coun-selor then records on paper at least two or three letters of each word as the counselee says them. At each blockage the coun-selor dots with his pencil by the word with the same rhythm the counselee was using. The majority of counselees will stop in the middle of this experiment and start talking. If this happens, the counselor should simply lean back in his chair and forget the whole procedure. The purpose has already been accom-plished since this was an attempt to help the individual get started talking again.

If the counselee does reach seventy-five to one hundred words, the counselor should then examine what he has on paper. He should not only examine the words that were blocked on but should also note the words that were repeated from three to five times. He should then take these words and ask the counselee to "rack his brain" to see if anything comes to his mind through these words. Invariably the counselee picks up new trains of thought that will furnish material right on to the next hour. Words repeated in association with one another will always lead to material of concern to the counselee.

A final suggestion on how to get through this "bogged-down" stage in counseling has to do with sharing on the part of the counselor. He need not be afraid to share his own experience, but he must be careful how he does this. He will let the person know that he is human, but he will also be sure the material he is sharing is used in an objective manner. For example, he may see close to the surface hostility which is making it diffi-cult for the counselee to talk. The counselor might say, "I don't know about you, but I know in my own case in growing up there were times when I thought my father was showing par-tiality toward my brother. He may not have meant it that way, but I still felt that he was partial, and it did influence my atti-tude at that time."

Many people feel that they are the only ones that ever felt a certain way. When they find that the counselor has experienced some of the same emotions they are struggling with at the mo-ment, an atmosphere is created which tends to free the person of his blockage. The best way for the counselor to tell whether or not he is sharing with a purpose is to ask himself if he is getting satisfaction out of what he is telling. If the counselor enjoys telling his experience and takes much of the time from the counselee, perhaps he should exchange chairs! The kind of sharing recommended here is specific, to the point, and not the kind that goes into great detail and description. There is nothing wrong with the counselor's taking responsibility for the coun-seling relationship at times, so long as in the over-all process he gradually withdraws and leaves the individual standing on his own two feet and not dependent on him for guidance in every small matter.

The Fourth Hour

Mrs. A. was on time for her appointment, was more neatly dressed than usual, and seemed much calmer than in previous inter-views. She exhibited fewer nervous movements with her hands than she had before. She began the interview this time by saying, "I am amazed at the way I have been talking to you." (Mrs. A. had a brighter expression than in any of the other interviews.) The coun-selor responded to this statement by saying, "How do you mean?" The counselee then proceeded to tell how all her life she had never been able to confide in anyone. She said she had never experienced a real companionship with her mother. The next oldest sister "bossed her around." "There are some things you simply don't talk to your father about when you are a girl." She also said that she hadn't found the really close companionship that she had expected to find in her marriage.

Mrs. A. then looked at the counselor and said, "I believe I feel closer to you than I ever have to any person." The counselor's response was, "All of us live in a shell to some extent, some more than others. Any time we bare our souls to another individual, we tend to feel much closer to that person. After all, you have shared a portion of your life with me so far as your confidence is concerned. Do the feelings you are having now remind you in any way of how you might have felt at one time or another toward your father?"

The counselee became emotional at this point and told how much closer she felt toward her father than to any other member of the family. There were times when she wanted to get closer to him, but for some reason or another she was unable to do so. Mrs. A. said she believed it was because of her mother and sister that she was unable to confide completely in her father.

Mrs. A. wept during the remainder of the interview. She told how she tried to restrain her emotions even at her father's funeral. She described in detail many of the circumstances connected with her father's funeral, weeping all the while. She was left out of the family council and was not allowed to have any part in making decisions concerning the funeral. She said that her sister just older than she had her way about everything. Though her father has been dead for several years, she still has feelings of missing him very much. When she thinks of him, she works very hard around the house in an attempt to get it off her mind. "He was the only one who ever showed any love toward me."

The conversation shifted to her husband, and Mrs. A. said she had not received the love and affection from her husband that she had expected out of the marital relationship. She thought that when children came along they might help to cement the bond between her and her husband. A few weeks after the birth of their second child, a girl, she saw a letter from his girl friend. She then realized why he had been so persistent in wanting to name the baby girl by a certain name. The name he had suggested was the first name of the girl friend he had been "running around with" during her pregnancy. Mrs. A held out for another name, however, and her daughter was not named after his girl friend. She said that she had not revealed this information about her husband to him until they had started coming for counseling.

The counselor asked Mrs. A. at the end of the interview if she had any better understanding of her feelings toward him. Her remark was, "I can see that I have not been sharing my inner feelings enough with my husband, and if I expect him to share with me, I must share with him." The counselor agreed with Mrs. A. and then made another appointment one week later at the same hour.

Mrs. A.'s remark about the closeness which she felt toward the counselor is indicative of transference or dependency feelings developing in the counselee. (Mrs. A.'s pregnancy probably accounts for her openness in expressing these feelings.) As the counselor suggested to Mrs. A., any time a person pours out his life to another he is going to feel much closer to that individual. The intensity of these feelings varies with each individual case and is governed largely by how well the person's emotional needs have been met in the past and are being met in the present. These feelings usually appear in the fourth, fifth, or sixth hour in the counseling relationship.

The counseling relationship is more secure now; possibly for the first time in her life Mrs. A. has experienced a deep interpersonal relationship with another human being. She has known understanding, love, and forgiveness from another member of the human race. Up until now she has been so preoccupied with her problem that she has hardly been aware of the counselor, except that she has found someone who seems to understand.

From this point on, the counselee's relationship to the counselor can become intensely important in her life. She appreciates what has been done for her and will tend to become dependent upon this experience. Transference, as it is called by the psychoanalysts, or strong dependence, must be handled correctly by the counselor, or else he will do lasting damage to the individual. The reason for this is very simple: any time a person is hurt by another person he is a little slower to make new relationships. This is true even in friendly social contacts. Therefore, the more intense the relationship, the more intense the damage.

What actually happens is that the deep feelings of a child toward his parents become attached in an irrational manner to the counselor. The problem involved, of course, is that the counselee is no longer a child, and if the counselor is of the opposite sex, these feelings can become more difficult to deal with. Hence it is important that the counselor deal with these feelings when they arise. Evidence of transference may be observed in the counselee's failure to bring out material which shows him in an unfavorable light, in his more frequent requests for advice, or in his showing an unusual interest in the counselor's private life. In the case of a woman who has a male counselor, it can be seen in her dress, tone of voice, or attempts to be more alluring. Between men and male counselors it may be expressed negatively in hostility and aggression, usually of a passive nature in the same manner as that of a boy toward his father.

Occasionally the counselor will observe false cures which are due to transference. For example, an individual who has some physical symptoms may lose those symptoms, perhaps in the fourth, fifth, or sixth hour. If the counselor attempts to move the appointments further apart, he will note that when the person returns the next time the symptoms have come back again. The following suggestions may be helpful in dealing with transference or dependency feelings:

First, the counselor will need to recognize what is taking place as early as possible. He will deal with these feelings as honestly and understandingly as possible. Since these feelings come as a surprise to the counselee and since they are a rather strange experience, more of the responsibility rests on the counselor. The subject should be approached with caution, but it should be faced. Especially is this true if the process of counseling is being blocked.

Second, it is possible to approach the subject from the negative standpoint. The writer was seeing a student nurse who always came to her appointments dressed in her uniform. For the fifth interview she wore a street dress. As the counselor sat down to start the hour, he said, "You know I forgot to tell you this in the beginning, but it is my job as a counselor to represent reality to you to the best of my ability. When I do this, it may many times bring up strong feelings in you. I expect that there have been times when you have wanted to pick up a book and throw it at me. What about this?"

The counselee was puzzled. Finally she said, "No, I haven't felt *that* way," and added in a very hesitant manner, "I have wondered if I did not feel too strong the other way." The counselor then said, "That is wonderful. That's the best thing I've heard yet. You mean, then, you do have some positive feelings toward me. Do you remember telling me, about two hours ago, how as a child you went through the living room a thousand times on your way upstairs? You said you looked over at your father sitting in a chair reading a paper and longed to go over and kiss him good night, but you never remember kissing him in all you life." Of course, the counselee remembered this and was able to see how these unexpressed feelings were now coming out in a relationship in which she felt understood.

Third, the counselor should remember that these feelings are not always brought out into the open and discussed. As has already been stated, it depends upon the individual and his background as to how intense these feelings become. It is only as these feelings get in the way of the growth of the counselee that they should be dealt with and discussed. Then, too, the more experience the counselor gains, the less he is likely to manage the total counseling relationship in such a way as to create dependency.

Fourth, the more responsibility the counselor takes for the counseling relationship, the more dependent the counselee will become. This is especially true if he is too directive and attempts to give advice and interpretation too readily.

Fifth, the scheduling of appointments may be used to meet the dependency situation. The counselor may praise the individual who is getting too dependent and say, "You are doing a good job now. What do you think about 'trying your wings' a bit and going an extra week this time?" Gradually moving the appointments further apart will help to break the dependency relationship. However, if this is poorly timed, it may cause a regression in the counselee. Well-timed interruptions can also be used by the counselor.

The feelings of the counselor should also be considered. Any time a counselor is allowed to "walk around" on the inside of another person's life, he tends to feel closer to that person. These feelings are called "countertransference" by the psychoanalyst. Such emotions will arise in some degree in every situation; one is bound to be more interested in a person for having known him. The feelings are intensified if the counselor has unmet emotional needs which he has not allowed himself to acknowledge. He may even encourage an attachment on the part of the counselee which is actually a form of idolatry; a relationship of this kind may be used to build his own ego. Of course, if the counselor has had any training at all, he realizes that the counselee's feelings are the same as those of a child toward a parent. He may hurt others and be hurt himself if he lacks understanding at this point.

When the counselor finds himself looking forward to a counselee's appointment or refusing to represent reality when he should for fear of hurting the counselee, he will be wise to deal with the situation honestly and openly. Otherwise, the counselee will recognize the situation and tend to manipulate the counselor by staying longer than the time allotted or calling him between appointments.

As the individual begins to trust the relationship, his unmet emotional needs from his parental background will be transferred to the counselor. How the pastor deals with these misaddressed emotions is a matter of basic ethics. The teaching of Jesus against overdependence on religious leaders (Matt. 23) can be used to help the counselee redirect his energies toward others and ultimately toward God. The counselor takes up his own cross, foregoes his desire to be ministered to, and in the name of the Lord Jesus Christ ministers instead.

Every pastor should be aware of this psychological principle whether he is in a counseling relationship or not. There are always people whose emotional needs are not being met and who will develop an unhealthy dependence on others if they are allowed to do so. A widow to whom the pastor ministered during a bereavement may need to ask him questions concerning her boys. A Sunday school teacher or music director may have more business than is necessary to talk over with the pastor. Rather than getting angry with these people, he should deal with them gently but firmly.

The Fifth and Sixth Hours

Interview Five: Mrs. A. had difficulty in getting a parking place and was fifteen minutes late in beginning this interview. It was evident from the beginning that she was more free of her physical tension and more relaxed than she had been during any previous time. She was elated as she described in detail how she and her husband had argued during the past week over one of the children. They were able to sit down later, talk out the problem, and come to an agreement between themselves. She said they had never been able to do this before, and she now believed it was because she always "clammed up." She then became more serious and said, "I have been doing a lot of thinking since our last two interviews, and I don't know whether you will agree or not, but I know what my trouble is. I had never realized before that I wasn't close to anyone when I was growing up. I never had anyone that I really thought loved me. Now I can see what I have been doing. All of my actions have been attempts to get love and attention." The counselor said, "How do you think this has affected your relationship to your husband and family?" "Maybe," said Mrs. A., "that is the reason why I have been so passive when I talk to my husband and family and fail to stand up for my rights. Maybe I was afraid I would lose what little love they did have for me."

The counselee felt that she had taken an important step during the past week when she refused to go to her sister's birthday party. Her sister had called her at the last minute as usual, and Mrs. A. simply had said that she was sorry but she had already made other plans. The counselor responded, "I believe you told me earlier your sister is nine years older than you. Let me ask you a question. How do you suppose a nine-year-old feels when a baby is born into the home and demands almost all the time of the mother for at least the first year?" The counselee said, "Well, I have never thought about that before. Do you suppose she started resenting me or was jealous of me from the early beginning?" The counselor said, "It could be. You know, the more understanding we get of another person, the more we can look out at the world through their eyes and relate to them without getting emotionally upset." The counselee said, "You know, I didn't brood over the birthday party as much as I have over such things in the past." The counselee said further, "I am going to continue to think about these things." An appointment was made at the same time a week later.

Interview Six: Two weeks intervened between this interview and the previous one because at the last minute Mrs. A. could not get a baby sitter. The counselee said that little had happened to her since the last visit because she had been so busy doing her house work and helping the ladies from the church fix up a new Sunday school department. She said that her church life meant a great deal to her. She told how, when she was a little girl, she had been to a Presbyterian Sunday school, but her parents did not attend church. Several years ago, following her husband's injury in an automobile accident, a Baptist minister visited with him and talked to the two of them. Later, when they moved to their present location, she joined the local Baptist church and her husband joined with her. The counselee then said, "You know, I felt closer to God in the worship service last Sunday than I ever have in my life."

Mrs. A. spoke of how close it was to the time for her baby to be born and mentioned the fact that neither her sister nor her mother had called her or contacted her in any way. She said neither of them had ever helped her when any of her children were born. "In fact," she said, "my mother has not been in my home to see me but one time since I have been married." The counselee said that she had come to the place where she was accepting this better than she had in the past. However, she did show some emotion as she spoke of how they did not care for her.

The counselee said things had been going well at home and showed real feelings of satisfaction about this. She said she had actually made a suggestion to her husband about a business deal he wanted to make and also about buying a lot, and he had accepted her suggestion. "This was the first time I have ever done anything like this since we have been married." An appointment was made for the following week at the same time.

It is clearly evident from the last two interviews that the counselee is making a better home adjustment and has lost most of the tension which caused the doctor to refer her in the first place. It is also obvious in the fifth interview that the counselor has become more conscious of interpretation. When to interpret and when not to is probably one of the most difficult problems in counseling. One cardinal rule to remember is that the counselor never be dogmatic with interpretations. He cannot force insight. The counselee may accept what the counselor has to say and still not gain insight emotionally or have the material "come alive," so to speak.

Every counselor should say to the counselee early in the relationship, "Don't accept anything I have to say unless it 'rings a bell' with you. After all, we are dealing with your life and your mind. If you don't see what we are talking about, it will not mean anything to you." If the counselor should say to the counselee, "Do you see any relationship between what we are talking about now and what you were saying last week?" and get a negative answer, he should go on to something else, as the counselee is not ready for this insight yet. In regard to interpretation, it is a good idea for the counselor to use such wording as, "It seems to me . . . ," or, "I don't know; have you thought of this . . . ?" or, "Why did you respond this way in this situation and another way in the other situation?"

When the pastor is preaching to a congregation, he hopes that he is presenting truth in a way that will be helpful. But when he is dealing with one individual in a counseling relationship, there is no excuse for generalizations and dogmatic attitudes. The counselor will remember that he is going alongside this individual, and if Christianity has anything to say to this life situation, it ought to be applied specifically.

The Seventh Hour

The counselee, Mrs. A., was on time and neatly dressed. She smiled frequently throughout the interview. She said she would be glad when the baby came, now that the time was so close. She mentioned again the improvement of things at home and said, "Things seem so different to me." The conversation was about her own family, especially her children, during this interview. She said she was absolutely determined that her children would have a better childhood than she had and that there was not going to be partiality or favoritism in her family. "My middle child has had some difficulty, and as I look back on it now, I know it was emotional." She said her oldest child has always had things to come easy for her in school, and she has to watch that this one doesn't boss the others around or make fun of them for not making high grades.

Mrs. A. said the middle child and the oldest child were at a neighbor's house last week and were offered some candy. When they got home, the middle child said, "I took the kind my sister wanted me to take." The counselee said she spanked her for letting the older one boss her around. "I wanted her to learn to stand up for herself and not be pushed around by her older sister as I was." The counselee then laughed and said, "Maybe I was really spanking myself for letting my sister push me around."

The counselee said she was proud of the fact that her children were free and open with her and came to her with their problems. "Even though their problems may seem awfully small, I try not to shame them or get impatient because I know one day they will have big ones. I never had anybody to talk to."

Mrs. A. said the children had asked a good many questions about sex, especially since they knew about the coming of the new baby. She always tries to answer them truthfully. "I was completely ignorant when I grew up and learned all I knew from the girls my own age in high school. It was hard for me to adjust at the beginning of my marriage because I somehow had the feeling that there was something bad about it." She said she didn't feel this way about sex any more.

Since the baby was due within about two weeks, the counselor and counselee discussed whether or not she needed to come back for further counseling. It was decided that she would not make a further appointment but would feel free to call after the baby was born in the event she felt the need for any further interviews. As she was leaving, she said, "I have wondered whether things have changed or whether I have changed, and I think it is me."

A summary of Mrs. A.'s background reveals a person who was probably unwanted when she was born. Her brothers and sisters were all married or about to get married when she came along except for one sister nine years older than she. This sister had dominated her as far back as she could remember. She never had a satisfactory relationship with her mother, and the relationship to her father was only partially satisfactory. She was basically a lonely individual who had never really learned how to communicate and therefore did not make a good social adjustment.

Mrs. A. talked out her heart and soul for the first time in an atmosphere of understanding; this made it easier for her to communicate with her husband and with others. She ventilated her feelings toward her family, especially the hostility she has against her sister; she made some application of her own childhood to that of her children and resolved to be a better mother to them. And, finally, she worked through her partially delayed grief for her father.

We see Mrs. A. experiencing confession, forgiveness, and the love of God in the person of her pastoral counselor. This enabled her to see her family in a new light of forgiveness. Her relationship to God was deepened, and she found a spiritual family in her church.

Nevertheless, this individual could have profited by several more hours of counseling. Actually we know very few details of her early life. We know nothing about her adolescent dating and courtship. If she had come back for further appointments, she probably would have relived more of her childhood experiences and perhaps would have reached the place that she could have worked through more of her feelings toward her mother.

The pastor should remember that there is nothing that will take the place of listening in counseling. The therapeutic value of talking in a carefully planned relationship is always amazing. To remember this will keep him from trying to force Christianity down over a personality. An individual who is bursting with hostility can gain a Christian perspective that has depth if he is allowed to relieve himself of these feelings. The pastoral counselor should be the love of God rather than talking about it. And because one person has shown kindness, human nature both within and without loses its former ugliness and the world becomes a better place in which to live.

By way of conclusion the writer wishes to make two suggestions. The first is that the pastor should not do multiple-interview counseling with women in a church study unless he has another employee of the church close by at all times. If he doesn't have a church secretary, then he should do longer-term counseling with women in his own home.

Secondly, in these two brief chapters on multiple-interview counseling seven interviews were used deliberately. The pastor should not go beyond seven to ten hours of counseling with any person unless he has had supervised training in formal office counseling. The only exception to this principle might be a situation in which he has the opportunity of working under the close supervision of a psychiatrist.

This writer has been working in a medical center for twelve years and has had the opportunity of spending thousands of hours in office counseling. This personal reference is given to emphasize the fact that this warning has grown out of personal experience as well as out of many contacts with pastors. About ninety per cent of an individual's actions are highly emotional and are not thought through calmly. If the pastor does nothing but sit with someone for twenty hours, certain emotional forces would come to the surface in the relationship that might be hurtful to the other person or to the pastor.

The law does not permit a medical doctor to go directly from the classroom to medical practice. He must have a year of supervised clinical experience. The same principle applies to the training of pastoral counselors. Skill in intensive office counseling does not come by reading a book or listening to lectures. The young minister who wishes to go beyond seven to ten hours in his counseling should go to a training center where he can have not less than a year of supervised experience. However, this case record and accompanying comments are included in this book in order to introduce the student, insofar as a book can do so, to the inner realities of longer-term counseling.

13. The Pastor as a Marriage Counselor

Samuel Southard

The pastoral counseling of men and women in marital conflict raises unique issues in theology, ecclesiology, church administration, and psychology. Theologically, Christians view marriage as a spiritual relationship. It cannot be considered apart from the biblical ideas of one flesh, the covenant relationship, and the danger of idolatry. Ecclesiastically, marriage is a concern of the church as an institution. A pastor cannot counsel a husband and wife without some thought for his official position and its effects upon this couple and the community. Psychologically, marriage is the most intimate and complex of adult interpersonal relationships. The counselor must certainly see two individuals; he must also observe a third factor, the quality of their relationship.

These aspects of marriage counseling are closely woven together. They are separated into three major emphases only for purposes of discussion. In the living situation, they flash consecutively into the pastor's view like the facets of a diamond as it is turned before a light.

The Relevance of Theology

Christianity is a family religion. The relationship of God to men is symbolized in terms which men and women can apply to their own homes. Three of these divine-human phrases are directly related to marriage.

One flesh.—The first type of human interaction which has a divine counterpart is the unity of personalities in marriage which is called "one flesh." [1] The love of husband and wife typifies the love of Christ for his church. [2] Christ cherishes the church, which is his body. A man is to love his wife as a part of himself. Why? Because marriage has made the two "one flesh."

This doctrine of one flesh articulates an essential quality of American marriage. A man and a woman are not to share only a kitchen table and a bed. They are also to participate in each other's dreams and disappointments; each must know the other's simple pleasures and complex problems. Companionship is an essential part of marriage in American culture. [3] When this intimate communication is missing, friction is as inevitable as in a motor without oil. Pastors often are puzzled because a good, moral family seems to be falling apart. Closer examination reveals an absence of personal feeling between husband and wife.

Here is one example. A mature woman was referred by her doctor to her pastor because, as she reported, "I guess I'm just sick of my family. My doctor says all these pains in my stomach start when I think of my home life." As the pastor listened, the woman told how she and her husband had gradually lost contact with each other. The marriage had grown so cold that when her mother died, her husband only said, "The funeral's tomorrow, and I can't get in touch with the boss. What a fix for me to be in!" The wife was deeply hurt but said nothing. When the pastor asked why she held herself in, she said, "Oh, I used to tell him, but he didn't listen. He would just shut me off. I'm sick of keeping all my feelings to myself, but what can I do?'"

After several interviews, this wife could unbend enough to

---

[1] Gen. 2:24; Matt. 19:3–6; Eph. 5:31.
[2] Eph. 5:21–33.
[3] In his 1958 lectures to the Southern Baptist Conference on Counseling and Guidance, Dr. David Mace stated that companionship is not an integral part of marriage in other cultures of the world today.

tell her husband how she felt about things. She was surprised to find that her husband also wanted to talk with her. He explained, "I would want to talk, but you seemed so self-sufficient. I thought you didn't have any feelings. I just never realized that we should depend on each other." There was nothing morally wrong with the marriage. The couple had merely lost the spiritual bond of personal communication which would make them one flesh.

The covenant.—A second doctrine which has family connotations is the covenant. The covenant of God with his people involves personal commitment, privilege, and responsibility.[4] The voluntary vows of a man and a woman include these same qualities. The deep love of God for men is mirrored in the personal bond of husband and wife. The open declaration of men's faith in God is paralleled in the pledge of abiding affection between a man and a woman. When self-seeking, disguised motives enter the relationship, the covenant between man and God is defective. The pure in heart seek one thing— God's love. The impure are weakened by internal conflict. They want many things and cannot decide for God alone.

So it is in marriage. The couple who regard each other's personality above all else have a secure foundation for all the storms of life. But when one or both have some hidden and tawdry but nevertheless powerful underlying motive for marriage, this rankling secret weakens the home like patches of sand in concrete pillars. It is difficult and painful to dismantle the marital relationship down to these hidden, unspoken forces, but only by this process can the couple regain a firm footing.

One pastor detected a defective covenant in a case of infidelity. The wife, a plain, home-loving soul, could not understand why her husband would leave her when she had given him the best years of her life. The husband provided an explanation in his hour with the pastor. "My wife helped me get

[4] Deut. 4:1 to 8:20.

started in business, and I'm grateful. But I've prospered, and now I'm in a position where she's just a drag on my career. I'm willing to give her a good settlement. All I want is a chance to keep up with my friends, and A. [the other woman] knows how to entertain them."

This man had not married his wife because of who she was but because of what she could do for him. When she had served that purpose to the limits of her talents and tastes, he was ready to use another woman as a steppingstone to business and social advancement. To him, marriage was not a personal covenant. It was a business contract.

Idolatry.—A third term of family and theological significance is idolatry. If one thinks only of a graven image, this danger seems far away. But images may be engraved on the heart as well as in stone. A man or woman may be as bound to the memory of a parent or departed loved one as a heathen is to the ancient superstitions of a temple cult. Idolatry is sometimes confused with the religious desire to honor parents. But a discerning pastor can usually separate the two just as Jesus did. Christ taught that a man should love his mother and father, but he also taught that a man should leave them to cleave unto his wife.[5] When a man is so dependent upon parents that it interferes with normal growth toward responsible marriage, something is wrong. There must be some leaving before there can be any cleaving.

This axiom is most often related to the early days of marriage. But it may also be applied to later marriages. A widow or divorcee may refuse to give up the image of the the one from whom she is separated. A memory is worshiped. A new spouse is helpless against a ghostly rival. But the pastor may firmly lead the idolator through the pain of a long-delayed grief experience. A person suffers at the full realization that a lover is gone forever, yet this agony lays a memory to rest and revives the

[5] Matt. 19:3–6.

mourner's sensitivity to living people. Marital idolatry may assume either of two forms. On the one hand, slavish conformity to a parent's wishes leads to the adoration of something less than God. On the other, a morbid memory leads to reverence of a dead ideal rather than to worship of the living God.

These theological terms—idolatry, covenant, one flesh—are living realities in marriage. They are not to be used superficially by a pastor. There are times when a counselor is tempted to offer generalized moral answers to marital problems. This must be guarded against by a twofold reminder. First, the byways of motivation are intricate. People in trouble defy direct, simple exhortations to their conscious will. Second, the outworkings of these theological truths in human personality run deep. They demand a reverent and analytical approach.

The Pastor's Position

As ministers seek to evaluate the deep stirrings of two hearts that are no longer rhythmical, they may call upon many resources. A reservoir of them cluster about the pastor's position as leader of a local church. Because of his sacred office, friends and relatives entrust to him information about a couple in distress. Through church activities and community work he has opportunity to meet all members of a family in trouble. His entrance into a disturbed home is assured because he alone among professional men is expected to visit his people in both illness and health.

One of the most promising advantages of the pastoral office is the opportunity to see all members of a family. A recent study by the National Institute of Mental Health illustrates this. A small research project was undertaken on psychotherapy for the family as a unit. The workers found that the fathers were key figures in the recovery of schizophrenic daughters. The mothers seemed bound to the daughters in their sickness. But when the father could firmly establish himself as a person in the family, then the mother gained strength. So long as he was passive and withdrawn from the struggle, there was little improvement.[6]

Ordinarily, a psychiatrist would have access only to the patient and the person who brought her in, who would probably be the mother. But a pastor would have opportunity to see each member of the family and let them discuss their problems with him. While the psychiatrist was treating a schizophrenic daughter, the pastor would have a vital contribution to make in his encouragement of the father. For example, the pastor might suggest, after he had listened for some time, that the father take his wife out one evening to relieve the strain. The mother might resist this and desire to go to the hospital, even though she had visited her daughter every night for five months. This unhealthy reaction can be broken when the father is supported by his pastor in his surge toward healthier patterns of living.

A second contribution of the pastoral office to marriage counseling is the sharing of information about people in trouble from friends, relatives, and other responsible persons. Because he enjoys their respect and trust, friends and family may share intimate details in the hope that the pastor may provide needed counsel. The minister's view of the problem is enriched by this community background. He obtains new perspective from the past and present events which are confided in him.

Although community opinion must be sifted and evaluated, it can make a pastor sensitive and sagacious when a husband or wife deliberately seek to deceive him. For example, after an Easter service a pastor was drawn aside by a grandfather who said that his son and daughter-in-law were in trouble again. He explained that the son had an uncontrollable temper and had been hospitalized on one occasion for nerves. Several weeks later a church officer asked for advice about a friend "who looks like he's mentally ill again." The officer identified his friend as

[6] Murray Bowen *et al.*, "Study and Treatment of Five Hospitalized Family Groups Each with a Psychotic Member," National Institute of Mental Health (mimeographed).

the son of the grandfather to whom the pastor had previously spoken. He added a good deal of marital history from his ten-year friendship with the disturbed man. On the following Sunday morning, a Sunday school teacher told the pastor that the teen-age granddaughter, who was in her class, was under great tension and needed help. In each of these contacts the pastor listened, asked if the son and daughter-in-law would be willing to see him, and offered to work with the interested persons in the stabilization of this troubled family.

On the same Sunday when the teacher spoke of the grand-daughter, the pastor was sitting in his study before the evening service. There was a knock on the door and the son, of whom so much had been said, came in. He was a forty-year-old man of distinguished appearance. Although he appeared to be pre-occupied, he was polite and coherent. He gave the pastor a precise, vivid description of the troubles he had endured from his wife and children. What he said sounded logical. The pastor wondered why he could not interrupt the man but assumed it was natural for him to complete his story first. When the son had finished, he asked the pastor to pray that their home would stay together and be Christian. The pastor assured him that he would do so, suggested that the man return during the week, and ushered him into the sanctuary where the service was about to begin. The man left immediately.

Two days later the daughter-in-law came to the pastor's study. She poured out a flood of frustration and suffering at her husband's hands. Her latest grief was his unwillingness to see a psychiatrist. "Oh," she said, "he can be so convincing outside the house!" The pastor did not know what to say, but the story she told was similar to the partial history he had received from others in the church. He therefore reinforced her desire to take her husband to a psychiatrist. He also suggested that she see one herself for the sake of her mental health and an understanding of her husband.

In the weeks that followed, the wife came for several interviews with the pastor. The husband refused to see anyone. Eventually he was hospitalized through legal pressure of his wife's family. The pastor admitted to himself that without previous information he would have sided completely with the son. His story was logical and convincing. Actually, his preoccupation, extreme conciseness, and unwillingness to be interrupted were signs of his illness.

If the pastor had seen this man and his wife on several occasions before and during the onset of illness, he would have been better prepared to evaluate their stories. This leads to a third value of the pastor's position: the relationship which he has with people before a marital crisis comes to a head. His contacts with the family in the home and the church give him some basis for judgment before the husband or wife come to him in subdued panic. Their anxiety may distort the reality of their situation. The pastor's previous observations will help all of them to see the problem in a steadier perspective.

A mother sought pastoral counsel about an unmarried, thirty-year-old daughter who had "wasted away to nothing." She reported that doctors could not account for the daughter's loss of energy, weight, and appetite. "Preacher," she said, "she seems to be lifeless, like someone grieving." The pastor heard this reference to grief and said, "Why, that reminds me of something. Has she been living alone since you remarried last year?" The mother said that she had moved out of the apartment which she shared with her daughter for seven years after the death of her first husband. Gradually the mother and pastor came to the realization that the daughter was grieving for the loss of her mother. The girl had given up thoughts of marriage and was reconciled to a life with her mother in the apartment. Now all that was gone. The pastor was sensitive enough to catch the reference to grief, but he also had a good memory. He had married the mother during the previous year and had visited the daughter and mother in the years gone by when they had thought to remain together in the apartment.

These prior experiences give the pastor unusual advantages in marriage counseling. A couple whom he has married may wish to come to him "because you were so interested in us and talked with us before the ceremony." A wife whom he has visited routinely in a pastoral call may arrive at his office six months later and say, "You asked such wise questions about me, my husband, and the reasons why we don't come to church. I feel that you'll understand if I tell you why now." The pastor's contacts provide information for him and confidence for his people that he can help in time of need.

Previous relationships, contacts with all the family, and information from interested persons are examples of the benefits of the pastor's position for marital counseling. There are other aspects of his office which may either help or hinder his therapeutic role. Among these are his religious authority and his function as preacher and administrator.

The recognized spiritual authority of the pastor may be helpful or harmful. The outcome will depend both upon congregational expectations and his own use of authority. Some parishioners believe that the clergyman should exert his influences to save all marriages. That is, he should hold people in legal deadlock. Behind this is the assumption that divorce is an unpardonable sin. A pastor may share this opinion and threaten, cajole, and otherwise manipulate persons into the semblance of marriage. But in such an atmosphere he is practicing coercion, not counseling.

Other pastors may reserve judgment about divorce until they have heard the story from at least two sides. They may stand by as a comforter to both parties and make no suggestions. Or they may help the couple to clarify their motivation for and against separation. Instead of pronouncing judgment, they may summarize the reasons which those involved have given either for divorce or reconciliation and say, "What decision will you make? I will be your pastor in either case."

The decision is sometimes complicated by the activity of one or both partners in the church. The pastor then confronts another influence of his office upon counseling—his function as director of the church program.

People will seldom consult a pastor who uses his administrative role for his own advantage. Some ministers dominate the nomination of church officers. They make it clear that laymen are to conform to the clergyman's standards. Church positions are viewed by such men as rewards for those whom they approve. Under this patronage system a leading layman would know that the revelation of personal difficulty to the pastor would lead to disfranchisement or impeachment.

Other pastors look upon church offices as opportunities for people to grow under Christian instruction and responsibility. For them the church is a school in Christian living.[7] Church officers are encouraged to talk with their pastor when they observe a genuine interest for their personal welfare. A Sunday school teacher burst into his pastor's study one Thursday morning to say, "I've been thinking about your prayer meeting talk last night. What you said about learning to control your temper is my problem. But if you had hard people to teach like I have, you'd blow up too. Of course, I can't show how I feel before them . . ."

The man unfolded a series of jangled relationships at home, work, and the church. The pastor asked him if his religious responsibilities made him feel better or worse. The man replied that he would enjoy his class if he just didn't have to do so many other things in the church as well. The pastor encouraged him to think of the one thing he most wanted to do and drop the rest. As the man left, he said, "You're the first pastor that ever took me seriously. All the rest just told me to buck up and get back to work."

Several weeks later the man returned to discuss his family tensions. The pastor saw him on five occasions for counseling.

---

[7] See the May, 1958, special issue of *Pastoral Psychology* on "Pastoral Counseling and Church Administration."

A chronic marital difficulty was not removed, but it was eased. The man found in his Sunday school class a deeper satisfaction. He was more relaxed in the worship services. Occasionally he would come to see the pastor when his hostility and anxiety began to mount up again, talk it out, and go away with the feeling that someone understood.

There are other aspects of the pastor's office which influence his ministry to people, but these have been chosen to illustrate how church relationships foster marriage counseling. Another discussion of "The Pastor as a Marriage Counselor" by Dr. Wayne Oates may be found in *Marriage and Family Living* [8] and in *Readings in Marriage Counseling*, edited by Clark E. Vincent. [9]

The Management of Interpersonal Relationships

The previous discussion of theology and the pastor's position in the church is essential for an understanding of the personal relationship between husband, wife, and counselor. People come to the minister with expectations different from those they have of doctors or lawyers. They look to him for some kind of spiritual guidance which will lift up the load of anxiety, indecision, frustration, and guilt which they may carry. Without an understanding of the theological dimension of the conversation, the pastor has partially failed in his relationship to suffering people. He has not seen himself as all that they would see in him. He has not helped the couple to grasp the intangible spiritual bonds which have torn loose in their conflict.

The official position of the minister also carries a host of implications for the relation of husband and wife. A man may be incensed because his wife has "run to a preacher." Another may be terrified that word will get out about family difficulties and thus undermine his position in the church. Or, more positively, both husband and wife may rekindle associations of earlier

---

[8] XVII (February, 1955), 1 ff.
[9] New York: Thomas Y. Crowell Co., 1957.

happiness as they talk with the pastor who had married them.

Because these involvements are often complex, they will be separated for the sake of clarity into tactics and dynamics of interpersonal relationships. "Tactics" will include the many initial questions of appointments, confidences, time, and referral. The section entitled "dynamics" will consider the interplay of personalities during and after a counseling hour.

Tactics.—The discussion of the pastor's position has already set the stage for the question, "How do I get couples to come to me when they're in trouble?" Specific reference was made to members of the family and friends who can convey the pastor's concern to the husband and wife. A second answer was provided in the illustration about a troubled Sunday school teacher. The pastor's contacts with people in the church organization lead them to him. A third solution was for the pastor to go to his people. Consistent, attentive pastoral visitation gives opportunity for many to open their hearts and awakens in others the desire for help.

A fourth opportunity for the pastor to pave the way for counseling comes through sermons and other talks. On the one hand, people are forewarned by the preacher who openly states, "I can't understand how anyone could get a divorce." They look elsewhere when he gives superficial, general, and absolute solutions to complex family problems. On the other hand, his sermons may convey understanding. It is true, for example, that a family that prays together will stay together *if* the atmosphere of prayer is an open, honest sharing of deep needs and a confession of petty irritations. People will listen if the minister can set prayer in that context and, also, deal sympathetically with the complex question, "Why can't couples pray together?"

Preaching that relates biblical truth to personal concerns is an open invitation for intimate conversation. Biblical passages on family relationships can be illuminated with sociological information and psychological understanding. Such exposition

will invite people to see their pastor and also provide information for their own solution of a problem.[10]

Sometimes a husband or wife will hint at trouble when they
see the pastor in church, at their home, or on the city street.
This is the time for the pastor to offer them the opportunity to
discuss their problem privately. Chapters 6 and 7 have provided detailed information about this, but there is one special
question to be considered in marriage counseling: "Does the
pastor see the couple together or separately?"

Separate conferences are essential in the first appointments
of both husband and wife with the pastor. A three-way conversation provides too many temptations for each party to portray
innocence and condemn the other. The pastor can be caught in
the middle as each one tries to enlist his support. Separate interviews, on the other hand, offer both a confidential relationship
and time for the pastor to ask questions. The climate is more
permissive, for the spouse does not need to defend himself
against his hostile mate. He can admit a fault without its being
used against him.

Sometimes husband and wife come together, and one waits
in the sanctuary while the other talks with the pastor. At other
times one may come alone and without the knowledge of the
other. Then another question arises: "Should I tell him that
I'm seeing you?" The answer is a qualified yes. The qualifica-
tion concerns the attitude in which the party reveals that he is
seeking help. If there is a tone of genuine relief in the counselee's
admission, the marital partner may begin to think that he might
be helped also. He may even volunteer a comment, "Well, I
thought you were getting some help, for you've been a *little*
easier to live with for the past few days." A humble answer will
turn away wrath, but a contentious use of an appointment to
show superior insight will drive the other party away.

[10] Many suggestions will come from David Mace, *Hebrew Marriage* (London: Epworth Press, 1953) and Ernest Groves, *Christianity and the Family*
(New York: The Macmillan Company, 1942).

Closely related to this is the problem of confidences. A pastor should assure husband and wife in their separate interviews that he will not reveal their words or attitudes to each other. If a husband who has not come to the pastor should meet him on the street and ask, "Is my wife coming to you to talk about us?" a simple statement is sufficient: "I have given your wife an appointment, but you will have to ask her about our conversation. If there is anything that you wish to discuss with me, I would be glad to see you."

Since couples often bring problems which require medical or psychiatric consultation, the minister should tell them in the first interview that, with their permission, he may call upon the services of others when it is necessary. When the pastor senses a need for referral as the interviews progress, he can tell the husband or wife that their problem requires specialized help from another professional person and suggest that they seek such help before their next interview. If they know no psychiatrist, gynecologist, or obstetrician, the pastor may write down the names of several, with telephone numbers, for them.

During the first interview the pastor can also explain that he is a friendly teacher rather than a judge. He will seek to develop understanding rather than to fix blame. Their decisions will be respected. He will not advise divorce or try to force them to stay married.

The pastor should also clarify the question of time. After the pastor has heard enough of the problem to see that it is intricate and deep, he should tell the couple that a solution will take time but that time spent in thinking quietly through their problems has helped many unhappy people. The number of interviews need not be decided on in the first interview, since no one knows exactly what lies ahead.

As the counseling relationship progresses, the pastor may see the couple drawing close enough to each other for a discussion of some problem of mutual concern. He may then suggest that they see him together. Or he may be confused by some separate remarks from each which indicate, in a cloudy way, that each wishes to be reconciled to the other. It is then time for him to bring them together and seek to clarify their conversation.

Dynamics.—Included in this section are some of the common tactical problems of interpersonal relationships in marriage counseling; beyond these there are deeper aspects of personal involvement. There is first the willingness of an individual to admit that he has a problem. Beyond this is the exploration of the stage of the marital conflict and the trials and solutions through which this couple has gone. Above all, there is the continual question, "How do these people relate to each other and to the counselor?"

Access to these dynamic problems comes through the counselee's willingness to see that he is in trouble. Some people explain marital strife, sexual impotence, or mismanagement of money as everyday occurrences of all people; they are not yet ready for counseling. Others frankly admit, "We've had problems before, but not like this. This is trouble that I can't see through. It has me licked." Trouble is something beyond the usual pattern of life which the person cannot control. When he sees this, he is ready for help.

Is it enough for him to admit this need? No. Some interviews bog down at this point. The counselee says that he wants help and asks the pastor to give it. What is the counselor to say? Now is the time for an investigation of the stage of conflict at which the couple find themselves. Dr. Wayne Oates has listed eight of these:

A. *Typical Adjustmental Conflicts:*
   1. Conflict over fear of pregnancy *vs.* wife's working
   2. Living conflict over definition of adequate routine; i.e., agreeing upon a schedule—work, prayer, eating, sleeping, sexual relations, social engagements
   3. Conflict over communication failure
   4. Conflict over in-laws, especially financial, housing, and vocational involvements.

5. Conflict over spheres of dependence and independence, masculine and feminine role definitions
6. Conflicts arising out of transferred or dated emotions
7. Revelation of a defective covenant

B. *The Stage of Serious Conflict:*

1. Assaults upon each other's integrity
2. Appearance of deception and withdrawal of the real selves; subterfuge
3. Stalemate of communication

C. *The Stage of Private Misunderstanding:*

1. Agreement upon their helplessness; total resignation at attempts to communicate
2. Individual isolation, loneliness, and anxiety of communication
3. Search for an understanding person
4. Alcohol, drugs, excessive spending, etc., as solaces; sexual deviations; pick-up type of sexual escapades

D. *The Stage of Social Involvement:*

1. Going to members of parental families for understanding; in-law involvement
2. Going to a third person of the opposite sex; extra-marital activity.
3. Development of community gossip
4. Going to a formal counselor

E. *Threats of or Attempts at Separation:*

1. Threats to leave
2. Socially acceptable separations: changing jobs for travel opportunities, going home for summer; entering military service, etc.
3. "Going home to mother"
4. "Kicking" one another out, especially for drinking

F. *Legal Phase:*

1. Going to a lawyer for advice as to rights
2. Private discussions of division of property, custody of children, etc.
3. Institution of divorce procedures

    4. Conflict over grounds for divorce or giving one another a divorce
    5. Social pressure from outsiders on either side

G. *Divorce:*
    1. Conflict over alimony, etc.
    2. Conflict over seeing children

H. *Postdivorce Bereavement:*
    1. Shock; "not me" feelings
    2. Numbing; loss of interest in other things
    3. Struggle between completely breaking and trying to reconcile the relationship; legal break not final; the question of remarriage
    4. Flood of grief, characterized by much hostility and repressed need to admire; sexual deprivation; economic insecurity
    5. The grief-work period: selective memory, reassociation, one working through of feelings; *loneliness;* popular expectations of divorcees
    6. The recharting of affections and discovery of new relationships; encounter of biblical dimensions of divorce; emotional readoption of children to meet needs left unmet by husband or wife
    7. Remarriage

By the time husband and wife have found where they are in this order of marital maladjustment, the pastor will know a good deal about their interpersonal relations. If he has been reflective with his questions, they will also have gained insight. From this point the pastor will rely on the suggestions for counseling given in chapters 11 and 12. But there will always be an additional factor in marital counseling. This is the quality of relationship between this man and this woman. The pastor is not seeing people in isolation; he is seeing people in relationship.

Pastoral counseling offers a unique opportunity to sense this added dimension. Unlike many doctors or lawyers, the minister often interviews both husband and wife. He will observe differences in their attitudes which would probably be undetected if one were seen in isolation. A wife sought counsel with her pastor after her doctor told her to "slow down." She was very active in church and civic affairs. Her conversation centered about the problem of adjusting her time so that she could fulfil obligations to clubs, classes, and social groups.

During the following week the pastor was drawn aside at a civic meeting by the woman's husband. He said, "M— tells me that she's been talking to you. I'm glad. She's never home with the kids. I guess she hasn't cooked a meal for me in a week." The pastor then began to see that the wife's activities might be an escape from her role as a wife and mother. This had not dawned upon him during his interview with her. Then he had thought of her health and subconsciously hoped that she would keep up valuable church activities and drop some in the community. Upon the pastor's invitation, the husband began a series of counseling sessions which revealed a seething cauldron of emotions at home. Meanwhile, the wife continued her protestations that husband and children existed in a well-run household. At first, the pastor saw that this fiction was necessary for the continuation of her club work. But as he continued to see the husband, he realized that the wife was fleeing from an unfeeling spouse and an inadequate parental relationship. Reflection upon conversations with both husband and wife gave rapid insight and broad perspective to the pastor's understanding of this couple.

The Never-Ending Adventure

These high points of marriage counseling may give the pastor a perspective from which he may see many other aspects of family relations which should be considered. This chapter has not attempted to cover all these, but several should be mentioned.

One is the problem of social class as it affects marriage. A thoughtful discussion of this is Talcott Parsons' "Age and Sex in the Social Structure of the United States" in *Human Relations* by Hugh Cabot and Joseph Kahl.[11]

[11] Cambridge: Harvard University Press, 1953.

The thorny issue of divorce also deserves attention. D. S. Bailey has provided an exegesis of Jesus' sayings about divorce in his study of the theology of sexual relations, *The Mystery of Love and Marriage*.[12]

Pastors who wish to pursue the many additional avenues through which the tangled trail of a couple may lead them may consult comprehensive works such as *Readings in Marriage Counseling* by Clark E. Vincent [13] or *Dynamic Mental Hygiene* by Ernest Groves.[14]

Of particular interest to Baptist pastors is *Premarital Pastoral Care and Counseling* by Wayne Oates.[15] This book discusses the pastor's relationship to the engaged couples within the context of the church and denomination.

[12] New York: Harper & Brothers, 1952.
[13] New York: Thomas Y. Crowell, 1957.
[14] Harrisburg, Pa.: Stackpole and Heck, 1947.
[15] Nashville: Broadman Press, 1958.

14. Calling in the Help of Other Counselors

A. Donald Bell

The magnitude of the counseling task and the difficulty of training church-related counselors indicates a need for help. Such help must mean that both pastor and other professional counselors in the community work together as a team. The pastor and other counselors in the community must keep the interaction of two-way referrals going on constantly. The multitude of people in any community who need guidance necessitates that everyone with the call and training in the field do his part. There are several things about this great co-operative program of helping people which are of particular interest to the church worker.

Some Principles of Referral

First, when a church leader refers a parishioner to a professional counselor in his community, he must not refer that person away from himself and his ministry. Rather, he must call in the help of the other counselors and retain his identity with the person whom he refers. Even a parishioner with an incipient psychosis needs the spiritual help and guidance of his pastor as well as the skilled therapy of the psychiatrist.

Second, referral between the church-related worker and the professional, secular counselor must be reciprocal. It must be a two-way referral. However, the referral by the professional to the minister is underdeveloped and retarded in this country.

Slowly but surely professionals in the field are understanding that part of the insight which the patient needs is a proper religious orientation. Some wise practitioners are referring patients whose problems are more spiritual and moral than emotional to an experienced and trained pastor for help. Many psychiatrists and professional counselors state that as many as 50 per cent of the referrals they receive come from local pastors. In fact, Dr. Robert Felix of the National Association for Mental Health estimates that about 40 per cent of the people who seek help for their emotional problems turn first to their ministers.

A third fact involved here is that many church-related workers are not aware of the professionals and institutions available in their communities. Man's attempt to help his fellows in critical times is not a new endeavor. Therefore, in many vocations and professions there have been systematized developments of skills and techniques for helping people with life adjustments. People related to schools, community and welfare agencies, and various professions are readily available for referral. Many times the church worker is not educated to this fact. Too, in some isolated rural areas there are virtually no professionals other than the public school person, the attorney, the physician, or the county social worker. Nevertheless, at reasonable distances there are county, state, and federal institutions of help as well as professional practitioners.

The Church Worker—A Key Person

The church worker must familiarize himself with these available facilities and personnel since he may be the first person in the referral reaction. This is true because of his unique position. Dr. John W. Drakeford lists six things about the church worker's unique position in this area:

1. A number of people in any community have an attitude of trustfulness and faith toward the religious leader.
2. The religious worker can take the initiative in visiting people when he sees or hears of danger signals.

3. The religious worker can often detect emotional difficulties when they are in their incipient state.

4. The religious worker is often familiar with the total situation in which the person is placed.

5. The religious worker may be the only one who can persuade the person to take a certain line of action, such as visiting a psychiatrist.

6. In some small communities he may be the only one who has any knowledge of mental health.[1]

All of this indicates the necessity of a pastor or minister of education's acquainting himself with facilities and personnel that may be helpful immediately upon moving to a new situation. Perhaps in his initial church survey he could note the possibilities that are in his community and also in nearby areas and metropolitan centers. It is unwise for the staff member to wait until he needs to refer a client to a professional person or institution before he becomes acquainted with them. One of the best investments of time the worker in a new situation can make is to acquaint himself with these sources of referral immediately. Therefore, when he must call upon them, his contact has already been made. He knows the personality of the individual or the institution, and thus the whole referral process can be better and smoother.

A pastor had been in a community for some time and was working with a marital case. He might feel the need for referral to a Christian attorney and had gotten acquainted with one. He could simply call his attorney friend and say, "John, I need some help," and continue to give a brief case history. This contact would also help when he discussed the referral process to the client. Such contacts are also one of the best means of preventing the danger of loss of client contact in the referral process. In a large city the church worker may not be able to be

---

[1] From an unpublished paper given at Second Annual Conference on Counseling and Guidance, Southern Baptist Sunday School Board, Nashville, Tennessee, October 2, 1957.

acquainted with all of the helping personnel, but he can at least make contact with one of each of the following: a Christian physician, a Christian attorney, a Christian public school person trained in counseling, and a certified psychiatrist whose views are consistent with the Christian life. The ideal here would, of course, be to have ready for referral a psychiatrist who is thoroughly Christian.

Many of the professionals listed above do not understand clearly the role of the pastor or other church staff member as a counselor. They have their own professional criteria as standards and many times feel that the church counselor has neither training nor standards. This is, of course, a false concept that can easily be remedied with clear information and better communication. A survey of college counselors was made recently by Dr. Charles Kemp of Texas Christian University. The results are comparable to those which probably would be found from a study of psychiatrists. Therefore, it will serve to illustrate the point.

1. Of the sixty-three college counselors who answered, only one rejected the idea of there being a special need for a religious worker as a counselor on college or university campuses.

2. Many went as far as to say such things as, "I believe that such a counselor is absolutely essential."

3. Most of those who replied indicated:
   a. The religious counselor should be trained.
   b. He should not attempt to work in areas in which he is not qualified.

4. One illuminating fact was that 65 per cent of these indicated that they would be willing to make available files containing tests, etc., to the religious counselors.

Thus another advantage in referrals to professional people who are already friends of the minister is that they will gradually see the worth of the church-related worker as a member of the counseling team in the community. Referring patients and clients back to the minister will be easier then. This underdevelopment—which has been mentioned above—is more obvious in America than it is in Britain, where several prominent pastoral counselors receive referrals from leading British psychiatrists and psychologists regularly. Such a return referral usually involves cases which are highly spiritual, moral, or ethical in content. Another point of interest is the fact that sometimes the professionals may have problems of their own in these areas and come for help to the minister or church counselor.

Such two-way referring of clients is based upon four factors:

1. A healthy respect for professional skills. This necessitates an understanding of the respective areas of help which each profession covers.

2. Personal friendships which make the referral process easier. The minister understands and appreciates the psychiatrist better if he is an intimate friend of the psychiatrist. So does the psychiatrist understand the pastoral and educational ministry better when he knows these men and understands their training, maturity, and level of proficiency.

3. A clear understanding of vocational limitations. It would be wise for every church worker to study carefully the ethical practices and standards of the medical profession, the creeds and standards set out by the American Psychological Association, and the standards of practice of the local bar association.

4. A true understanding of the team concept in counseling through interprofessional meetings. Counselors within the church and out of the church need to understand clearly the differences between the role of the professional counselor and the role of the church counselors.

Differences Between Professional and Church Counselors

Let us first look at definitions: The professional counselor is trained for and spends his life in the full vocational career of counseling. His frame of reference is altruistic but not necessarily religious. He is a secular, professional worker.

The church counselor is trained for and spends his life in a full-time ministry of religion to which he has been called. His counseling may play a major or minor role in this total ministry. He is a called, vocational worker.

Some other contrasts between the two areas of counseling are:

1. The counselor-client relationship is different because the church counseling explicitly involves a direct reference to God.

2. Professional counseling profits by the very professionalism which church counseling avoids. The latter alienates any evidence of the shingle, the diploma, and the clinical milieu.

3. The professional may be trained to deal with psychotic cases with depth-therapy and/or medication. The church counselor finds his field of service in the vast level of everyday spiritual, family, vocational, and social problems.

4. Professional people have a written and fixed code—often taken by oath—which is based on the ethics of the professional group. The church counselor's code is not formally stated, but though informal, it is on an even higher level—that of Christian interpersonal relations.

5. The professional counselor is protected by the laws of most states from dangerous involvements in cases. The church (evangelical) counselor is not protected by the laws of most states and enters into the intimacies of people's lives with some degree of risk. He does so, however, because of a spiritual calling to help others and exerts as much tact and care as possible.

Examples of Referral

The pastor of a metropolitan church has been dealing with a child who is having difficulty adjusting to school and church. The pastor has done all he feels able to do in the case, but he knows about the child guidance center in his city. It is supported by the Community Chest and provides psychiatric and social help for children and parents at a nominal fee. He has visited the center, is acquainted with its clinical director, and is able to call the center for the mother of the child and tactfully make arrangements for aid as well as to orient the mother and child for the new therapy.

Tom Wilson is student director in a small college town. He is helping a student with a rather serious personality problem during several counseling interviews. He has also referred the student to the teacher of psychology and the several deans of the college. This cross-referring has helped, but the student's personality pattern seems to have psychotic characteristics. The staff members, led by the student director and the boy's family, arrange, with the advice of the college physician, to get the student to the state mental hospital for an examination period. The referral process has been achieved skilfully because the student director was familiar with the professional services supplied by the state and he knew his state's mental health laws.

A missionary was faced with a case of family disharmony in the migrant group with which he worked. The husband and wife were at the point of divorce, and several children were in the home. The missionary was very interested in family counseling, and although he had dealt with the case for some time, he felt the need of professional help in this crisis stage before the family moved on.

When he had first come to the area to work, he had become acquainted with the welfare agencies in the nearby city. He had visited the family service center and knew the staff members. It was easy to get the couple to a counselor of the service center who was a well-trained Christian woman. She picked up the case where the home missionary left off.

These are but a few examples of the fine way the church worker can use the professional services available, if he knows about them and has taken time to make proper contacts. Every full-time Christian worker owes it to his calling to familiarize himself with the counseling facilities available when he moves to a new field of service. Also, more church leaders ought to serve on the boards of the community institutions, some of which have been mentioned.

A *Misunderstanding in Church Counseling*

A basic problem which has limited the co-operation between professional and Christian counselors is the current misunderstanding about the initial contact of counselor with client. Many professionals criticize ministers for counseling those who come to them for help; pastors are not sufficiently trained according to professional standards. However, these counselors are oriented to the idea of the client's coming to the minister because he has set up a practice and makes himself available to his work. The church counselor, however, is in the position of having people come to him for help even though he does not set himself up as a trained counselor. He must do the best he can, for frequently he is the only person available when people find themselves in crisis situations. He attempts to help and refers when he reaches his limit of ability. People will come to Christian workers for help; they always have, and they always will. Christian love and compassion must make up for specialized techniques the minister lacks.

This misunderstanding is, however, indicative of some mistakes church counselors have made. Therefore, let us look at some hazards involved particularly in the case of the church-related worker's referring to the professional.

The first characteristic of poor referral is seen when the pastoral counselor continues a counseling relationship beyond his limit of ability, training, and experience. It is a dangerous thing not to refer the counselee to a specialist soon enough. Every church counselor needs to be familiar with the symptoms of mental illness. These symptoms are listed briefly and concisely in several leaflets which can be obtained from the National Association for Mental Health, Inc., at 1790 Broadway, New York 19, New York. Detailed discussions of such symptoms can be found in reputable books in the field of mental hygiene, abnormal psychology, basic psychiatry, and textbooks in mental health and personality adjustment. However, the counselor needs specialized training in college and seminary so as to be able to recognize symptoms. The counselor must be consciously and constantly aware of his responsibility here. Usually there will be no one to tell him when his ability reaches its limit in a particular case. He will have to surrender the counselee to a professional counselor on his own initiative, although he will want to retain contact, as has been mentioned above.

Poor orientation of the counselee for referral is another hazard, particularly when the referral must be to a professional such as a psychiatrist. Many people are still sensitive to such specialists, and proper, tactful orientation must take place. If the referral is to a mental health clinic or a child guidance clinic, the pastoral counselor must again spend some time in preparing the parent and the child for this new contact. There will be cases where the counselor is unable to lead the client to proper preparation for adjustment, and he may have to call in help just for this task of orientation. If a minister of education is counseling a person who gives evidences of deep neurotic tendencies, he may not be able to prepare the client himself for professional therapy and may have to call in the pastor to assist. At other times a family physician will be very helpful. In fact, if there are signs of psychosis, the laws of many states simply require referral by a general practitioner.

The precise techniques used in referral are adapted to the personality, prejudices, and understanding of the counselee himself. Usually it is wise to be straightforward and frank with the client. However, in many cases the counselor will have to be very tactful and may have to work through members of the family in order to secure proper referral. Usually when the counselee is ready and prepared to go to a professional, he ought to get an appointment immediately. Here there is always the problem of getting appointments when they are needed. Again, a previous friendship with the professional may help in this instance.

A third danger is a forced referral. Many times the counselor who is not sufficiently trained will become overeager to get the client to additional help. Such anxiety is, of course, justified when the case is definitely an emergency. Otherwise, the counselor will have to be patient in adjusting the person to the new situation. Very few other counselors will want to have a client who comes to them by referral because he has been made to do so. In fact, a psychiatrist will often ask, "Does the patient want to see me?" Therefore, unless the situation is an emergency, the counselor should be patient in the preparation for referral and ought not coerce the counselee into it.

In the fourth place, the minister would want to be very careful about referring a person to a fellow counselor or professional who is not properly qualified and trained. Although psychiatrists have been carefully regulated by the American Medical Association and the laws of most states, there is still much laxity in the control of the field of counseling and psychology. Usually a psychiatrist is in private practice and a member of the local medical association or attached to a reputable institution such as a hospital or a clinic. Usually a psychologist of any kind is attached to a reputable institution. There are a few psychologists who offer a general practice in the field of counseling and psychotherapy. These are very rare and should be investigated before referral. Normally the clinical psychologist is attached to a hospital, clinic, or guidance center. Many qualified counselors are attached to family service agencies, planned parenthood centers, and welfare agencies. In such instances the person referring may have to depend to a great extent upon the reputation of the agency to which the practitioner is related. Many times a family doctor in the church membership can give the pastor or other staff member assistance in checking on such qualifications. Certainly a pastoral counselor would not refer a person to those who practice all sorts of healing arts but who have no academic or organizational qualifications. He ought to be particularly careful of the practice of mystics, spiritualists, and devotees of all sorts of metaphysical groups. A rather complete national survey has been made of such unorthodox practitioners and is recorded in detail in the book *Where Do People Take Their Troubles?* [2]

A fifth hazard of referral is involved in an abrupt referral to a professional who is unknown by the person referring. Previous contact should have been made with the psychiatrist or counselor, since personal information about him can be used by the pastoral counselor in the referral orientation of the person. Such friendships are invaluable and fit in several aspects of the whole counseling process, as has already been mentioned.

A sixth dangerous practice is referral to a professional who is scientifically qualified but who is not oriented to the Christian point of view. Many lay people feel that anyone in the various psychological therapies is necessarily unchristian and irreligious. This of course is not true; some leading psychiatrists and counselors are acceptable in their spiritual beliefs. The pastor will want to be certain in this area, of course. The first choice would be to refer to a well-qualified specialist who is a dedicated Christian. The second choice would be to refer to a qualified specialist who, though broad in his religious concepts, is at least not inconsistent with the Christian view. Referral to a non-Christian and irreligious therapist would, of course, be a last resort.

A seventh possible danger is referral to a reputable counselor sponsored by a group which is not reputable. This is an unusual situation, but it has been known, and the pastoral counselor should be sure that the group or institution sponsoring the counselor is a worthy one.

A final hazard in the referral process has to do with the personal reputation of the counselor himself. In all vocations the human element is evident. People get into trouble. It would probably be unwise for a pastoral counselor to refer a person to a practitioner who is well qualified and who is even a church

[2] Lee R. Steiner, *Where Do People Take Their Troubles?* (Boston: Houghton Mifflin Co., 1945). See also Wayne E. Oates, *Where to Go for Help* (Philadelphia: Westminster Press, 1957).

member but whose personal and moral standards are not of the best. When this unfortunate situation happens, the client's disturbed condition is aggravated rather than helped.

Members of the Helping Team

The first group of those who are members of what is called "the helping team" includes lay persons whose professional training may be limited but whose practical experiences and maturity compensates to some degree. They would include:

1. Mature Christian adults who might be friends of the person in need of help.

2. Experienced parents who can help—particularly in the counseling of children.

3. Volunteer workers in the church who have had experience in dealing with people. These might be Sunday school teachers, youth workers, deacons, mature women in the organizational life of the church, and qualified workers in community groups such as Parent-Teachers' Association, Boy Scouts, Girl Scouts, boys clubs, and others.

Another group of team members includes those working in full-time Christian vocations where counseling may permeate many of their functions:

1. Other pastors, ministers of education, ministers of music, age-group directors, and other church staff members.

2. Teachers in home and foreign mission schools.

3. Chaplains in military service and helping institutions, particularly hospitals.

4. Deans, residence hall counselors, and student workers in Christian schools and children's homes.

5. Workers in Good Will Centers, mission houses, and denominational publishing houses producing literature related to personal problems.

6. Fieldworkers of denominational boards as they confer with local workers about local church and organizational problems—which always entail personal problems.

The third group of team members includes professionals who work with people in various aspects of human relations. These include some of the most significant members of the team who many times, though not employed by church groups, inject a definite Christian frame of reference into their work:

1. Practitioners who deal with the deeper dynamics of the neurotic and psychotic patient: (a) psychiatrists, who hold the M.D. degree, have had psychiatric training including a residency in a mental hospital, and pass the examinations of the American Psychiatric Association; (b) psychoanalysts, psychiatrists who undergo extensive psychoanalysis themselves and then have training in a reputable school; (c) psychologists, who hold the Ph.D. in the field plus sufficient clinical work to be approved by the American Psychological Association; and (d) psychiatric social workers, who have the Master of Social Work degree, a two-year course including supervised clinical experience, plus additional clinical experience in psychiatry, and are approved by the American Association of Psychiatric Social Workers.

2. Clinical and testing psychologists in hospitals, clinics, and schools. (The qualifications are similar to the above for psychologists.)

3. Welfare agents with federal, state, county, and municipal governments.

4. Trained counselors with family service agencies, the American Red Cross, planned parenthood clinics, etc., who usually hold the master's degree in social work or psychology.

5. The staff members of guidance or mental health clinics, including psychiatrists, clinical psychologists, psychiatric and general social workers, and caseworkers who deal directly with the clients.

6. Psychologists and counselors in institutions—penal, corrective, custodial, and medical; also, personnel directors in business and industry.

7. Public and private school counselors and deans; also teach-

ers of psychology. These school guidance officers may be the only available help in small communities. They usually hold the M.A. or Ed.M. in guidance and membership in the American Psychological Association.

8. Legal and law enforcement personnel including attorneys, judges, peace officers, school attendance officers, and court workers.

The matter of fees is difficult to discuss since practices are not uniform. The psychiatrist's fees are tabulated by the half-hour or hour of psychotherapy. They must be computed on a comparison with minor surgery—not an office call with a general practitioner. Many states have diagnostic and out-patient treatment centers which are tax supported. Here there are either no fees or minimal charges. Although these centers may be distant from the patient's home, they usually have excellent staff psychiatrists and fine facilities.

State and county mental hospitals provide prolonged treatment. These are state supported and referral is by a psychiatrist, two general practitioners, or other commitment designated by the laws of the particular state. City or county mental health or child guidance clinics are usually supported by United Fund or Community Chest and offer services of psychiatrists, clinical psychologists, and social workers at a token fee. Psychological aid is often available free or at minimal fees at counseling centers of colleges and universities. Legal aid normally requires stipulated fees, but if the minister will contact his local bar association, he can find out how his parishioners can obtain financial help when needed.

Most social workers are connected with welfare agencies which receive their support from sources other than fees. Ministers never accept fees for counseling.

How to Measure a Counselor's Worth

In counseling, as in every area of human relations, it is difficult to make accurate evaluations. Many people who have a good technical background in the field of counseling are unable, because of personality difficulties, to do a good job. Other people with a minimum of formal training seem to be so made up that people will come to them. Certainly the ideal in measuring the worth of the counselor is to consider both aspects of the role—training and personality. Some of the hazards of referral above may serve as general guides in evaluating a counselor, and there are more specific tests. For example, the seven tests given by Dr. Wayne Oates in his book *Where to Go for Help* are concise and specific. They are:

1. Who sponsors your counselor?
2. Has the person been in the community very long?
3. Has the person been adequately trained for his task?
4. Is the counselor a person of basic spiritual integrity?
5. Has the counselor been reasonably successful in dealing with other people's problems?
6. Does this person promise much and do little, or does he promise little and do much?
7. Can you trust this person basically? [3]

The evaluation of local helping institutions is not as difficult a task. Most of these will be affiliated with national groups of good reputation. They fall usually into the general categories previously listed.

Detailed lists with addresses, qualifications, and spheres of function of each profession and institution can be found in several sources. Some of these are Dr. Oates' book mentioned above; *The Family Problems Handbook*,[4] available at most social agencies; and Steiner's *Where Do People Take Their Troubles?*

[3] Oates, *op. cit.*, pp. 32–37.
[4] Arnold W. Holmes, *The Family Problems Handbook* (New York: Frederick Fell, Inc., 1952).

15. Ways to Learn Pastoral Counseling

John W. Drakeford

The task of counseling is so different from the normal work of the minister that some specialized training is required to adequately prepare him for this task. There was a time when the minister was looked upon as the best educated person in the community; as such he became the source of all knowledge and very often an authority in the life of that group of people. Even if this idea has not carried down to this day, the fact still remains that a successful minister is characterized by a definitely outgoing personality and a positive manner. In fact, in some circles the minister must be dogmatic to get any following. This may all be very well from the viewpoint of leadership, but it is not the attitude which makes a good counselor. A really good counselor must be anything but dogmatic; he must be receptive, permissive, and nonjudgmental, with a sensitivity to the emotional overtones communicated by the counselee. Above all, he has to learn to stop talking and listen to others for a while. For the vigorous minister this is not an easy thing to do. Much of the art of counseling can only be learned by careful study. In this chapter we will indicate some of the ways in which counseling skills can be developed.

There are a number of techniques for learning these newer skills, but it can be conveniently stated that there are two basic approaches to the learning of pastoral counseling. The student may begin by making a study of personality and its dynamics, then go on to a study of the theories of counseling, and finally study and practice the specialized methods used in pastoral counseling. The other way of learning is to begin by studying actual counseling situations and getting the feel of the give and take of the experience. As these are studied, the student will gradually begin to see the importance of the theory and dynamics of personality and get to know them from a sense of need. This latter method has much to commend it from an educational point of view and is recommended by some of the most outstanding authorities in the field. The reader's choice of method will be influenced by a number of factors, but an effort is made in this chapter to suggest sources from which material may be gathered in respect to either of these approaches.

Knowing the Significant Literature

Whichever approach is used, the student will at some time or another want to consult some of the books in the field. For this purpose a number of books are suggested. The list is somewhat abbreviated and rather elementary, but it could form the basis for a vocational religious worker's library. In this listing the simpler books are placed first.

BONNELL, J. S. *Psychology for Pastor and People*. New York: Harper & Brothers, 1948.

MAY, ROLLO. *The Art of Counseling; How to Gain and Give Mental Health*. New York: Abingdon Press, 1957.

HULME, WILLIAM E. *How to Start Counseling*. New York: Abingdon Press, 1955.

WISE, CARROLL A. *Pastoral Counseling, Its Theory and Practice*. New York: Harper & Brothers, 1951.

DICKS, RUSSELL L. *Pastoral Work and Personal Counseling*. New York: The Macmillan Company, 1949.

OATES, WAYNE E. *The Christian Pastor*. Philadelphia: Westminster Press, 1951.

JOHNSON, PAUL E. *Psychology of Pastoral Care*. New York: Abingdon-Cokesbury Press, 1953.

HILTNER, SEWARD. *Pastoral Counseling*. New York: Abingdon-Cokesbury Press, 1949.

———. *Preface to Pastoral Theology*. New York: Abingdon Press, 1958.

Approaches to Personality:

WOODWORTH, ROBERT S. *Contemporary Schools of Psychology.* London: Methuen & Co., Ltd., 1951.

JOHNSON, PAUL E. *Personality and Religion.* New York: Abingdon Press, 1957.

OATES, WAYNE E. *The Religious Dimensions of Personality.* New York: Association Press, 1957.

Counseling Theory and Technique:

WARTERS, JANE. *Techniques of Counseling.* New York: McGraw-Hill Book Co., Inc., 1954.

ROGERS, CARL R. *Counseling and Psychotherapy.* Boston: Houghton Mifflin Co., 1942.

————. *Client-Centered Therapy.* Boston: Houghton Mifflin Co., 1951.

Specialized Counseling Areas:

YOUNG, RICHARD K. *The Pastor's Hospital Ministry.* Nashville: Broadman Press, 1954.

CLINEBELL, HOWARD J. *Understanding and Counseling the Alcoholic.* New York: Abingdon Press, 1956.

SKIDMORE, REX A., GARRETT, HULDA VAN STREETER, and SKIDMORE, C. JAY. *Marriage Consulting.* New York: Harper & Brothers, 1956.

JACKSON, EDGAR N. *Understanding Grief.* New York: Abingdon Press, 1957.

HAMRIN, SHIRLEY A., and PAULSON, BLANCHE B. *Counseling Adolescents.* Chicago: Science Research Associates, Inc., 1950.

Writing Up Relationship Experiences

One of the most valuable ways of learning to counsel is to write up a verbatim report of a counseling experience with another person. Hiltner calls these "contact reports." The pastor writes up some experience which he had with a person in his church. As much as possible he writes it up word for word. Later he reviews the material and studies the record of what he said, what the church member said, the way he felt, and the way the other person felt. Some things will immediately become obvious to him, but it will be of greater help if he can confer with a more experienced and better trained person who may be found near his church.

The would-be counselor will soon find that this procedure is not easy. However, some rough notes can be jotted down during the conference or immediately after it has taken place. These can be expanded later. Practice will lead to a person's remembering more material than he would ever have thought possible. There is always the problem of forgetting things, but this should not unduly concern the counselor-trainee. Many writers in the field believe that the individual is not ready to face things that cannot be remembered; some motivating force pushes them from consciousness. When he is ready to learn them, it will be possible to recall them.

As in all record keeping, great care should be exercised in the use of people's names. It is best to use some sort of code as well as to make sure that no one has access to what should always be treated as confidential documents.

This procedure is somewhat crude, but it has considerable value for the learner. It is of utmost importance that the reports should be as close as possible to verbatim. Most authorities are agreed that interviews put into indirect language are not nearly as valuable.

Study of Interview Material

Most books on counseling or pastoral counseling are liberally sprinkled with case histories. These constitute good basic material of counseling experiences which will generally repay study. One of the best examples of such material is found in the latter part of Roger's *Counseling and Psychotherapy*,[1] where a complete record of a counseling experience is presented. In terms of specific pastoral counseling, Seward Hiltner has prepared a case book, *The Counselor in Counseling;*[2] in this book

[1] Carl R. Rogers, *Counseling and Psychotherapy* (Boston: Houghton Mifflin Co. 1942).

[2] Seward Hiltner, *The Counselor in Counseling* (New York: Abingdon-Cokesbury Press, 1952).

various aspects of a counseling experience are demonstrated in terms of the cases presented.

As in any other study procedure, it is not enough just to read this material. Each case should be read critically. The would-be counselor should ask himself, "What are the counselee's problems?" then, "What did the counselor attempt to do about these problems?" and finally, "What indications are there of the success of the outcome in terms of the original problem?" If the case is read in this way, it gives the reader the feeling of standing off and looking objectively at the process that takes place in counseling.

There are refinements of this procedure which are helpful for the student. In Snyder's *Casebook of Non-Directive Counseling* [3] are a number of cases which can be used for study. The appendix of the book includes a case with the counselor's responses omitted. After trying to take the role of the counselor and fill in the appropriate responses, the student can consult the verbatim report given earlier in the book and compare his responses with those given by a competent counselor in an actual counseling situation. This type of technique is described in Seward Hiltner's book *Pastoral Counseling*.[4] His technique is to tell the group of the circumstances under which the interview took place and then give each member a small mimeographed report of the counseling session minus what the pastor said. The student then writes in the responses which he would have given. A student anxious to learn can get much from reading the various responses given and Hiltner's evaluation of them.

It is well to remember that there are some shortcomings involved in this technique. Hiltner suggests that there are three defects in this method of learning through studying interview

---

[3] William U. Snyder, *Casebook of Non-Directive Counseling* (Boston: Houghton Mifflin Co., 1947).

[4] Seward Hiltner, *Pastoral Counseling* (New York: Abingdon-Cokesbury Press, 1949).

material: (1) the temptation to get some details of the method without understanding or inwardly accepting the presuppositions apart from which methods are meaningless; (2) the temptation to declare that psychological dynamics are irrelevant; (3) the temptation to develop a theory of dynamics which goes along with the interview material but omits important considerations that cannot be seen in the material. If the student has these facts in mind, he can avoid the pitfalls mentioned here and get a well-balanced approach to the counseling procedures and theories.

Clinical Pastoral Education

One of the most successful ways of learning to counsel is by taking a course in clinical pastoral education. "By and large clinical pastoral training is by far the quickest, simplest, most comprehensive and least expensive way to get a toe hold in learning counseling." [5] Clinical pastoral training has been defined by Hiltner as "a procedure whereby theological students or ministers are brought face to face with individual people in a situation which is susceptible to supervision from the pastoral point of view and in which, through the use of various participant devices—such as interview material and compilation of case histories—both the dynamics of human conduct and the pastoral ways of dealing with it are learned, and learned together." [6]

This training is usually taken in an institutional setting where the student may live from six to twelve weeks. Half of the student's day is spent in visiting and interviewing the patients or inmates. The other half is occupied with writing records, conferring with the chaplain, and attending regular seminar discussions. An idea of the possibilities of this type of training can be gained by examining the goals agreed upon by the Institute

[5] *Ibid.*, p. 246.
[6] *Ibid.*, p. 244.

of Pastoral Care and the Council for Clinical Training. In *Pastoral Psychology* of January, 1958,[7] these are stated as:

1. To enable the student to gain fuller understanding of people, their deeper motivations and difficulties, their emotional and spiritual strengths and weaknesses.
2. To help the student discover more effective methods of ministering to individuals and groups, and to intensify his awareness of the unique resources, responsibilities, and limitations of the clergy.
3. To help the student to learn to work more cooperatively with representatives of other professions and to utilize community resources which may lead toward more effective living.
4. To further the knowledge of problems met in pastoral care by providing opportunities for relevant and promising research.

Some writers, such as Hiltner, have indicated that they can see clinical training spreading beyond the institutional setting. However, Hiltner sees in a hospital setting a number of advantages. These would include: (1) People can be seen more frequently than in the parish, so there can be more contacts in the same amount of time. (2) People in a hospital are confronting difficulties; if the student wants to learn how to help, he can learn much by understanding people at such points as tend to make them open to new sources. (3) The supervision of training in a hospital is easier. (4) The student sees plainly that the pastor is not the only professional worker who can help people, that he needs to co-operate and work with the physician, the nurse, and all others who come with various skills to the person in need.

Students in Lutheran theological seminaries have an organized program of clinical pastoral education under the auspices of the National Lutheran Advisory Council on Pastoral Care. Southern Baptist professors and chaplains in seminaries and hospitals have recently organized the Southern Baptist As-

[7] "Opportunities for Study, Training, and Experience in Pastoral Psychology—1958," *Pastoral Psychology* (January, 1958), p. 28.

sociation for Clinical Pastoral Education. The constitution and by-laws of this association are included in this book as the Appendix. The first president of this association was Dr. John M. Price of New Orleans Baptist Theological Seminary. A thorough description of the programs of clinical pastoral education among Southern Baptists is found in the *Encyclopedia of Southern Baptists*.[8]

For those who might be interested in clinical training it is of interest to note that there is a type of organization which conducts programs independently of, but in co-operation with, theological schools. These organizations offer training in a large number of centers which are accredited by them. They are:

The Institute of Pastoral Care, Inc. Inquiries about the various centers which this organization supervises may be obtained by writing to Rev. Otis A. Maxfield, Executive Secretary, Institute of Pastoral Care, Inc., 50 Elm Street, Springfield 3, Massachusetts.

The Council For Clinical Training, Inc. Inquiries should be addressed to Miss Emily Spickler, at the council office, 2 East 103 Street, New York 29, N. Y.

Observation

In the development of the intangibles that have to do with counseling it is important that the student have opportunities to watch an experienced counselor at work. Hamrin and Paulson state, "As the teacher learns most about teaching by observing and practicing in the classroom, a counselor learns most about counseling by watching others counsel and practicing himself once he has the theories in mind. Preferably he should watch a counselor more expert than himself at work." [9]

Such a situation is not easy to arrange. Sometimes with a

[8] Wayne E. Oates *et al.*, "Pastoral Care," *Encyclopedia of Southern Baptists* (Nashville: Broadman Press, 1958), II, 1073–79.

[9] Shirley A. Hamrin and Blanche B. Paulsen, *Counseling Adolescents* (Chicago: Science Research Associates, Inc., 1950), p. 143.

counselee who is feeling particularly secure it is possible for a
third person to be present, or in a well-equipped building a
special room with one-way glass may be utilized. However,
there will always be a certain artificiality if a stranger is present, and the closest thing to reality is a sound recording of a
counseling session. This enables the student to catch the inflec-
tions of the voices and feel something of the relationship which
comes to exist in the give and take of a counseling session.

An excellent recording of an interview which is slanted toward the minister is produced by Pastoral Psychology Books of
Great Neck, New York. It is a re-enactment of a series of pastoral interviews conducted by Rev. Clinton Kew of the Marble
Collegiate Church of New York City. The editorial comments
on the recording could be of great help to the student counselor.
The Educational Testing Bureau has both tape and disc recordings of a series of interviews called "The Case of Jim." This
is not so well done technically and is not in a church setting,
but it has the additional advantage of a booklet with it. This
booklet contains a verbatim report of the interview. With this
booklet in hand there are increased possibilities of learning, and
such a procedure lends itself to a group situation.

Experiencing Personal Counseling

It is quite common in a number of the social science disciplines to have some sort of therapeutic relationship as a part of
training. The psychoanalyst is required to be analysed himself
in a process which may take a considerable period of time, and
the prospective social worker has this sort of relationship with
the teaching supervisor, who analyses what happens in each
practice interview and helps the student understand something
of his own personality traits.

A number of the leaders in the clinical counseling movement
advocate each prospective counselor's undergoing a period of
therapy. Paul E. Johnson states, "It may well be the responsibility of theological school to include in their services to stu-

dents some sort of therapy." [10] This is in line with the findings of workers in secular fields. In describing the training program conducted in the Counseling Center at the University of Chicago, Carl Rogers tells how the students were given an opportunity to have personal counseling. At first only a few of them took advantage of this offer, but those who did were so pleased with the results that they made a strong recommendation that there should be more stress on this aspect in future programs. In later groups some 80 per cent of the students took advantage of this opportunity and found it a significant part of their training.

The man who is in seminary will probably find many such opportunities open before him and should make the most of them. If a would-be counselor is serving on the field, he will possibly be able to find some trained minister who would be happy to give some of his time to counseling, and the outcome could be very rewarding to both of them.

Group Work

There is a tremendous enthusiasm among ministers and other vocational religious workers to learn more about counseling, and with the right sort of leadership much can be done to help. Sometimes a group of vocational religious workers can meet together, or the members of a pastor's conference can prepare a plan that will lead to helpful experiences in learning counseling. Any of the techniques previously mentioned in this chapter could be utilized in such a plan, but there are some methods which are particularly suitable.

Some groups of pastors and religious workers have found one-day conferences very helpful. For an occasion such as this other professional people can be called upon to help. These may include psychiatrists, social workers, and psychologists. If there is a college in the vicinity, it is often possible to get professional

[10] Paul E. Johnson, *Psychology of Pastoral Care* (New York: Abingdon-Cokesbury Press, 1953), p. 268.

people connected with it to co-operate. The program of such a conference which was held for one day was as follows:

Minister's Counseling Institute

Morning Session

9:00	. . . . Registration
9:45	. . . . Devotional and Statement of Purpose
10:00	. . . . "Counseling Theories"
	James Smith, Ph.D.
11:00	. . . . "The Minister and the Psychiatrist"
	Sidney Hover, M.D.
12:00	. . . . Luncheon

Afternoon Session

1:30	. . . . "Community Social Services"
	Anne Thousard
2:00	. . . . "The Distinctive Role of the Minister"
	Joseph Harris, Th.D.
3:00	. . . . Demonstration of a Counseling Interview
	Rev. Harry Fosher
4:00	. . . . Panel Discussion
5:00	. . . . Benediction

Another way to have a one-day conference is to secure the co-operation of a chaplain in a nearby hospital. These men are generally most willing to co-operate in a venture like this. The chaplain can arrange a one-day meeting like the one outlined above, or he can make a variation by having the group visit the hospital for a series of seminars on some six or eight successive Mondays. Gatherings like this, which involve members of a number of professions, are particularly valuable. They not only help the pastor but also facilitate the understanding of the doctor, psychiatrist, nurse, and social worker and make much easier the whole ministry of referral.

Role Playing

Role playing has been defined as "the acting out of real or imaginary situations involving relationship between two or more persons." [11] Although it is here thought of primarily as a method of teaching, it should be borne in mind that such techniques as this are therapeutic media themselves. Psychodrama, a device of psychotherapy whereby the person acts out his personality problems, has made a very real contribution to helping people in their emotional problems.

Role playing as a way of teaching counseling has a number of advantages:

1. This procedure can give the individual an opportunity not only to hear about techniques and theories of counseling but also to observe the dynamics of a counseling situation.

2. Playing a role before an audience makes an individual self-conscious and consequently aware of his actions in a new way. Becoming sensitized to his own actions, he has a tendency to analyze them and evaluate his techniques as a counselor.

3. Through observing and participating in role playing, would-be counselors develop a greater sensitivity toward the emotions of other people and an insight into the problems people bring.

4. Role playing teaches the student the important skill of putting himself in the other person's place in order to understand why the other person reacts as he does in a particular situation.

5. If the group is taking turns at playing the role of counselor or counselee, each one has either had his turn or is waiting to participate. This rotation of roles causes certain factors to operate:

a. The ones who are waiting their turn take full advantage of the opportunity to see what the participants will do and so learn to eliminate errors from their own performances.

b. People who have already participated are either elated or disappointed with their efforts and are only too ready to find and point out the good and bad points in the current session.

[11] Robert O. Strufling, "Role Playing in Counselor Training," *Teachers College Research* (1954), p. 429.

c. Very often the person who has just played the role of the counselor takes the role of the counselee in the next session. For him this offers the stimulating experience of feeling the difference between the counselor's and the counselee's position in the interview.

6. Above all this method of teaching has the sound virtue of getting people to learn by doing.

However, despite these advantages there are a number of things that the leader of the group needs to watch for in the use of role playing. To save from an unhappy experience the group leader should remember:

1. Coming out in front of the group to take a role can be a threatening experience. Therefore, it is wise for the leader to select as participants early in the experience people who are secure and confident. Seeing others in action will encourage other members of the group to take part later.

2. The leader should be careful to make sure that the members of the group do not confuse role playing with acting. He should emphasize that this is not a test of acting skill and that the participant should not worry as to whether he played the part correctly or not. He should remind the group that the whole purpose of this experience is to improve counseling skill.

3. It is wise to insist that in the role-playing session fictitious names be used, and both the participants and the observers should continue to use the fictitious names which were used in the counseling session. This tends to focus attention on the role playing and not upon the individual participant. Talking about a role is far less personal and threatening.

It is most important that the members of the group who are watching be made to participate. They should be told that it is necessary for them to make observations. Argyris suggests that there are a number of reasons why observation is important:

1. Much of the value of role playing depends upon the discussion after the session. Naturally this in turn depends upon the observations that the audience makes.

2. If the group members have been hard at work observing during the session, they tend to have more interest in their observations and feel more attached to them. Therefore, they tend to defend them more strongly during the evaluation.

3. The leader can use the observations to show the members the differences in people's observations of an identical situation. For example, the leader may ask two members to read their observations as they have written them. The group is then asked to evaluate the differences.

4. The group realizes, through practice, the difficulty of observing and recording human behavior even in a simple situation.

5. Some members who are not acting may laugh or make fun of the participants. The possibility of this is greatly reduced if the audience is hard at work.

6. The participants tend to do a better job if they see that the audience is also working. Furthermore, it makes the actors feel that they are doing something important and not merely making believe.

7. The feeling of being important tends to eliminate any ham acting which may otherwise occur. Incidentally, ham acting may be a defense against portraying a certain role. It is not necessarily an indication that a person is trying to be smart.

8. Observation may help the group continue role playing, since the actors usually want a chance to observe and the observers a chance to act. This statement naturally gives rise to question of what is to be observed. Argyris suggests that the leader should help the group arrive at a decision as to what should be observed. If this is not possible, the leader may:

   a. Give the group a list of some of the questions to be asked during the evaluation period. This gives the group some idea of what they should observe.

   b. Give the group members preplanned forms which serve as a guide for observation.

   c. Allow the members to note anything they think is important. The members may then discuss their selections after the role playing has finished.[12]

That such a technique is of value is underscored by Dr. Carl Rogers. According to his suggestions, there are three variations of this role playing that will be of use in teaching vocational religious workers.

The first is simple role playing. A pastor takes the role of someone in his church with whom he is familiar. Another pastor takes the role of the counselor, and they proceed with the session. Speaking of such procedures, Carl Rogers says: "As described, this device may seem artificial, but it develops a surprising amount of reality and at times it becomes just as real for the counselor as actual therapy." [13]

In the second method an experienced person takes the role of the counselee. This is even better, for the experienced person can put himself in the place of someone with whom he is working and thus make the situation more vivid as the would-be counselor tries to help him. This "counseling" may be carried on either in front of a group to provide materials for discussion or with an individual in private. Such a procedure not only provides an experience of value for the student but also helps the experienced counselor to gauge the progress of the student. Rogers comments: "It is a particularly good basis for observing and experiencing the student's attitudes as they operate in therapy. When the 'instructor-client' says to the student, 'I felt as though you were thinking so hard about what you were doing that you weren't much interested in me,' or 'I felt as if you were telling me what my attitudes were rather than trying to get into this thing with me,' such expressions of feeling have real impact." [14] This getting to know how one is seen and ex-

---

[12] Chris Argyris, *Role-Playing in Action* (New York: Cornell University, 1951), p. 16.

[13] Carl R. Rogers, *Client-Centered Therapy* (Boston: Houghton Mifflin Co., 1951), pp. 468–69.

[14] *Ibid.*, p. 469.

perienced by the counselee is of great value. From such an experience as this the pastor can learn almost as much as he
would in an actual counseling situation without any feeling of
responsibility which would come from a real situation.

In the third situation pastors counsel each other. The pastor
selects a fellow preacher with whom he feels at ease, and they
team up for a counseling experience. One becomes the counselee and the other the counselor as a problem is talked out. The
situation may then be reversed, or another choice of a partner
made. It is highly improbable that there will be any depth in
this experience, but it gives something of the "feel" of the situation. Sometimes it is possible with people as mature as pastors
for them to have a third person present as an observer; the role-
playing counselor is then able to discover how his work seems
to a neutral party. This whole activity is made more meaningful
if the sessions can be recorded and listened to, discussed, and
evaluated.

We would conclude that the main thing is for the minister to
really want to learn to counsel, to see that instead of an irksome
duty counseling can become a meaningful opportunity to help
people. Many factors will determine the sort of training that a
minister can get: available time, geographical location, finances.
But if he really wants to learn, he will surely find a way.

Part IV

Pastoral Counseling and the Ministry of the Word of God in Christ

The whole perception of pastoral counseling which sustains all the authors of this book is that pastoral counseling is in deed and in truth a form of the ministry of the Word of God in Christ. The communication of the gospel, the experience of prayer, the interpretation of Scripture, and the exposition of Christian doctrine all permeate the practice of pastoral *counseling. Pastoral counseling worthy of the name is vital participation and responsible involvement in the lives of other people as the Holy Spirit brings them new life in Christ. Therefore, this section is devoted to the work of the pastoral counselor in relation to the communication of the gospel through prayer, the interpretation of the Scriptures, and the setting forth of Christian doctrine.*

16. Pastoral Counseling and the Communication of the Gospel

James Lyn Elder

In the Great Commission Jesus instructed his followers to go forth into the world and make disciples (this could be as well translated "discipline the world"). That is to say, the early Christians' task was not simply the proclamation of a message but the effective, persuasive proclamation of it, which is a different thing. The gospel had not been published as Christ intended until it had to some degree been received or at least responded to by the hearers.

The "communication" of the "gospel"—both of these terms are in need of careful definition—includes at least three things: the setting forth of Christian experience in comprehensible ways; the creating of a tension between the hearer of the gospel and the ideal which it sets up; and the response of the hearer in terms of an embracing movement toward the ideal, i.e., the initiation of a process in which the hearer translates the Christian idea into his own personal idiom, giving it expression in terms of his own life situation. Only when this effective relationship between the gospel and the hearer has been achieved may the Christian message be said to have been fully communicated.

In biblical times sexual union was spoken of as knowledge. A man did not "know" a woman nor she the man until, in the profound intimacy of intercourse, they had "experienced" each other. It is in terms of this deepest possible sense of unitive knowledge of the Christian ideal that the communication of the gospel defines its task.

This is suggested repeatedly in scriptural figures of speech such as that in which the disciple is represented as a branch and the Lord, who is the true content of the gospel, as the vitalizing vine. A similar metaphor is used by Paul in portraying the relation of Christ and church as that of bride and groom (see the comment above on the nature of ultimate knowledge as interpenetrating union). Or, in other figures, the Christian is spoken of as being "in the Lord," or as having Christ in him. All these ideas reinforce our understanding of the object of the gospel as being not merely an intellectual or moral change, and certainly not simply an institutional alignment, but rather a profound and thoroughgoing alteration of personality in the direction of Christlikeness.

Because of the long-standing use of the term "preacher" to describe the Christian minister, and because of the continuous emphasis given to religious education, there has been a widespread assumption in our religious culture that communication is almost entirely a matter of preaching or teaching. Associated with this is a directive, one-way concept of one person—the preacher or the teacher—somehow putting something into another simply by "telling him." This is perhaps an unfair oversimplification of the current idea, but it is sufficiently true to have some validity. The hearer of the gospel is thought of in this context as being to a large extent one who passively receives instruction or one who, robot-like, responds to exhortation.

The entrance of counseling into what Dr. Hiltner calls the "communicating perspective"[1] of the ministry points up the interplay of personalities that takes place in all true teaching, preaching, and counseling. It underlines the active role played in the communicative process by the one to whom the message

---

[1] Seward Hiltner, *Preface to Pastoral Theology* (New York: Abingdon Press, 1958).

is being given. Especially does it reveal value in the use of interview in the communicative process, completing as it does the cycle begun by teaching, in which the Christian ideal is comprehensively presented, and continued by preaching, in which emotional persuasion is added to intellectual conviction. Counseling aims squarely at helping the individual to whose head and heart teaching and preaching have made their appeal to make the fullest and most complete "digestive" response to those appeals. Perhaps the following interview will help us to see how this and other communicative objectives are achieved in counseling.

An Illustrative Interview

Tom Jarrett, a seventeen-year-old church member, knocked on the pastor's door. Mr. Miller, the minister, answered the knock. He and Tom greeted each other warmly and sat down in the study. After a few general remarks they got to the purpose of Tom's visit: he faced the need to decide which college to attend, and this in turn was related to his vocational choice. Some conflict had arisen between his father and himself about the latter. The interview continued:

Tom: So you see, Brother Miller, I'm in a pretty tough spot. If I do what I want, I know my father will be angry. But if I do what he wants me to do, I can't possibly be happy.

Pastor: You feel that no matter what you decide one of you will get hurt.

Tom: Yes, I do. Dad has had his heart set on my going into the insurance business with him ever since I can remember. He's talked about it more and more all the time I was in high school. I've known for some time it wasn't what I wanted, but I just couldn't tell him.

Pastor: I see.

Tom: I guess the thing really came to a showdown last fall when I took a high school course in journalism. It was just an introductory course, but it showed me how much good or harm a newspaperman can do. And then I thought of something you said in one of your sermons about the many different ways we can witness to our faith. Right then I knew that newspaper work was for me.

PASTOR: You feel that in journalism you can do not only the thing you would like most to do but also something to express your spiritual convictions?

TOM: Yes, I do. And I know that that is what I'm going to study. I just wish I didn't have to upset my father, though.

PASTOR: You'll make the choice you feel is best so far as your life work is concerned, but at the same time you wish it didn't conflict with your Dad's plans.

TOM: That's about it. You know, I just thought of it—isn't this something of the same problem Christ faced when he started preaching? His family wasn't too sold on the idea, were they?

PASTOR: No, the New Testament tells us that they actually thought he was insane at one time.

TOM: But the thing is, as I remember it from Sunday school, he went on preaching and later his family, or some of them at least, saw that it was best.

PASTOR: And you're hoping something like this will happen in your case.

TOM: Yes, I think so.

Counseling and Christian Expectancy

There is an "expectancy inherent in the gospel," Carroll Wise reminds us, which counseling has the responsibility to implement.[2] Put into other words, this means that such an interview as we have just witnessed between Tom and his pastor should do something to make more real to the boy the resources of his faith.

That there is an expectancy in the gospel is obvious; the word itself means good news. The primary reference is not wholly to the past, however, but to the present and future as well. It is not simply what has happened that comprises the gospel but what can happen again. The wonderful possibilities of the present are always stressed. Perhaps we may make this more clear by asking certain questions concerning gospel expectancy as it related to Tom Jarrett. What had the gospel encouraged

[2] Carroll A. Wise, *Pastoral Counseling: Its Theory and Practice* (New York: Harper & Brothers, 1951), p. 3.

him to expect, and how did counseling implement that expectancy in his case?

In the first place, Tom had a justifiable Christian hope that he would become a person in his own right, apart from his family or anyone else. This does not mean, of course, the cutting of all family ties, but it does mean the establishing of oneself as an autonomous being. In Tom's case this was related, as it often is with young people, to a vocational decision and this in turn to the choice of college.

Furthermore, Tom had the right to expect his life to count for Christ, to contribute something to the kingdom of God. He had been encouraged by his church to think of himself as a world-changer for God. His vocational interest is directly related to this spiritual concept of himself.

It is evident, isn't it, that Tom's talk with the pastor helped him to realize, or to begin to achieve, these expectations? The process may not soon, if ever, be completed, but the boy is helped on his way. What teaching had set before him as an ideal and what preaching had persuaded him to embrace, counseling helped him to take in and to incorporate effectively into his own life. What elements within the interview specifically contributed to this desired end?

In the first place, the interview itself is a drama of redemption. It contains interpersonal warmth, permissiveness, and encouragement. It is the most favorable possible climate in which insight and growth may be achieved. What a greenhouse in which light, temperature, and humidity are carefully controlled is to a plant, so the gracious atmosphere of counseling is to a growing soul.

In the second place, the pastoral counselor, as a mature person himself, is of help to Tom's spiritual development. (A mature person is one who, his own needs having been largely met, is able to meet the needs of others.) If preaching is, as someone has said, not simply the preparation and delivery of a sermon but of a man, counseling is even more so. It has been suggested by a well-known therapist that the healing interview is 95 per cent personality and only 5 per cent technique. Mr. Miller is himself what he is trying to help Tom to become. In counseling the minister presents himself as an object of identification, saying with Paul, "Be ye imitators [or representers] of me, even as I also am of Christ" (1 Cor. 11:1, ASV).

In the third place, counseling assists the communicative process by giving the individual both the opportunity and the encouragement to put into words the feelings and thoughts half-formed within him. Not until a person can verbalize to some extent his inner experiences can he be said to know them. Good teaching does this to a large degree, but counseling, inasmuch as it deals intensively with the individual, does it even more.

Perhaps an illustration from the area of botany will clarify this. The growth of a plant begins when food and water press on the surface cells of the root. As tension increases, these cells open to admit nourishment. It is then drawn by assimilation up into the plant to be changed into stalk, leaf, and fruit. Counseling aids the digestion of those nutritive concepts, ideas, and ideals which, through preaching and teaching, have been made to press on the roots of the soul. Without such assistance the assimilative process would be achieved much more slowly, if at all.

Fourthly, counseling helps to make real, as it did to Tom Jarrett, what it means to be a person in one's own right. The attentiveness paid by the pastor to Tom's statements and the permissiveness extended the boy in letting him discuss what he wished and in the manner he wished—these and other elements of the interview combined to strengthen Tom's sense of individuality and his awareness of himself as a person of value without reference to his family or anyone else outside himself.

The Holy Spirit in Counseling

Thus far counseling has been presented almost as though it were a purely human undertaking. No reference has been made at all to the role played by the Holy Spirit in the procedure. To discuss Christian counseling without some such statement is, as someone said with reference to something else, "*Hamlet* with Hamlet left out."

The Christian minister understands the Spirit of God to be operative in all that is done in obedience to him. This is to say, wherever the commands of Christ are taken seriously and the goals he indicated striven for, there the Holy Spirit is in action.

The pastoral counselor assumes that if he is working for a Christian objective in a Christlike manner, the Spirit of God will fill out that which is lacking and complete the work. The minister's feelings, thoughts, words, and actions with reference to the counselee will be imbued by the Divine Presence. The Christian assumption is that every step made in the direction of likeness to Christ is ultimately the fruit of the Spirit at work within the counselee. In true pastoral counseling there is no point, no moment, at which the Holy Spirit is not effectively present. To speak of psychological laws of insight and growth is but to indicate the near edge of the work of God in human experience.

Summary

"Communicating the gospel" means the effective inworking of Christian ideas and ideals into the life of persons. Teaching and preaching tend toward this end; teaching makes its appeal primarily to the head, preaching to the heart.

Communication is complete when the person with whom teaching and preaching have done their best is helped to respond and to resolve the tension in the direction of the ideal by assimilating and digesting what has been presented to him.

The person of the counselor, the gracious warmth of the interview, the encouragement and opportunity given one to put his deepest thoughts into clarifying words—all these elements of counseling combine to help the counselee appropriate for himself the treasure of the gospel.

And through all that is said and done in the interview the Holy Spirit is at work. His presence is manifest in the Christlike results achieved. His power is depended upon by the minister and church alike for success in counseling.

17. Pastoral Counseling and the Experience of Prayer

Wayne E. Oates

Pastoral counseling, when properly understood and practiced, is in and of itself a total experience of prayer. Prayer is the native hue and resolution of the man of God who dedicates hours of time to one person, who listens to that person with fulness of attention and abandon, and who searches with that person for an over-all meaning and purpose for his life under God. This spiritual pilgrimage, which is commonly known by the somewhat pedestrian term "pastoral counseling," *is* the "soul's sincere desire, unuttered or expressed" for both counselor and counselee.

Prayer and the Third Presence in Counseling

Not only the counselee but also the counselor tends to feel alone in the process of counseling. The Holy Spirit becomes the Third Presence which breaks down the middle walls of partition that cause both counselor and counselee to feel alone. The Holy Spirit becomes the power who creates communion. We can call this "rapport," "a relationship of a trusted motive," "empathy," or "client-centeredness," depending upon which technical set of books we read. But in the faith of the pastoral counselor this is that work of the Holy Spirit which helps both the counselor and the counselee to understand in his own language the truth that God would have them both know.

This Third Presence keeps the pastor at his best in probing

his own motives for being a counselor. He does not fear to be met by and to meet his counselee in openness and sincerity when he consciously practices the presence of the Holy Spirit in what he does as a counselor. Furthermore, he has a keener sense of responsibility for the counselee, not just as another "case" nor as a person "with problems" nor even as a "prospect," but as a person for whom Christ died. He is less likely to act irreverently, facetiously, or flippantly or to depend upon his charm, his cleverness, or his prestige. Rather, he is more likely to take the attitude of openness so characteristic of a little child and seek to learn from the person who has sought his aid. For, in fact, the counselor begins anew with each counselee, learning of that person's uniqueness before God.

Again, this Third Presence is the pastoral counselor's main assurance against using the counselee for his own self-gratification, self-enhancement, or self-defense. This person will be an end in himself and not a means to the counselor's preordained objectives. The counselor's love will be unconditional and non-exploitative; it will be devoted to the person's good and not merely his own. In other words, the pastoral counselor who feels himself to be an instrument of the Holy Spirit will be a counselor who ministers, not one who counsels in order to be ministered unto. God, unto who all hearts are open and from whom no secrets are hidden, will cleanse the inspirations of the minister's heart so that he may worthily serve the Heavenly Father and magnify his name through counseling.

Exploring the Counselee's Prayer Relationship

A unique characteristic of pastoral counseling is that the counselor has the primary responsibility for dealing with the counselee's capacity to communicate with and relate to God. The heart of this capacity is the experience of prayer. Therefore, the pastoral counselor will routinely take a primary interest in what the counselee has to say about his prayer life. This relationship should be explored with sensitivity, skill, and spiritual understanding. All that can be learned concerning prayer from the Bible will be exceptionally helpful.[1]

The important thing to look for in the exploration of the prayer life of the counselee, however, is the quality of the relationship between the person and God. This knowledge gets the counselor to the center of pastoral counseling as a ministry of reconciliation. The counselee may feel hostile toward God, and his resentment may be rooted in the accumulated feelings of rejection from all spheres of his life. He may have withdrawn from God and begun to build an imaginary world in which he himself is all-powerful. Therefore, he cannot stand any frustration, disappointment, or disillusionment from other people. Or, again, he may feel that God has left him and will not return. Such feelings could be rooted in his bereavement of a loved one who was for all practical purposes an idol to him. The process of counseling may well become for him a bridge over which he may walk to God out of his bereavement.

The counselee may say that he can no longer feel close to God and that his spiritual life is cold and lonely. When the counselor compares this with all his other relationships, the counselee's apathy and coldness applies not only to God but to all other people as well. The counselor cannot rush this person into an artificial experience of prayer; he may do well to assure him that he will pray for him for a while. Rather, through the warmth and sustaining grace of his own consistent affection and understanding the counselor can gradually restore some of the feelings that were anesthetized by shocks and blows this person has received. A mother who saw her only daughter attempt suicide, for instance, understandably cannot pray. Such a situation will take time and sustaining patience on the part

---

[1] I have dealt with this in more detail in my own book, *The Bible in Pastoral Care* (Philadelphia: Westminster Press, 1953), pp. 108 ff. Furthermore, careful study of the spiritual experience in the great classics of devotion such as Thomas a Kempis' *Imitation of Christ;* Jacob Boehme's *The Way of Christ;* Augustine's *Confessions;* Bunyan's *The Pilgrim's Progress;* and others, will yield real assistance to the pastor as a counselor.

of the counselor. An unmarried girl who has just learned that she is pregnant is shocked and numbed, and the pastor is insensitive who expects her to have certain feelings, especially the deep remorse that will come later.

But, on the other hand, the dependent person who expects God to give him a ready-made answer may demand that the pastor pray *for* him. The pastor may be put into the position of requiring this person to stand on his own two feet before God and do his own praying. He will do so with gentle firmness and trusting confidence. But, nevertheless, he will not become a crutch for the person to use. Nor will he let the chronically dependent person use prayer as a sedative, an opiate, and a placebo. He thinks of prayer as a way of life and not as an addiction whereby to avoid life. This attitude is particularly relevant to the Baptist view of life, in which ritual in prayer, repetition in prayer, and heavy symbolism in prayer are somewhat restricted and often completely absent. The Christian Science practitioner can use repetitions of reassurance to accomplish not healing but symptom restriction. This is something which appeals to the dependent personality who needs constant reassurance.

Again, prayer can well be a form of manipulation, both of the counselor and of God. Witness the demands that are laid upon pastors to pray for other people in ways which do not take the personhood of the other people into consideration at all. Also, prayer can be a means a person has of maintaining a "sticky fixation" upon the pastor long past the time he should have been moved into a more mature perspective of him. These are extractive and manipulative attempts of counselees to get something out of God, the counselor, or other people without any sense of personal responsibility.

But more often than any of these, prayer may be that quest of the spirit of counselor and counselee for a new meaning for the life of the counselee. It may be the comradeship of two people, both of whom perceive themselves as sinners in the hands of a loving and revealing God in Christ. Prayer may well be the revelation of a new and deeper level of personal honesty, in which the counselee is enabled to confront himself with more courage and self-understanding wrought out of a quiet communication of a God that understands and empowers. Prayer also may be toward the latter phases of counseling a sense of triumph and completion in which God is glorified for the new hope that has come out of despair, the new purpose that has come out of pointlessness, and the new satisfaction that has come to a previously unhappy marriage. In the final analysis, then, prayer becomes the conservator of all the gains that have come into being in counseling.

Some Techniques of Prayer in Pastoral Counseling

The timing of prayer is extremely important. In the earlier phases of a single-interview counseling situation the pastoral counselor is wise to leave the initiative on the counselee for any formal expressions of prayer. But he should be exceptionally alert for references to difficulties the person may have been having in his prayer life. A formal prayer at the end of a single-interview encounter may render tremendous support and make the conference unforgettable for the counselee.

In the earlier phases of a longer-term, multiple-interview counseling relationship the chances are strong that the pastor will use prayer most effectively by simply telling the person that he will be praying for him and telling him what he will be praying. He can say: "I will be remembering you in my own personal and private prayers. I want you to know that I will be praying that you will be given courage to face both yourself and your world and that you will become aware that you are not alone but that God is with you."

Prayer, Pastoral Counseling, and Evangelism

In the central, detailed inquiry of longer-term pastoral counseling the barriers between the person and an effective relationship with God and with the significant persons of his world are the stuff of which the conversations are made. As the person faces up to his own limitations, he sloughs off his feelings of worthlessness before himself and other people. He frankly confesses his own sins before God; he deals with the barriers under the grace of God. This *is* evangelism, as a person discovers new life in God as revealed in Christ and interpreted by the counselor, particularly in his own personal reactions toward the counselee. Often this relationship results in a spontaneous and profound conversion experience.[2] But evangelism is the work of a minister of reconciliation as he enables an individual before God to deal with the barriers that separate him, estrange him, cause him to condemn himself, and threaten him with destruction apart from the love that knows no barrier in Christ.

Prayers of Commitment and Vows of Dedication

In the closing phases of a longer-term counseling relationship certain decisions will have been made about many areas of life. They tend to be brought into focus in a new commitment to God. These decisions are also coupled with tangible evidences of new growth, sustaining insights, and reassuring discoveries. The counselee-counselor relationship then becomes more specifically and formally one of prayer. The psalmist speaks to the point again and again of such feelings and needs, as in this example:

I waited patiently for the Lord; and he inclined unto me, and heard my cry.
He brought me up also out of an horrible pit, out of the miry clay, and set my feet upon a rock, and established my goings.
And he hath put a new song in my mouth, even praise unto our God. . . .
Many, O Lord my God, are thy wonderful works which thou hast done, and thy thoughts which are to us-ward: they cannot be reckoned up in order unto thee: . . .

[2] See Wayne E. Oates, *Anxiety in Christian Experience* (Philadelphia: Westminster Press, 1955), for examples of this.

I have not hid thy righteousness within my heart; I have declared
thy faithfulness and thy salvation.

(Psalm 40:1–3, 5, 10)

Many such Psalms catch up the specific feelings of the counselee. In preparation for a concluding interview the pastoral
counselor may do well to get a small paperback edition of the
book of Psalms and mark it for the future reading of the counselee. Thus, in the phase of reconstruction and guidance the
counselor begins to teach the counselee to pray. The counselor
cannot leave this task undone or refer it to others, whether he
is preaching, teaching, or counseling. When he assumes this
perspective of his task, he feels genuine comradeship with the
Master, who himself first taught men that they should always
pray and then taught them how to pray.

Danger: Prayer as a Means

A stirring word of warning must follow any discussion of how
to pray. Prayer is a relationship. It is not a tool or a resource
or any such means to some other end, however worthy that
end may be. Communion with God, more so than any other
relationship, has many dramatic and awe-inspiring side-effects,
such as healing, relaxation, and peace of mind. But these are
not the purpose of prayer. Communion with God is the love of
God for his own sake alone. We like to say that "the family
that prays together stays together," but keeping the family together is not the primary purpose of praying. Christians are to
love God for his own sake and his own sake alone, and then all
such good values such as a family that stays together are added.
This becomes painfully apparent in counseling with a person
who is a devout Christian but whose marriage has collapsed.
If he had made a happy and successful marriage the intention
of his prayers, his relationship with God would have been
broken when his marriage failed. In turn, it might well be said
of him that his religion was an idolatry of his marriage partner.

Furthermore, when the pastoral counselor deals with secular therapists of one kind or another, he hears them saying that "religion" is a "resource" which is helpful to a patient in his struggle for help. Prayer thus can become a means to well-being and is judged as being valid in terms of its practical results. Yet this idea can lead the pastoral counselor into some very shallow thinking about the meaning of the life of prayer. Unless the pastoral counselor and his counselee are genuinely convinced of the truth of the relationship of prayer, they may find themselves in the position of attempting to cure one false way of life with another fictitious one. Therefore, it is extremely important that prayer life be considered by the pastoral counselor as being intrinsically real and worthy in its own right apart from any lesser goals it may achieve.

The Goals of Pastoral Counseling and the Life of Prayer

The pastoral counselor must see goals of pastoral counseling itself very clearly. If prayer is to be relevant at all to the work of pastoral counseling, the goals of counseling must be deeply compatible with the character of prayer. What, then, are the goals of pastoral counseling and how do they relate to the life of prayer?

Self-confrontation.—One of the major objectives of pastoral counseling is enabling the counselee to face himself as he really is. He is called upon to lay aside his subterfuges of self-deception and to see himself, not merely as he hopes that he is, but indeed as he actually is. This self-confrontation is essential to meaningful prayer, also, and is a vital part of genuine repentance. Whether counselor and counselee are engaging in formal prayer or not, both of them are essentially engaged in the spiritual exercise of prayer when they each confront the other and cause each to confront himself.

Achievement of insight.—A second goal of pastoral counseling is the achievement of insight into self and the meaning of life. Karl Menninger is right when he says that a genuine experience of prayer can bring to an individual a more fully orbed understanding of himself and a firmer grasp upon the nature of human existence. Here again the nature of prayer and the objectives of pastoral counseling are profoundly compatible. The pilgrimage upon which counselor and counselee embark together as they quest for the meaning of life is a comradeship of prayer. The objective of the achievement of insight which motivates all good pastoral counseling is also intrinsic to the meaning of the life of prayer.

The stimulation of spiritual maturity.—Self-confrontation and the achievement of insight contribute to the growth of the mature Christian. Spiritual growth means that vital changes are taking place in the life of the individual. We often say that "prayer changes things," but the pastoral counselor spells this out in detail by asking the direction which the changes take. Is the person learning to speak the truth in love and to grow up into Christ who is the head? This is the transcendent objective of all good pastoral counseling.

The establishment of durable relationships.—Harry Stack Sullivan has said that one of the characteristics of the mature person is that he has the capacity to establish lasting or durable relationships. This is one of the objectives of pastoral counseling: to help people do just this. The spiritually immature person breaks his relationships with people as soon as he no longer has any use for them. But the spiritually mature person works faithfully at the business of establishing relationships on grounds upon which they can permanently stand. In this sense prayer and pastoral counseling have another meeting place. We like to think of prayer as being a relationship between man, who lives from generation to generation, and God, who lives from everlasting to everlasting. Therefore, when two people pray together, they are praying in relation to each other in such a way as to be caught up into an everlasting dimension of existence. Prayer becomes that gauge by which we measure all other relationships, and pastoral counseling becomes that process whereby we learn to live with one another in order that our prayers be not hindered.

Communing and relating.—Finally, one of the major objectives of all good pastoral counseling is the development of the art of communion and the skill of relating. Pastoral counseling has moved through several stages of development in the past two decades. At first we thought of counseling as handing out final answers to people. We thought of ourselves as failures unless we had the right answer for every conceivable problem. Then we moved into a second phase of understanding, namely, we learned to listen. We thought of pastoral counseling as letting people talk and getting things out of their systems. This helped more than just giving advice, but we found many people whose much talking covered up rather than revealed or relieved their difficulties.

Then we moved into a third stage of our understanding of pastoral counseling; we became aware of the importance of the life history and developmental processes of the individual's personality. Here we became enamored with diagnosis and developmental theories. But suddenly we discovered that we could have a thorough collection of information about a person's life and never have met him face to face as a person, joined minds with him as a fellow human being, nor appreciated him in terms of his own understanding of himself.

Consequently, we turned to a fourth phase of counseling, that of learning how to communicate with the person and to appreciate the powerful forces of relationship interacting between the counselor and the counselee. This has thrust us into the accent of pastoral counseling as recent as our last breath: the importance of communing with and relating to the counselee. As we come to this important goal of counseling we once again find ourselves more intimately involved in pastoral counseling as an experience of prayer. For this is exactly what prayer is: communion with God, removal of barriers of relationship to God, and approaching with boldness the throne of grace.

Therefore, we can see that the goals of pastoral counseling and the goals of prayer, rightly perceived, should be the same. In both instances we have the ministry of the Word of God in Christ as the whole counsel of God.

18. Pastoral Counseling and the Interpretation of Scripture

D. Allen Brabham

The shepherd role of the pastor, the closeness that exists between pastor and parishioners, and the working of the Spirit through Scripture afford pastoral counselors an ideal teaching opportunity. The preaching method has its definite advantages over the one-to-one counseling interview when a large group is involved. But faulty communication can come between preacher and hearer, and since preaching does not offer that close interpersonal relationship necessary for maximum learning, the individual needs of the parishioners may not be met. Small group study or counseling also has its advantages. In a small group the leader is closer to the individual, and more participation by members of the group is possible. Through this participation the needs of the individual are more nearly met.

Nevertheless, when the one-to-one relationship of pastoral counseling is compared to both preaching and teaching, an even more ideal learning experience is presented because most communication barriers are absent, expression of real feeling is more apt to occur, and the two become one through the "commonness" which is experienced when two people are present with the Master. If this then be true, Bible teaching and interpretation find the most ideal environment in the counseling relationship. Much Bible teaching can be done in the verbal use of actual Scripture passages, stories, and parables and through the attitudes existing in this oneness which more nearly approximate the relationships the Master experienced in his pastoral ministry.

Mentioning some incorrect and correct uses of Bible interpretation from the pastoral counseling viewpoint may help approach the ideal teaching-learning situation just described.

Incorrect Uses of the Bible

The pastoral counselor may use the Bible as a lever to coerce his counselees into a position which would supposedly be a solution to the problem, or he may at least use it in an attempt to point the counselee in the direction of a predetermined goal. This use of the Bible is to wave it around in the counseling interview like a wand of authority. He may use the Bible to extend his own authoritarian feeling or unconsciously to give him an escape from responsibility. The dependent counselee may accept such an authoritarian use and feel comfortable in doing so. If the advice is good, the counselee may become a parasite; if the advice is incorrect, the dependent counselee may feel that he has not been understood, that the Bible has not helped, and that the counselor cannot offer further aid. Thus further relationship is deterred.

The dangers involved in such a use of the Bible are: first, the pastoral counselor may be by-passing the true feelings and the true needs of the counselee; second, the pastoral counselor, though unaware, may be merely meeting some of his own personal needs for security; third, the counselee may rebel against the counselor if advice fails; and fourth, the Bible may be put in a bad light. The Bible does possess therapeutic authority, but it may not be within reach for individuals with severely damaged emotions. The emotional structure within the person may have to be rebuilt so the Bible can be offered therapeutically and successfully.

The Bible has much symbolic power in both helpful and unhelpful ways. The concern here is with the misuse of the Bible as a symbol. The disturbed person seeking a solution to a problem will turn many times to the Bible because it is a symbol of wholeness, health, and unity. Unfortunately some pastors, religious leaders, and parishioners look to the Bible as if it were a fetish. "If you will read the Bible, it will help you," said the student-counselor. Or the parishioner might exclaim, "I read the Bible hours each day, but I still cannot feel God's presence."

Positive reading of the Bible is not the entire answer. Many people expect the Bible to heal them without their knowing what their trouble is and/or without their having to share in the responsibility of becoming well. This may also be true of the pastoral counselor. His use of the Bible as a fetish may indicate the shirking of all responsibility under the guise of the power of Scripture. Whether this use of the Bible aids the parishioner or not is sometimes of little concern to the pastoral counselor; his task is completed by admonishing, "Read the Bible; it will help you."

Once the pastor or religious leader determines that use of the Bible is appropriate and that this is the appropriate time to use Scripture with a given counselee, then selected Scripture passages may be used. Scripture may focus upon the particular type of problem on which the counseling is centered, as well as upon the emotional tone, capacity, and potential of the counselee. The pastoral counselor would not wisely use Psalm 37:3-5 with both the impatient and the lonely counselee. If the parishioner's emotions would allow him to accept this passage, the impatient counselee would likely find patience. The lonely person might find the pastor too assuming; he cannot be certain enough God is present for him to "trust," "delight," or "commit" himself for consolation.

Coercion is another principle which is seen often in counseling and unfortunately too often in the pastoral counselor relationship. The pastor, to meet (unconsciously) his own agressive needs, sometimes feels that he must superimpose his solution of the problem upon the counselee without considering the conscious or unconscious needs of the counselee. In this type of relationship, for instance, the pastor may give his own scriptural interpretation rather than allowing the counselee the freedom to present his or her interpretation.

Coercion all but demands conformity. When conformity is imposed upon disturbed parishioners, they may react like ambivalent adolescents—which they may be emotionally; therefore, they rebel, submit, or become anxious.

These coercive, demanding approaches tend to hinder the counseling relationship itself. They ignore the living relationship in favor of the letter of the Scripture. When used by the pastoral counselor with every counselee, these methods and their underlying principles may merely cover up his insecurity with his traditional authority as a Christian leader. Many religious leaders hide behind such methods and principles instead of becoming responsible teacher-counselors who release creative power within the counselee.

Why is the Bible misused? Why is the best tool the Christian worker possesses often used carelessly? Why is the Spirit quenched? Some answers to these questions have been given above. However, additional reasons may be suggested: ignorance of the Bible attitudinally, factually, historically, spiritually, and psychologically; lack of thought; inability to sense the real needs present in the counselee; failure to wait for the proper time in the interview to present the Bible; failure to wait until the problem has been fully defined; and the use of the proof-text approach to solving problems of the counselee.

In summary, the pastoral counselor who wrongly uses the Bible usually does so to meet some personal need which he feels in the interpersonal relationship between himself and the parishioner.

Correct Uses of the Bible

The counselor should be permissive enough to learn the actual nature of the problem presented by the parishioner. He should be aware enough to sense the symbolic meaning of the Bible to the parishioner. He should be informed enough to know the Bible historically, factually, spiritually, and psychologically. Knowledge of these things enables him to be person-centered in his approach and, thereby, be a better interpreter of the Bible. "Here he will find the 'attitudinal orientation' suggested by modern therapists extremely relevant, as he seeks to become a 'person-centered' Biblical interpreter to individuals." [1]

The pastoral counselor, in dealing with an individual, will only use the passages concerning death, the wrath of God, punishment, or condemnation—to mention a few—when the person has the capacity to accept such through trust. Some parishioners may feel that God has already done these things to them through their present problems because of some previous sin or unfaithfulness.

The pastoral counselor, however, may find appropriate Scriptures which illustrate the love of God, God's presence, confession of sin, profession of faith, repentance, comfort, and courage. These are very helpful to guilt-laden individuals and more nearly approach the positive method of Jesus. These Scriptures communicate that God loves, comforts, understands, and reassures. The pastoral counselor, by using these words of comfort, will more nearly identify himself with the Father of mercies and the God of all comfort, and a therapeutic understanding of God will be communicated to the parishioner.

Scripture may be used as an aid to prayer. Two factors are involved here: first, prayer enables the parishioner to move beyond himself and the pastoral counselor to God; second, the parishioner is allowed to become himself in his own relationship with God, not in the relationship the pastoral counselor has with God.

The pastoral counselor may also correctly use the Bible by verses, stories, or parables to illustrate the problem involved.

[1] Wayne E. Oates, *The Bible in Pastoral Care* (Philadelphia: Westminster Press, 1953), p. 72.

This confronts the pastoral counselor and parishioner with biblical characters and reality. This confrontation can enable the counselee to identify with God, self, and other important persons. Such identification is necessary to every person, especially in the pastoral-parishioner counseling situation.

Something has been said of the misuse of the symbolic power of the Bible. Now attention should be given to the correct use of the Bible as a symbol. The evidence that a Bible is in a room communicates a great deal. A Bible carried by a person as he walks the street communicates that the bearer is a religious if not Christian person, that this person—to some people—is a minister, and that this person is a witness of the gospel. D. L. Moody said to carry a Bible a mile is to preach a sermon a mile long.

Listed below are some Scripture passages which should be helpful in the counseling relationship.

Courage—Joshua 1:1–9; 2 Timothy 1:7
Discouragement—Isaiah 40; James 5:7–8, 10–11
Doubt—Matthew 14:31; John 20:25–29
Death—John 14:1–6; 1 Thessalonians 4:13–17
Failure—1 Corinthians 3:11–15
Forgiveness—Matthew 18:21–35; Luke 17:1–4
Fear—John 12:42
Hate—Ephesians 4:31; 1 John 2:9; 3:15
Happiness—Matthew 5:3–12; John 15:11–17
Patience—1 Peter 2:19–23; James 1:3–4, 19
Death desired—Job 6:8–11; 7:1–3, 15–16
Unanswered prayer—Luke 11:5–12
Suffering—John 15:18–25
Worry—Psalm 37; John 14:27–31

Principles of Biblical Teaching in Pastoral Counseling

Counseling as done by religious workers often becomes a form of biblical instruction. This teaching relationship necessitates sound principles of teaching. All of these principles cannot be discussed in detail. The more important ones, however, shall be mentioned as they relate to biblical interpretation in counseling. The method or methods utilized by the pastoral counselor will determine the principles involved since principles always are inherent in or underlie methods. Both methods and principles will be determined to some degree by the personalities of the religious leader and parishioner involved.

Participation.—Mutual participation is a general principle of biblical instruction within every pastoral counseling situation. Pastoral counselor and parishioner face each other in a common search for wholeness. Both participate, or the relationship is not a healthy one, and neither sound teaching nor counseling occurs. Involvement is a direct result of participation. Being involved creatively, for instance, in a spiritual or personality problem where Scripture can play a large part enables both the pastoral counselor and the parishioner to learn the meaning of the Bible.

Jesus used the principle of participation and involvement on many occasions by means of questions. On one such occasion he asked, "Whom do men say that I the Son of Man am? . . . But whom say ye that I am?" The question motivates thinking by stimulating the physical and mental processes necessary to learning. Participation and involvement are deepened when the counselor is sensitive enough, as was Jesus, to know that the question is in the mind of the counselee and fearless enough to build a relationship so well established as to lead the person into self-revelation. As Jesus revealed himself to people, they in turn were encouraged to reveal themselves to him.

The result of such participation and involvement is sharing. In fact, in our encounters with Christ and in turn with our counselees, sharing is but an outward expression of inward involvement, a part of the general principle of participation. Participation, however, may take forms other than mere verbal sharing.

The pastoral counselor may well be the one upon whom the successful carrying out of this principle depends. Being willing to participate himself, the counselor will so set the counselee at ease that participation, thus involvement, and thus sharing will be natural. Both individuals in the interview will feel free. When this is accomplished, growth as indicated in the story of Zaccheus will be seen. Jesus knew that more than curiosity motivated Zaccheus to participate in the actions of the crowd even to the extent of climbing the tree. So the Lord took the initiative by recognizing Zaccheus and inviting himself to abide in Zaccheus' home. Salvation came, and Zaccheus immediately made fourfold restitution to those he had wronged. This courageous act of Jesus set vital forces of participation into powerful motion.

Listening.—Listening is another cardinal principle which promotes sound teaching in counseling. Listening affords the pastoral counselor the opportunity to learn—to learn who, what, and where the counselee is. By listening he learns what the counselee knows about the Bible and how he relates his problems to the Bible. By listening the counselor learns the spiritual status of the counselee and can thereby decide what Scripture verse, story, or parable might be most helpful to the counselee. Jesus was and is a good listener. Cannot this be noted in the relationship between Jesus and the centurion as recorded in Matthew 8:5–13?

Observation.—Observation as a teaching principle takes into account the facial expressions, bodily movements, posture, and appearance of the counselee. These are physical observations and may be symptomatic of the emotional tone, ability, stability, and potential of the counselee. Other observations are necessary also such as the tone of voice, speed of speech, and flavor of words. These traits denote whether the counselee lives in a gay or gloomy atmosphere and determine what is demanded of the pastoral counselor in meeting the needs of the parishioner. On many occasions observations will go beyond the physical or verbal into the realm of feeling. In a long pause the pastoral counselor and parishioner may be observing and weighing the feelings expressed. Is it not possible that Jesus quietly observed the Syrophenician woman before he spoke to her? After she had spoken and poured out her problem, the Scriptures report that "he answered her not a word." Could this not have been a period of time, short or long, for physical and emotional observation by the Master and the woman? Even with the disciples' interruption, Jesus was able to communicate understanding because the woman went on to worship him and seek help.

Example and identification.—The principle of example should be present in the counseling relationship. Jesus on many occasions presented principles by which his disciples should live. He went further than verbalizing the principles; he put the principles into action by example. He not only said to forgive seventy times seven, but when the adulteress was brought before him he said, "He that is without sin among you, let him first cast a stone at her." After no man accused her further, Jesus said, "Go, and sin no more."

The principle of identification would of necessity follow as a result of example. The pastoral counselor must be an example of someone. Therefore, because of his role as a symbol of God in our culture, he is identified with God. Many persons will identify him as God. In the state of "peeping insight," a counselee said, "You are God to me. Even though I have felt that God has condemned me, I know he must be like you. I believe that sometime in the future, I'll come to see and know him as I have come to see and know you." Did not Jesus point men beyond himself to the Father? Did he not use sayings which pointed people beyond himself (someone they could see) to spiritual truths (which they could not see)? He said, "I and my Father are one" and "No man cometh to the Father, but by me." Paul and Barnabas said to those who would deify them: "We are men of like passions with you."

As these principles are seen in the attitudes and actions of Jesus, these principles should be seen in and thus taught by the pastoral counselor, especially in his use of the Bible. If the pastor communicates a desire to participate, to become involved, to share, to listen, to observe, to be an example, and thus to understand, love, and accept,[2] he will identify himself with the properties that set the stage for an empathic, therapeutic relationship. This type of relationship will be most valuable to the counselee in the reception, interpretation, and utilization of the Scriptures. The pastoral counselor, in other words, becomes that which is necessary for the meaningful use of the Bible.

Person-centered Attitudes and Scripture

Some of the principles which undergird the person-centered attitude and method have been mentioned above. Principles that complement sound biblical teaching in pastoral counseling seem to relate closely in attitude and philosophy to the person-centered procedures of counseling. These complementary procedures and principles also seem to relate closely to those inter-personal relationships of Jesus that are recorded in the New Testament.

Comparative principles and procedures.—Many Christian counselors have been amazed to find characteristics in secular counseling similar to those found in the Bible. Some critics think that Christian leaders have failed to avail themselves of the truths in the Scriptures by allowing secular disciplines to point out spiritual truths which have been at the finger tips of Christendom throughout the centuries.

The Scriptures reflect Jesus' respect for the dignity and worth of individuals as created by God, disregarding who they were. Jesus understood, loved, and accepted the breast-beating women, the blind, the deaf, the soul-thirsty Mary who sat at his feet, and the learned Nicodemus who seemingly played the coward by coming to the Master at night. Jesus allowed the breast-beating woman, Mary, and Nicodemus to be the creative souls they were born to be, and in that creative, loosing freedom

[2] Carroll A. Wise, *Psychiatry and the Bible* (New York: Harper & Brothers, 1956), pp. 117–19.

each one found himself. Each one came to see his inner self as it really was. Through this new respect and worth for themselves they became what Jesus wanted them to be. They fulfilled the will of God in their lives by being allowed to be honest, congruent, and transparent in the presence of God. Respect for persons involves creativity, freedom of choice, self-discovery, and self-respect. Through the pastor's respect for individuals, the transforming grace of God may be experienced by those who are seeking salvation, courage, assurance, or comfort.

C. B. Eavey used an interesting term, "mental set," [3] which correlates with the much-used counseling phrase "meet the person where he or she is." By this term Eavey meant the total condition of the person at the existential moment of the counseling relationship. What are the past and present experiences of the person? How is the person reacting to these experiences? Translating this idea into Bible interpretation within pastoral counseling, the counselor might ask the following questions: Where is the parishioner in relation to his knowledge of the Bible? What have been the past experiences of the parishioner with the Bible? What is the parishioner's present attitude toward the Bible? What is the parishioner's present interpretation of the Bible?

Perhaps these questions should never be asked the parishioner directly by the pastoral counselor. However they should be asked in the counselor's mind to enable him to know the person's "mental set" toward the Bible. David Belgum implied that the counselor should consider the attitude and background of the counselee before using the Scriptures.[4] Jesus made this truth evident when he said to his disciples, "I have yet many things to say unto you, but ye cannot bear them now." The

[3] C. B. Eavey, *Principles in Teaching for Christian Teachers* (Grand Rapids: Zondervan Publishing House, 1940), p. 118.

[4] David Belgum, *Clinical Training for Pastoral Care* (Philadelphia: Westminster Press, 1956), pp. 52–54.

Master sensed what spiritual truths his disciples could and could not discern.

Jesus so loved people that he sensed the needs of all. In this sensitiveness he communicated acceptance, understanding, humility, and above all, love. This respect for others is the true losing of oneself to find oneself, as a pastoral counselor, that parishioners may by losing themselves find themselves. The previous statement is biblical language; however, when modern therapists speak in terms of respect for others, accepting others, allowing the person the freedom to be himself, and meeting the person where he is—are not these therapists expressing similar truths in different language? Here is something of the same challenge for the pastoral counselor, especially in Bible interpretation, that the Saviour faced in the cross.

Teaching through "feeling" communication.—Participation, involvement, identification, sharing, "mental set," and respect for persons are of necessity important. However, through what avenue does the pastoral counselor utilize these to aid the parishioner? "Since feeling is deep and strong in all that any human being does and thinks, the feeling phase [of learning] exerts even greater influence." [5] Oates expressed something of the same thought when he wrote that the pastoral counselor must have some "feeling entree" into the context of the parishioner's life if Scripture interpretation is to be adequate.[6] Carl Rogers, perhaps the major advocate of teaching and counseling through "feeling" communication, wrote, "Few problems are solely intellectual in nature. . . . The intellectual factors . . . are often childishly simple. It is the unrecognized emotional factors which are usually basic. These emotional factors are most quickly understood by the client and the counselor if the counseling recognizes and follows the pattern of the client's feelings." [7]

[5] Eavey, *op. cit.*, p. 225.
[6] Oates, *The Bible in Pastoral Care*, p. 73.
[7] Carl R. Rogers, *Counseling and Psychotherapy* (Boston: Houghton Mifflin Co., 1942), p. 132.

A parishioner comes to the pastoral counselor perplexed over choosing between two interpretations of a Scripture passage. As the parishioner talks, the pastoral counselor discovers the pattern of indiscrimination throughout the parishioner's relationships with parents, siblings, and friends in every area of life. Then it is that the pastoral counselor sees "that the true configuration of his [the parishioner's] problem begins to appear in terms of its emotional elements." [8] The expression of these emotional elements by the parishioner and the acceptance by correct reflection of these feelings on the part of the pastoral counselor should bring insight.

If feeling is so important, then feeling is an ideal avenue of communication for biblical teaching and pastoral counseling. Jesus on many occasions taught and counseled his disciples by sensing their feelings. In the tenth chapter of Mark, after the story of the rich young ruler, Jesus conversed about trusting in riches rather than in God. The disciples, whom Jesus called children, asked the question, "Who then can be saved?" The disciples did not understand the Master, and verse thirty-two records that they were "amazed" and "afraid." The same verse records that Jesus took his disciples aside and told them of "what things should happen unto him." Jesus was sensitive to the insecure feelings of his disciples and answered them by saying, in effect, "My death and resurrection shall give you reassurance and hope."

Conclusion

The pastoral counselor must be well versed in the Bible, in effective teaching and counseling principles and methods, and in current social problems as these relate to his parishioners. Even more important, the pastoral counselor must know himself well enough as a person that he will not fear to know his parishioners as persons. If the pastoral counselor possesses the

[8] *Ibid.*

above insights, he will interpret the attitudes and values of the Bible in such an effective manner that these attitudes and values will be seen in the changed lives of those with whom he has counseled. After all, lives changed for greater service in the kingdom of God is the goal of pastoral counseling.

19. Pastoral Counseling and Christian Doctrine

Samuel Southard

Theological questions begin at the moment a person makes an appointment with a pastoral counselor. Why does this individual wish to see a minister? Is it because he senses a religious dimension in his life, or does he consider the pastor a competent counselor who will not charge him a professional fee? When a pastor asks, "I wonder why you come to me as a minister?" he is moving into a basic theological problem. If naturalistic humanism is right, then the counselee must look solely to himself for a standard of loyalty. The Christian understanding of God, sin, and salvation would be both irrelevant and untrue. On the other hand, if Christianity is right, then this man's beatitude depends upon a surrender of himself to God as revealed in Jesus Christ.

The main issue at stake in relating pastoral counseling to Christian doctrine is how to present forthrightly the claims of the gospel and yet be sensitive to individual attitudes and personal needs. Sometimes it is the pastor who relates human need to God's answer in Christ. At other times, as in the following example, the counselee brings up the question of his faith. The interview began as a young man told his pastor:

JOHN: We've broken our engagement, Ruth and I. It's so sudden, such a shock.

PASTOR: Have you ever had anything like this before—a great disappointment?

JOHN: No, and it's kinda hard to take.

PASTOR: Makes you think hard about many things, I know.

JOHN: Yes. It makes me think a lot about religion. I wonder if I am a Christian. I try to do right. But I've never joined a church.

PASTOR: How did you happen to think of being a Christian right now?

JOHN: Well, one of my troubles is always trying to get people to like me.

PASTOR: So?

JOHN: So, maybe I try too hard with some people and am not really the man I am. A Christian ought to be a true witness of his convictions to everyone.

PASTOR: To everyone?

JOHN: Especially the family. I laugh off what they say. They don't really know me any more.

PASTOR: Well, that's an important point, that a Christian is true to himself before others.

JOHN: But how am I to tell my parents, "You're wrong"?

PASTOR: Does it have to be with words? How about attitudes?

The conversation continued for some time. Through it all two themes crossed and recrossed: John's emotional involvement with his parents and the demand that he be himself through the challenge of Christ. The psychological and theological aspects of his personal decision were inextricably entwined.

Pastoral counseling includes theological convictions. These convictions may result in both positive and negative judgments. Superficially, a novice in counseling may think that he is being client-centered when he expresses no judgment and is consciously aware of none. But a deeper understanding of himself and reflection on the basis of mature experience will bring his own judgments to light. As Hannah Colm has pointed out, the depth of the counselor's acceptance of a person can be measured by the depth of his judgment. The counselor accepts a person in spite of what he knows both himself and his counselee to be.[1] The counselor who is willing to evaluate and bring to light his own judgments about the counseling relationship will

[1] "Healing as Participation," *Psychiatry*, 16 (1953), pp. 99–111.

help to encourage deeper understanding by the counselee of his own feelings and the way in which people react to him.[2]

When a counselor, by his detachment, gives the impression that nothing really matters, he is refusing to face the counselee as a person. A woman who was a patient in a Baptist hospital asked the chaplain of the hospital to lay his hands on her head and pray for her when he first visited in her room. The chaplain began to ask the woman about her church relationship and the value of prayer in her life. After she had made several evasive responses, he pointed out that prayer could sometimes be used to cover up problems instead of to help in facing them. The patient immediately said that she had no spiritual or emotional problems that she needed to confess. However, she did continue to press for "the laying on of hands" by the chaplain. He declined on the grounds that he did not see sufficient agreement between them about the meaning of prayer and healing. She demanded to know why he did not believe as she did and stated that she would call another chaplain or pastor if he did not meet her request. The chaplain said that he meant nothing personal by his refusal to lay hands on her, but that was not the way that he prayed. The interview ended with the woman's offering the chaplain some of her books on spiritual healing.

The chaplain who conducted this interview was then struggling to reconcile his desire to be a person with his nondirective theory of counseling. When he reflected on this interview, he recognized that he had not presented his own view of prayer in a positive manner. Instead, he had withdrawn in the face of the woman's attack. Although he had made it clear that he could not agree with her, he had not clarified his own belief concerning prayer and offered to pray with her after that manner. He had hidden himself behind a therapeutic technique.

The pastor's awareness of his own judgments does not mean immediate condemnation of his parishioner or himself. The per-

[2] H. Walter Yoder, "Judgmental Attitudes in Pastoral Counseling," *Journal of Pastoral Care*, 9 (Winter, 1955), pp. 221–24.

sonal convictions of a Christian stand under God's judgment and are continually subject to reappraisal. In many ways the pastor gives witness to what he believes in that he respects the witness of other persons to what they believe. Here again, doctrine is related to counseling. The counselor who says that he can never pass judgment on another individual may never have solved the problem of God's judgment upon his own life. He may fear that his opinions would get out of control and he would act in the place of a god before others. If this is so, it should be examined. If, on the other hand, a counselor knows from personal experience that he is under God's judgment, then with humility and faith he can present his own conviction in a spirit of love and self-control.

Because judgments are inevitable in pastoral counseling, the theological presuppositions of the minister and the counselee are a part of their therapeutic experience.

The Dialogue Between Counseling and Theology

The relationship of counseling to theology may be described as a dialogue. The pastor begins with theological presuppositions. He then gathers the personal data of his own interviews with people and the clinical research of others. These supply him with new material for theological questions and answers.[3]

Some people cannot accept this interplay of personal experience and Christian doctrine. The pastor may see this conflict in himself or in parishioners who are rigidly devout people. Within there is a seething conflict that demands personal attention. Without there is a façade of religious certainty. Such people are crustaceans in reverse. Their shell is not developed to keep enemies out but to keep their emotions within! Here is one pastor's example:

Mrs. A. stopped me in church after my sermon and said she wondered about my statement that the Holy Spirit worked through

[3] Seward Hiltner, *Preface to Pastoral Theology* (New York: Abingdon Press, 1958), p. 220.

human personalities. She said she had always understood that God works directly in the human heart without the intervention of any other person. I told her that the Bible continually referred to the fact that the Holy Spirit worked through teachers, preachers, and healers. She said that she was glad to have her thinking cleared up at that point.

That evening Mrs. A. again stopped me after church to say that she had a light problem which she would like for me to pray about because she hoped that it would be resolved within a week. I told her that prayers are most effective when we have some idea as to what we are praying about. She said that she was unaccustomed to ask anyone for help even in prayer. She had always believed that God was sufficient for all her needs without the help of men. I told her that there are times when men of God may do him service by listening to the heart-felt concerns of people. She said that perhaps she might call on me sometime.

On the following Sunday Mrs. A. came to see me during the Sunday school hour at the church office. She said that she would like to talk to me about a chronic problem with her husband.

Mrs. A.'s cautiousness was based upon both theology and psychology. The doctrine which she had always accepted was an individualistic type of theology which stressed the believer's personal relationship to God and said very little about his relationship to the fellowship of believers. Psychologically Mrs. A. was seeking to overcome her resistance to an admission to anyone that she had a problem. Her energy in the past few years had been directed toward concealment of the tensions in her home relationship. Seeking help would be a partial admission that her work was not successful.

A true dialogue requires listening as well as talking. A pastor must be attentive to the voice of human need calling to him through the distraught and fragmentary thoughts of his parishioner. When he can clearly identify the problem, he is prepared to look with the person for the right answer. Unfortunately, a pastor may be more concerned for his speaking than for his listening ministry. He may be so anxious to bring the Word of God that he does not hear the words of this man. Consequently, there is no dialogue, only intersecting monologues. Here is an example:

Roy and Mary asked their pastor to call. When he entered the home, Mary told him that they wanted to do something about the way they were living. Roy was not a Christian. Mary had been divorced. She told the pastor that her first marriage was at a young age and that she was deeply sorry for her haste and immaturity at that time. But now Roy's sister was telling Mary: "You are living in adultery and committing the unpardonable sin. You have two living husbands. You cannot be saved." Mary felt that she wanted a Christian home for her children. What could she do?

The pastor replied: "Life does get complicated at times, doesn't it? That is what Jesus came to do—help us tie together the broken threads of our life. Mary and Roy, do you believe God's Word, the Bible?"

ROY AND MARY: We do.

PASTOR: Let us then see what God has to say about this problem of yours. May I have your Bible? Let us read 1 John 1:9. What does it say? *all sin.* Not just one, or two, but *all.* Not all but adultery, but "If we confess our sins, he is faithful and just to *forgive* us our sins." Let us look now at John 3:16.

ROY: What is the unpardonable sin, then?

PASTOR: Just what the Scriptures say it is—wilful rejection of his Spirit and giving the devil credit for what God is trying to do. When Spirit moves your heart, Roy and you say, "I cry easy," or "I just feel that way," or "The preacher just wants another addition today," or "There is no need to make a fool of myself." A continuation of such wilful rejection will harden your heart and cause you to be forever lost.

ROY: When I feel that way, is that the Holy Spirit?

PASTOR: The purpose and work of the Holy Spirit is to convict men of their sins.

MARY: God will forgive me, then, for what I have done, won't he?

PASTOR: John said, "If we confess our sins, he is faithful and just to forgive us our sins."

ROY: Do you have to make public confession?

PASTOR: Roy, let's read Romans 10:9–10. (*They read together.*)

MARY: I sure feel better about things.

PASTOR: Mary, are you willing to do what God says? If you are not satisfied and want to become a Christian and a Baptist, then you may come forward at your first opportunity and make that known.

MARY: That's what I want to do. I'm coming next Sunday.

The conversation ended as the pastor exhorted Roy to come with his wife and join the church.

How is this conversation to be evaluated? From the pastor's point of view, it was satisfactory. Both Roy and Mary did join the church several weeks later. But did the pastor hear all that this couple wanted to tell him? No. He heard what he wanted to hear. He cut their thought to fit the pattern of his theological presuppositions. Then he gave answers which were true but so general that they might have been used without specific knowledge of these people. As a result of this inattention the pastor did not hear the problem about Roy's sister or Mary's guilt over an earlier marriage. A sensitive pastor would have sensed the strained relationship between the sister-in-law and Mary. Why had such absolute condemnation been pronounced by Roy's sister? This vital question was ignored. Also, Mary's reference to a previous marriage received no direct reply from the pastor. He did not investigate the ways in which she was more mature now, nor did he congratulate her for recognizing the immaturity of her impulsive actions in the past.

One may object that this judgment is too hard. Are not the Scripture passages used by this pastor true and applicable to all men? Yes, the Scriptures are true, but the pastor has not applied them to the specific needs of this couple. Instead, he has followed an outline which would be used in a sermon to a hundred people with a hundred different problems. He did not need to listen to Roy and Mary to say what he said. In fact, he didn't listen; he said it.

Roy and Mary want a *personal* Saviour. They need to feel that they are heard, that their individual wants are supplied. When a pastor enters into a dialogue with them, he can draw out their intimate desires and lift them up to God. By the example of their two-way conversation, he can teach them how to ask God and his people for specific help and receive it.

The Objectives of Theology in Counseling

How does this dialogue take place? What objectives must be kept in mind as the minister listens to human need and relates it to theological truths? There are several guiding principles which will bring the doctrines of the faith to bear upon the specific patterns of a personality.

First of all, a spiritual prescription should follow a spiritual diagnosis. The pastor must have some understanding of the problem before his theological answer can be specific and significant. An attractive young woman came to her pastor with a question about divorce. She had been married for a year and wanted to know if it was right for Christians to separate or divorce one another. The pastor did not immediately plunge into a theological discussion of the teaching of Jesus and Paul about the marital relationship. Instead, he asked the young woman why this question had come to her mind. She then began to pour out a story of progressive disillusionment in her married life.

She said that she always had expected that her husband would go to church and pray with her. The pastor asked her what she expected in a husband. She said that she would like to marry someone who was as strong as her father, but she did not want someone who would attempt to dominate her as her father had. She then told of a tragedy in her home which had changed her relationship to her father. The pastor asked: "How was your faith of help to you in that time of great crisis?" The young woman told how she learned to see her father as a person and had begun to have more sympathy for her mother. Then she brightened up and said, "Perhaps I learned some things about patience and the stubbornness of my own will at that time that should help me to get along with my husband now. Perhaps I should try to understand him a little better before I judge him so harshly."

In this interview the pastor dealt with theological issues. He asked about the relationship of faith to personal crisis and the connection of prayer to her personal expectations of others. The types of judgments which she passed upon men, especially her father and her husband, were examined more closely. All these problems are related to the great doctrines of faith, prayer, love, and judgment. The young woman responded to these questions because they were centered upon her personal difficulties.

The pastor did not take up the original problem which seemed to be such a burning theological issue. This was the question of divorce. He freely admitted that he did not know enough about the relationship of this couple to state the possibilities of divorce. Therefore, he could not give a relevent theological answer.

Patient and sensitive timing were all important in this interview. There were some important theological answers to be given, but they had to wait on the emergence of the significant questions in the young woman's conversation.

Secondly, pastors should be sensitive to the spiritual significance of illness, personal failure, and tragedy. Sometimes a pastor is so unsure of his ability to relate doctrine to personal need that he overlooks these crisis experiences. A man who was to undergo serious surgery was visited by his minister. When the pastor reminded him that he had been a faithful member of a Sunday school class for many years but had never joined the church, his wife interrupted the conversation to say, "But he does trust in Jesus, and that's what really counts. I know he trusts in Jesus." The pastor said that he understood. He then moved quickly to a question about the physical condition of the patient. After a few remarks he offered prayer and left.

The minister missed the opportunity of asking how trust in Jesus would help this man to face the operation that was impending. The wife was anxious to reassure the pastor about the faith of her husband. How could faith help her in this time of crisis? The wife was giving a religious answer, but it did not seem to calm her fears. Nor did the pastor see any evidence that trust in Jesus had given strong assurance to the husband. The opportunity for these questions was almost thrust upon the pastor, but he avoided them.

A more perceptive pastor seized a similar opportunity to relate illness to spiritual growth. He was visiting a fifty-year-old member of his church who had just undergone several weeks of diagnostic tests and was now wrestling with the decision of whether to undergo surgery. She told the pastor how her faith gave her much strength and beatitude. The pastor replied, "It is wonderful to hear this. I know that it has not been easy for you to achieve it." The woman looked up at him, smiled, and said, "You preachers really do know what we are up against, don't you? Yes, it has been a long struggle. At first I thought that I could not stand to wait until all those tests were through. Then I was filled with fear that the answer would be 'malignant.' I guess I have never learned to trust in God any more than during this experience." The woman then described how she had learned to talk about deep things with her husband, how she had appreciated anew the tenderness and affection of her children. She had always done things for others in the church, and now she was learning how refreshing it was to be ministered to by others. This was the first time that she had ever been willing to let other people do anything for her.

There had been significant changes in this person's life because of the crisis through which she was passing. Because the pastor was sensitive to this situation, he was able to draw out these new treasures of the spirit. The woman was strengthened in her spiritual growth because her pastor had seen and rejoiced with her in her fresh appreciation of God and man.

Thirdly, theology helps to give eternal significance to the common ventures of life. A man's job can be one of these ventures. An individual may see no meaning in what he does. As he talks with the pastor, he may be filled with despair because he is doing things for people rather than with people. The minister can remind him of the great Reformation doctrine of vocation: faithful performance of any honorable task is worthy of God's praise. An illustration of the use of this doctrine may be seen in the conversation of a fifty-year-old man with his pastor. The man felt drawn to a Bible school where he might gain preparation at night for "full-time Christian service." When the pastor asked what was wrong with his present job, the man replied, "Oh, it's the same old thing. I have continual conflicts with the people at work. Thank goodness one of them will retire next year. It's not bad all the time, but when I am having trouble at home, too, I just can't stand it. Don't you think I ought to be doing the Lord's work?"

The pastor suggested that this man was already performing many adequate services for God. He was a faithful Sunday school teacher and was presently concerned about the decision of his fourteen-year-old son, who had joined the church. As long as he stayed in his present position, he could support his family, assure his son of a good education, and continue his work in the church. The man stated that never before had anyone made him feel that these parts of his life were significant. He became more reflective and spoke of his hurry from his Sunday school class to the choir. He thought that perhaps if he could be more relaxed before church he might get more out of the service. The pastor nodded in agreement. As the parishioner went out the door, he grasped the pastor's hand and said, "No one ever took these conflicts of mine seriously before. I hope that I can come back and talk to you again."

Although the parishioner did not return for further interviews, he resigned from the choir on the following Wednesday evening. His outlook seemed to be improved, for he was more relaxed during the morning worship service and would shake the minister's hand and smile vigorously as he left the church.

If the minister has thought carefully about the relation of the Christian faith to human existence, there will be myriad opportunities to show people how they are serving God in daily living.

Fourthly, theology may also be used explicitly in the diagnosis of a personal problem. A pastor may begin to see the rele-

vence of a doctrine of the church to a problem which the parishioner presents. If he immediately asserts, "Ah ha, this is the
answer," his impulsiveness may short-circuit the person's opportunity for insight. But if he can muster the grace and humility
to suggest a specific theological proposition as a partial solution
to the problem, then he may be heard. People want their pastor to work with them on their problems. If he can hear them
out, participate in their thinking, and honestly express his opinions, they will know that he is concerned for them. Therefore,
as the minister is thinking with his parishioner, he may say,
"It seems to me that what you have just said is closely related to
Jesus' admonition that a man must leave his father and mother
and cling to his wife."

Such a conversation as this actually occurred with a young
man who could not make up his mind to get married. He kept
coming up with many thoughts about going to the mission field,
working in his father's business, taking care of his mother, or
going somewhere for graduate study. All these questions seemed
to evade the major problem. Was he willing to tell his mother
and father that he was in love with a certain young lady whom
he had promised to marry? Was he going to marry her or not?
The pastor cut through the mass of excuses which the young
man gave by reminding him of Jesus' words about marriage. At
first the young man was taken aback and could only answer that
he was sure his parents would allow him all the freedom that he
desired. When the pastor pressed the point of the young man's
own decision, there was a gradual change in attitude. The man
admitted that he had never really made decisions for himself.
Although he was restive under this, he had enjoyed the security
of his parental home. He was quite uncertain about his ability
to support a wife and to be a man both with her and among his
contemporaries.

Thus by the judicious use of a theological truth the pastor
brought his parishioner to the heart of the problem. Because
the pastor was reflective, the young man could think carefully

and honestly as well. It took time, and there were many anxieties to be overcome. But the young man was in time strengthened to make his own decision because his pastor had the strength to grasp at a possible solution of the difficulty, presented it with unvarnished honesty to his parishioner, and let the young man look at this possibility with patience and perseverance.

Finally, a specific theological doctrine may have an obvious and direct relationship to part or the whole of a personal problem. This is placed last, after the admonitions concerning diagnosis, dialogue, and spiritual sensitivity. Yet it is of importance. The pastor is a religious authority. After he has heard the person out and perceived the problem, his reflective judgment carries weight. If it is correctly placed, the person is stabilized and strengthened.

A business woman came to her pastor with a perplexed spirit. An attractive woman of forty, she had been proposed to by an outstanding citizen whose wife had died two years previously. Would it be right for her to marry him, since she had a child by a previous marriage? In questioning her, the pastor was soon satisfied to know that she loved this man, their relationship had been of a high moral quality, her child wanted him for a "daddy," and she was ready to do half-time instead of full-time work in her dress shop. What was the problem, then? Was this woman seeking routine approval from the pastor, or did she have a deeper problem?

The pastor drew forth the rankling secret by gently suggesting that she had been most co-operative in her answers and yet he felt constrained to ask one more thing: How did she feel about her previous marriage? The woman cast down her eyes and said, "I don't know what to say. Is it wrong for me to remarry? My first husband is living in a mental hospital. He's been there for ten years. About fifteen years ago I found that he was running around with other women. It hurt me terribly, for I really loved him. Then he began to abuse me. I took it myself, but couldn't bear to see him hit the boy. Finally his mother and I persuaded him to see a doctor. The doctor advised hospitalization for mental illness, but he wouldn't go. Finally we had to take him to a hospital. He's still there. I've often thought that love would have cured him. But I *did* love him. I don't now. We're divorced. Is it wrong for me to remarry?"

In the next few minutes the pastor asked more about the home conditions with the former husband and the doctor's opinion. He found that the woman had finally divorced her husband when she saw that he was hurting the son emotionally as well as physically. "Also," she said, "I was near the breaking point. I wasn't any help to my boy or to myself." The pastor told her that although she had responsibility as a wife, she also had a God-given obligation as a mother and as a person. Neither her son nor herself should be destroyed. Upon competent medical advice, she had done the best she could at that time. "But," she said, "I was always taught divorce is wrong."

The pastor summarized the biblical teachings on divorce for her, pointing out that a spiritual bond had been broken and that she and her husband could no longer have lived together without serious personality disturbance to the entire family. She had sought treatment for her husband, and he had refused. She had looked at her own failures. What more did she expect of herself? With relief she replied, "I feel so much better talking to you about this. I never saw it in that light. I mean, that I didn't have all the responsibility and that God does forgive people when they are divorced. I'm sure he does now."

The pastor had taken a chance. Only on a few occasions should he be so positive, so sure of an answer. But this was one of those times. Her present relationships had been explored and found to be full of hope. Her past had come into view and seemed to have little to hinder her remarriage beyond the residual doubt about divorce. His careful examination and authoritative judgment closed the door of the past so that she might look unhindered toward the future.

When a pastor sees theology and psychology in a vital dialogue and when Christian doctrines spring alive from the face-to-face encounters of counseling, he may have the assurance of a workman who is not ashamed because he rightly handles the word of truth. He has brought the sacred things of God to the human situation of his people with reverence for their personalities and assurance of God's concern.

Part V

Pastoral Counseling
and the Educational Intentions
of the Church

The calling of the Christian pastor is a calling to the threefold task of preaching, teaching, and healing. The healing work of counseling as done by the Christian worker, however his particular task in the church may be defined, always takes place in relation to his work as a preacher or teacher who works faithfully to prevent tragedies before they arise. The more we do the work of individual counseling, the more intensely concerned with education and prevention we become. Therefore, this section of this introduction to pastoral counseling is appropriately devoted to pastoral counseling and the educational intentions of the church.

The educational and therapeutic psychologists have given us working designs of the processes of personality development without which we could not function effectively as counselors. John Price will treat this important part of the counselor's preparation. The growing person as dealt with by the pastor and other religious workers is involved in the educational ministry of the church which either aids or hinders that growth. Professor Rutledge deals with this programming of the educational intentions of the church as it relates to counseling. Great portions of the counseling work of the religious counselor are done with small groups. Both Professor Price and Professor Bell will come to grips with the processes of group counseling and the training and counseling of group leaders who help the pastor and minister of education as lay counselors.

The more a pastor does the work of a counselor, the more he moves out of the "additive" and into the "multiplication" stage of counseling. In other words, he finds himself working less and less with the totally helpless persons of the community and more and more as a counselor of the counselors who in turn help the more or less helpless. He follows Jethro's guidance to Moses by dealing with the larger and more strategic task of counseling counselors. This will be dealt with by Professor Oates.

20. Personality Development and Pastoral Counseling

John M. Price

The religious counselor finds it vital to relate the psychology of personality development to his work and to his own life. The personality of the counselor as well as the growth possibilities of individuals and groups being counseled is coming in for closer evaluation.

The religious leader molds many types of groups in the variety of roles he is assigned as counselor, teacher, and preacher. Preaching to and teaching groups, as well as counseling with them, are processes which are changing in method and style, if not in message, because of discoveries in the area of personality development. Furthermore, the organizational and administrative work of the churches presupposes a knowledge of personality development. The psychology of leadership and learning, as well as of church staff and voluntary group harmony, require this knowledge.

The discussions of the processes and procedures of pastoral counseling which appear in this book presuppose a knowledge of personality development on the part of the counselor. Counseling requires the ability to relate to people. This relationship will rarely take place without some self-awareness and self-knowledge on the part of the counselor. These discoveries of self will come in many ways and on numerous occasions but will be increased more rapidly by the counselor's knowledge of his own development. The counselor will be able to "feel into" the situation through which the counselee is going when he is able to see, though not necessarily analyze, the developmental picture being portrayed.

Developmental understanding, furthermore, is an aid to a better understanding of the varieties of Christian response. This would include the various types of conversion experience. Two young girls in a church were not able to make a profession of faith no matter how thorough the invitation and in spite of numerous expressions of willingness on their part. During a visit to their home the reasons for their confusion became apparent. They were trying to make their feelings fit their father's preconceived notions. What he expected would not happen to them primarily because of the many differences, such as age, sex, social setting, and previous actions, that made them so glaringly different from the people their father wanted them to become.

Developmental knowledge will also shed light on such questions about religious experience as these: Does religion present a healthy approach to life, or is it an escape? Does man create, as Freud implied, a father-figure (God) as a means of meeting some need for security? Why do some religious people have nervous breakdowns? Does religious activity aggravate the problem after such a break? Can a person truly become a mature personality if he is seriously religious? How can God hold us responsible for our sins when the early development of our lives takes place with very little choice on our part?

Just as the medical, educational, and social science fields have realized the need for viewing the person from many vantage points, so have the fields of religious work, religious education, and the special activity of counseling. In the 1700's, when religion and science became separated, the tendency to fragmentize man became intensified. From about 1850 to 1900 the field of psychology made some unusual efforts to give a one-factor explanation of man. However, during the current century the psychologists have led the way in seeking to see man as a total person. This idea of oneness has been hard to accept, but is the more generally held view today. The medical doctor cannot treat the physiological man alone, nor can the religious leader seek to win his soul irrespective of the many other facets of his being.

The development of the religious worker's own life will so strongly color his interest and ability as a personal or group counselor that much self-awareness will need to go into his preparation. As he gains self-understanding through personal appraisal of his motives for being in religious work and his strong desire to help people, he will in turn be able to see more clearly the mixture of selfish and unselfish reasons. The discovery will come in many ways. Some of these are personal introspection, practice in helping others under supervision, and group interchange on the part of others studying personality development and counseling.

A Developmental Theory: Psycho-Dynamics

There are many theories of personality development. Very strong today is the special emphasis on the capacity to love and to feel other emotions and how it develops. This field is called psycho-dynamics; one interpretation is pictured below.[1] Upon this framework the following discussions will be developed.

The pastoral counselor cannot afford to overlook the feeling behind the expressions of a person with whom he is working. These feelings will very often be subtly interrelated to the past. Giving the counselee the time, patience, and freedom to explore these possibilities constitutes the first and sometimes the major portion of the counselor's task.

As the chart on p. 256 shows, the quest for a more mature personality will usually lead each individual through several stages of emotional development. Babies need much security in their emotional quest for proper food, air, and comfort. They are dependent on and interested in only those who can help to-

[1] Wilborn G. Hollister et al., Education for Responsible Parenthood (Raleigh, N.C.: Health Publications Institute, Inc., 1950), p. 6.

General Patterns of Emotional Growth

Note: We vary widely in our rate of growth and ages at which we reach new stages. Often our growth is irregular, sometimes fast and sometimes slow. Usually it is impossible to tell exactly when we pass from one stage into the next. Note that the emotional life of the adult includes all previous stages of love development.

P*—Crush on opposite parent

P—Crush on same sex parent

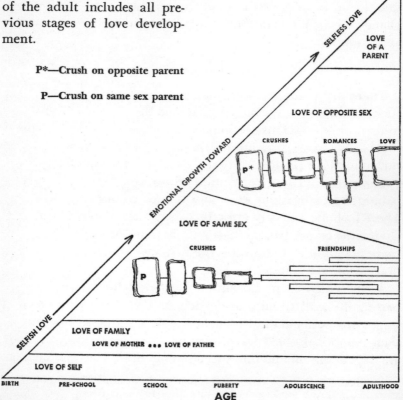

SELFLESS LOVE

LOVE OF A PARENT

LOVE OF OPPOSITE SEX

EMOTIONAL GROWTH TOWARD

CRUSHES   ROMANCES   LOVE

P*

LOVE OF SAME SEX

CRUSHES   FRIENDSHIPS

P

SELFISH LOVE

LOVE OF FAMILY

LOVE OF MOTHER ••• LOVE OF FATHER

LOVE OF SELF

BIRTH   PRE-SCHOOL   SCHOOL   PUBERTY   ADOLESCENCE   ADULTHOOD

AGE

ward these ends. They are not, during this stage, nearly as loving as their parents hope and imagine.

From babyhood until near school age children gradually move from self-love to loving mother, father, siblings, and others in the home and other groups around them. Learning to love both parents equally comes gradually. If the parents love one another, this will move along naturally. If such a love does not exist, there will be difficulty in achieving balance in learning to share affection. What happens here affects every relationship and will do so throughout each life.

While the pleasure nerves are developing in early life, so physical abilities are developing in the control of elimination. Conflicting attitudes on the part of the parents at this time and at other stages of body exploration, discovery, and examination may cause unusual interrelations of these processes. A child may seek pleasure, attention, or even try to manage his parents through these activities. This is especially true if his parents display surprise, impatience, shock, or shame. The wise parent helps the child through proper attention and affection until other interests prevail.

From around six years of age until adolescence, children fix their emotional attention on those of the same sex. These are strong feelings, both open and subtle, and are essential to healthy personality growth. The religious leader should not shun nor misuse this fact. "They are brief, over-done and deep at first, under better control and longer lasting later; toward older people first, toward children of our own age later. . . . Our first crush often follows or is a part of our learning to share love with our parents." [2] In addition to this relationship to parents there will be "primary substitutes," such as teachers, preachers, and leaders. There will also be "secondary substitutes," such as television characters and distant heroes. The chums, clubs, and groups of the child's own age follow.

[2] *Ibid.*, p. 8.

In the adolescent period the individual will return to his first love—that of the opposite sex. The young boy may approach his mother after having combed his hair and put on a fresh shirt. As he kisses his mother for one of the first times that she can recall in some time, she may feel that "the prodigal has returned." She may take advantage of his return and try to re-establish his dependence, or she may treat him as a soon-to-be adult and live before him the good qualities of womanhood that are within her. She will aid his steps through the substitute groups and on through friendships, dating, and into mature love. The father will in turn aid his daughter in the same way.

Learning, from deep crushes to thrilling dates, will cause love to proceed from a romantic fling to a mature love—one that is more stable, complete, and lasting toward one person. Only then can maturation through the several stages of parenthood take place.

From the cross-sectional or age-group standpoint, certain common religious traits and capacities are demonstrated by the group in general. At the same time, there will be unusual positive feelings in some individuals. In others, even at an early age, apparent retardation and negative reaction to many religious expressions and ideas will appear. Literature, methods of approach, and the personality of the teachers or leaders will be governed by these facts. In particular, the counselor will be sensitive to the proper development, or lack of it, which has taken place. Specifically he will try to note the personality traits of the person at hand and the particular stage of identification (self, family, parent of the same sex, parent of the opposite sex, etc.) of the individual. Next, he will note specific areas of confusion or conflict which might exist. Only then, and through a patient counseling atmosphere, can some of these incomplete steps be faced and worked through. Most important of all, these growth feelings of love, or the lack of them, will continue to affect the religious outlook.

The degree to which a person has developed in the capacity

to love may greatly affect his ability to understand and love God. It may be that a person fears, hates, mistrusts, or feels ashamed of one or both of his parents. These attitudes may make him feel guilty and unworthy of being loved and may be demonstrated in his church life by extreme selfishness or a "no" attitude. They may also show up in an attempt to divide and rule. The person may still be trying to get the attention and security that was not properly presented or available years before.

It may be that hate, fear, and disgust are so deeply ingrained now that the individual finds it hard to trust and love God. In counseling, such a person may declare, "I hate God." As this person sought to become like a parent, he may have been so hurt by the one with whom he sought to identify as to leave him crippled in his ability to love. One such person dared to express these feelings about God. This individual was frightened even by the expression of such deeply hidden thoughts. The actions of an immature, sadistic, alcoholic father had left such scars that made it difficult to feel any other way toward God. Gradually the individual was able to move into different feelings toward this Father God and in time was able to truly love God as well as forgive the pathetic parent who had done the harm.

Space and time will not permit detailed explorations of the light that personality development might have on the sense of right and wrong at each level of emotional growth. Many attitudes and actions deemed openly sinful and wrong might be appraised in this light, however.

A fifteen-year-old girl in a church in which the writer taught demonstrates this possibility. A teaching program was being held in her home. Her parents were very active in the church, and her father was unusually busy, often day and night, in his profession. She demonstrated by her longing looks at her father, who was preoccupied, distant, and unavailable, that she strongly needed closer comradeship with him. About a year later she ran away and secretly married a forty-five-year-old man who was twice divorced and had children by each marriage. This crush met her girlhood need of love and belonging which her father could and should have supplied. The father was disgusted with her and felt violent toward the man she married. He did not see that his lack of love and attention were involved at all. The right and wrong elements in this matter were complicated, to say the least. They should have been appraised in the light of all these factors and not placed on the shoulders of the girl alone.

Some Ingredients in Personality Make-Up

In the emphases on the development of emotions, as described above, much is being said today about the home atmosphere. The effects of this intangible ingredient are both obvious and subtle.

The attitudes existing in the atmosphere of parent-child relationships also have strong determining influences at every stage. Tension on the part of one parent, as well as the existence of pressure and strife between parents, affect the child at any age. Many problems in later life can be traced to the air of unrest. The trouble does not have to stem from a particular event but can be the result of daily anxiety. The concern for a way of life in the home that will produce feelings of democracy, freedom, and a sense of belonging are stressed in many writings.

Some of the particular approaches that radiate unhealthy attitudes might be mentioned. First, the rejection of a child or children is a common one. The parents may demonstrate selfishness and immaturity when they feel the child gets in the way of their happiness. They might feel anguish over an untimely arrival. A child may be rejected because his parents feel inferior, inadequate, and unable to meet the responsibility of parenthood. The parents might overdominate, overindulge, and overprotect the child to hide their own true feelings. These actions only cause more uncertainty and anguish in the child.

Second, due to a lack of success and achievement, real or imaginary, the parents might project their own ambitions and goals onto the child. They will imply that they want the best of everything for him, but they hope to have these things for themselves through the child. Quite often the child does not have the talent, ability, or interest in such ambitions. He is given the choice of open rebellion or meek submission.

Third, many times the relationships of a child to the other children of the family constitutes a major adjustment. This adjustment influences the person's attitude toward himself and later peer groups. Again the parents may aggravate the matter through ignorance, indifference, or partiality. Working through these unsolved relationships in later life will not be easy, but patient counseling can help immeasurably.

Fourth, family insecurity, as described above, may stem from such problems as economic pressures and transient living. Usually the attitudes within the parents toward these facts and not the conditions themselves do the damage.

Early studies in psychology strongly emphasized the physical person and the effect of inherited tendencies. More emphasis today is on the psychological atmosphere surrounding the growing person, although heredity is not ignored. Social psychology has taught the powerful effects of the group or groups involved in the person's life. The role or roles he chooses to play, as well as those he finds he must play, will affect his development.

Some Major Facets of Personality

Many interesting facets of personality should be studied by the religious counselor, including the following:

The physical basis of personality.—From the standpoint of inheritance, the value and necessity of good organic equipment and basic intelligence are obvious. These must exist, else there are serious limitations. The person's reactions to his physical make-up are important in conjunction with the four following factors:

Such inherited factors as size, color of hair, or baldness will inevitably produce reactions. A person's size may cause him to be meek or domineering. A "red head" may develop a temper just because it is expected of him. Especially in adolescence, the individual may tend to build his personality around his appearance, whether it is attractive or unattractive. Worshiping self may cause a dependency on personal strength, power, or beauty that will change or decline with time. These changes may not be anticipated and may leave the person void of an integrating force.

When physical limitations such as deformities exist, the person may or may not compensate in a healthy way. He may either use the problem as a protective measure or be strengthened by it. One student came to a school with extreme physical deformities. Those around her felt repulsed because of her appearance. She had faced her problem, and in overcoming it she was able to put people at ease. Thus she earned her rightful place in the group. Her strong personality far outweighed her physical deformities.

Acquired physical changes, both organic and structural, may cause unusual personality changes. Such changes caused by sickness, disease, or accident demand a re-evaluation of the personality. The person may grieve, feel guilty, and wonder if God is punishing him. He may, to the contrary, become more mature.

Another unique physical factor affecting personality is the glandular structure. The pituitary gland located at the base of the brain may produce variations in body size. The thyroid gland, located in the throat area, may produce a stepped-up or an apathetic approach to life. The adrenals on the kidneys are called on to help produce unusual temporary strength. The pancreatic gland behind the stomach controls the sugar supply in the blood. The reproductive or gonad glands cause many variations in both sexes. Much about personality can be explained by these potent physical factors. Some feel that personality is greatly determined by these glands.

Basic urges and drives.—The following basic urges and drives are outstanding in personality development: self-preservation, possession and accumulation, social or group desires, projective or self-assertive actions, reproductive or sex drives, and the desire for unity or oneness. Especially important will be the degree to which the person shapes these into a meaningful, healthy, and constructive pattern.

Temperament and personality.—Temperament, whether inherited, acquired, or both, will be a strong conditioning factor in personality. For centuries man has attempted to develop classifications of temperament. Especially Jung's terms "introvert" or "turning within" and "extrovert" or "outgoing" are in common usage today. People do show marked differences here which will affect their religious experiences.

Personality structure.—The structure of the personality is also a major concern in developmental understanding. The conscious activity is only a small part of mind function. The super-ego, representing a person's sense of right and wrong, is of major concern. A person may vary from having a pathological "blind spot" or seared conscience to an extremely morbid and continuous state of guilt. The religious counselor will not approach these problems with logic, persuasion, or explanation but will help the person to discover the hidden conflicts in his life. These conflicts may be in his unconscious or subconscious reservoir, and although the feelings present there may be real or imaginary, they will color and shape the person's current or conscious actions. Personality change and improvement will require an understanding of these and other ingredients.

Normal Personality Development

The word "maturity" must be defined or qualified, for there are almost as many variations of meaning for it as there are people who use it. William James said one was adult when he became twenty-five, for probably by that time 95 per cent of his actions had become habitual.[3] The bewilderment as to where

---

[3] William James, *The Principles of Psychology* (New York: Henry Holt and Co., 1890), I, 121.

maturity begins is reflected in the following story. A college student visiting in the home of one of his professors sought to make conversation by asking, "How old are you?" of his host's little son. "That is a difficult question," answered the young boy, removing his glasses and wiping them reflectively. "The latest personal survey available shows my psychological age to be twelve, my moral age four, my anatomical age seven, and my physiological age six. I suppose, however, that you are referring to my chronological age, which is eight. That is so old-fashioned, however, that I seldom think of it any more!"

The most satisfactory picture of a maturing person is one that shows adequate movement along mental, emotional, social, and spiritual lines. If the person is making satisfactory advancement along the path from self-love to outgoing love, some of the following signs of development will begin to appear. These are some of the criteria mentioned by D. R. Gorham, G. S. Dobbins, Harrison Elliott, Luella A. Cole, H. A. Overstreet, and others.[4] Luella Cole says, "Probably no one is wholly mature. Most of us certainly retain one or more childish traits, even though we may be quite well aware that they are childish."[5]

Intellectual achievements in personality development.— Only those with some brain limitation, brain changes by surgery, or disease of the nervous system fail to mature to some degree. Our concern here will be with the intellectual attitudes rather than with biological or social determinism. However, the following criteria of maturity have stood the tests of time and experience.

The mature person has the capacity to make decisions. The mature person is able to make up his mind. Authority of another cannot be relied upon completely. He will decide and not

[4] Luella Cole, *Attaining Maturity* (New York: Rinehart & Co., Inc., 1944); G. S. Dobbins, *Understanding Adults* (Nashville: Broadman Press, 1948); Harrison Elliott, *Solving Personal Problems* (New York: Henry Holt & Co., 1936); D. R. Gorham, *Understanding Adults* (Philadelphia: The Judson Press, 1948); H. A. Overstreet, *The Mature Mind* (New York: W. W. Norton & Co., 1949).

[5] Cole, *op. cit.*, p. 14.

remain in a state of crippling anxiety. He accepts responsibility for and stands by the decisions he makes.

The mature person bears the results of action. Having made a decision, this person will accept his portion of the responsibility for the success or failure of his actions. Failures can be accepted without lasting depression, and successes can be borne without undue pride.

The mature person views himself critically and objectively. This action requires a certain amount of basic intelligence but is not guaranteed by its existence. It involves a willingness to accept self-discoveries. Few, if any, people can have complete self-insight, but the maturing person will succeed to some degree. This is not just a one-time experience but rather a continuing daily process. This soul searching, long advocated as a basic necessity in Christian growth, is strongly emphasized in counseling as well.

The mature person adjusts to circumstances beyond his control. A person need not give up or give in to adjust to circumstances over which he has no control. One man decided to be a preacher during a revival. He was forty-five and had one son ready for college and another in high school. His job was meager, and by the end of the week he was already showing signs of anxiety over how difficult it would be to break away, go to school, and in general rearrange his whole pattern of life. Two years later he had all the appearances of a man with real maturity. He described the cycles he had been through and the changes he had made in order to preach. It became evident that he could not leave his work and go to school. He had adjusted to this and accepted the circumstances he could not change. He had become active in establishing several mission churches and Sunday schools in the surrounding territory. Here was a maturity that was enviable.

Emotional maturation in personality development.—Man operates on the level of feeling in making life's choices as much as he does on the intellectual plane. Such positive emotions as love, trust, and faith affect choices he makes. He must also face the influence of unhealthy fears, perversions, and anxieties. The type of personality, the strength of character, and the health of mind will be greatly governed by the emotional patterns developed.[6] Patterns of progress can be judged by criteria such as the following:

Immature people have a low frustration tolerance. "When a small child is angry, he strikes out at once and discharges his anger. . . . An adult can be angry for quite a while without showing it very much. In the case of an adult a temper tantrum is evidence only of infantile capacity to bear the stress and strain of life." [7]

The more mature person experiences mild feeling contrasts. The child can change from one extreme feeling to another in minutes. The adolescent with the many chemical extremes going on within can match them with a wide range of moods. The maturing person can maintain a fairly even balance between inferiority and self-confidence, despondency and a sense of well-being. This is because he has learned to adjust to the realities around him.

The mature person has interests similar to those of others in his group. All people carry over some concerns of the past improperly treated or hidden away in the unconscious. Any person may temporarily regress on occasions. However, a notable preoccupation with social or group activities similar to those of groups younger than a person's age level may call for careful attention.

The mature person has a maturing affection or love capacity. The developmental theme might be pointed to again. From extreme self-love to love of others, especially one of the opposite sex, is the normal pattern. If this is not completely achieved, the

[6] Ernest Ligon, *Psychology of Christian Personality* (New York: The Macmillan Company, 1935), p. 13.
[7] Cole, *op. cit.*, pp. 39–40.

maturing person is at least secure enough to give of himself to others around him.

Social outreach in personality development.—Social maturation will be evident in several areas.

A mature person has satisfactory family relationships. "There are two common types of immature reactions to the problem of achieving independence from the parental supervision. The submissive person who is as dependent upon his parents as the average child, and the person who is in a flaming revolt against his home."[8]

The mature person has a healthy sex outlook. Frequent heterosexual crushes, homosexual relationships, and promiscuity are obvious announcements of immaturity. A healthy outlook here will embody personal, social, and moral acceptability and balance.

The mature person has satisfactory group relationships. Social outreaching implies the ability to lead and follow, to give or to receive, and above all, a sensitive concern for others.

Ethical perspectives in personality development.—Though opinions vary widely as to what would constitute healthy moral, ethical, and spiritual development, most sound scientists would agree that a basic philosophy of life should exist. Such a philosophy would mean that one should be motivated by some moral standards, should be tolerant of others, and should have an integrating force strong enough to hold the personality intact. "Briefly, integration is the condition of personality in which all of the emotional attitudes are harmonious and mutually helpful, thus permitting all of one's natural energy to be directed toward one end. Thus, integrated action is coordinated action in an organism or machine. Each part contributes its portion to the whole, all parts are mutually interdependent upon one another."[9]

[8] *Ibid.*, pp. 60–61.
[9] Ligon, *op. cit.*, pp. 14–15.

Summary

Personality development has many implications for pastoral counseling. It holds many facets of truth for the counselor both in his personal life and in his approaches to people. It can explain the resistance that some might have toward Christian truth. Through study of personality development the learning processes at different age levels can better be understood. The problems of doubt can be handled, both from an individual and group standpoint. Matters of sin in general and hate in particular need exploration in the light of developmental knowledge. Many harmful and destructive actions can often be understood and dealt with from this vantage point.

Responsibilities of right and wrong at different age levels, although complex at best, can be seen more clearly through the study of personality development. It would be a serious mistake to explain them away by blaming developmental factors. However, an awareness of the awesome complexity of personal responsibility is made more clear. Ways and means of building into life the capacity to love need to be explored. Here adequate tools to approach God in faith and love are found. Also, the counselor can better recognize when such essential personal ingredients are missing. The varieties of religious experience are better understood. The pastoral counselor will be enabled to recognize a maturing Christian personality and will be able to enjoy the experience of his own personal growth.

21. Pastoral Counseling and the Educational Ministry of the Church

Pastoral counseling is an educational means in that it affords opportunity for the individual to learn about himself, thereby setting off an educational and growth chain reaction in which he learns about and better relates himself to his own small group, his family, his church, society, and God. Pastoral counseling is also educational in that it often is involved, along with other educational procedures, in the process of problem solving. In any consideration of such a counseling-educational endeavor, two facts need constant re-emphasis. First, all religious workers, lay as well as professional, can and should be pastoral counselors in one sense. Second, the activities constituting the work of pastoral counselors are not limited to those involving serious emotional situations. They involve intellectual problems as well. They involve much that should produce general educational, spiritual, and developmental results.

Religious workers who work in an educational capacity with groups cannot be expected to be highly trained in all phases of psychology and counseling. However, the professional leaders in the church need to be well trained, and, in turn, in their counseling leadership they need to train others. These workers should be trained to the extent that they will be familiar with basic counseling principles and can help in developing a counseling atmosphere, which should prevail in all the educational activities of the church.

The classroom teacher in the secular educational program is coming to be regarded as a child's most significant counselor. It is likewise true that the most significant counselor in any system of religious education is that teacher, leader, director, superintendent, or other worker who is in closest contact with individuals within the organization or group.

There are organizations in most churches which minister to those who have been thwarted in their emotional development. They have perhaps been pressured into skipping a developmental stage or have regressed from some area of growth because life at that point has been unbearably unpleasant for them. Some understanding of personality development and some use of group and/or individual counseling in the educational program of the church would help the person to grow and to overcome his problems. In many such cases there is counseling value in just the relationships that are established within a group. This is significantly true if the group is led and developed in such a way as to create an air of permissiveness which allows freedom to express, freedom to withhold, freedom to seek, and freedom to grow.

Counseling opens the door so that education, particularly religious education, can enter. Counseling is a means of making a personal, educational application of theology and the life-developing principles of Christianity. Many individuals have needs which could be classified as religious needs that are produced because of a lack of interpersonal or group activity. These needs can be satisfied in group situations. Many of these needs could be satisfied in church-related group situations such as Sunday school, youth groups, and other organizations.

A pastor's counseling ministry, teaching ministry, and preaching ministry should be regarded as inseparable. They are parts of the same thing, each supporting the other. Many of the recorded interpersonal relationships of Jesus could be said to be preaching. They could also be described as counseling. Therefore, while engaged in one activity, he was also teaching, preaching, and counseling. The pastor's ministry today could be characterized as a preaching-counseling-teaching ministry with much less distinction between the three phases than is usually made.

In attempting pulpit counseling a minister will find it difficult to achieve complete permissiveness in his preaching, but the direction or aim of the preaching can be person-God-centered instead of being centered on the problems of the preacher. Such an aimed pulpit ministry will produce 1) sermons indicating understanding; 2) sermons identifying problems; 3) sermons dealing with and meeting needs; 4) sermons indicating the worth of the individual; 5) sermons majoring on an attitude of acceptance more than condemnation; 6) sermons stimulating inquiry and arousing intellectual and spiritual curiosity; and 7) sermons generating faith, love, security, forgiveness, and peace.

The pulpit ministry which makes the listener feel that he is being talked with instead of at and which makes the listener feel that he and his own problems are more important than the preacher's problems is likely to be counseling-teaching-preaching. A pastor's counseling ministry outside the pulpit reveals the need for his counseling ministry in the pulpit.

Some Educational Group-Guidance Ministries

The church, through its program of work, proposes to deserve its place in the community by helping people. Many people attend the services of the church because they have problems and are expecting to receive help from religion. This has always been so. Helping people who already have great problems is at the very heart of the ministry of the church. However, more good with less effort for more people could likely be accomplished in a program designed to prevent as well as solve problems. Numerous churches are now working from many different approaches toward this preventive type of ministry. Some such efforts are highly structured and specifically aimed at the prevention of one specific type of problem. Others are more general in scope, working toward the development of the total personality of the individual. Such generalized efforts are justified on the basis that if personality growth can be promoted to a point of high individual and interpersonal competence, major problem areas would not be a threat to the highly competent individual.

Any activity, therefore, conducted or sponsored by the church or its organizations which promotes individual or group growth is religious educational guidance in the prevention of major life-limiting problems.

Special efforts at educational group guidance ministries in a church often center in or relate to such terms as vocational guidance, premarital and marital education and preparation, family life education, mental hygiene, and alcohol education. Of course, if there is any degree of success in the efforts pointed specifically in the direction of any of these areas, there is automatically a corresponding degree of success in developing an over-all competent personality.

Vocational guidance.—A high percentage of the problems disturbing young people are directly or indirectly related to the difficulties they face in choosing a vocation. The church, in its educational counseling ministry, can be of great assistance to its own youth and the youth of the entire community by promoting a helpful program in this troubled area.

The church has a legitimate concern for the vocational interests, not only of its youth, but also for such interests of those of all ages. Family problems, church problems, and personal personality problems are often inseparably related to forced, poorly chosen, or unpleasant vocational relationships. Since young people are more readily reached in a program of vocational guidance, vocational counseling is slanted toward them.

Much that will have value in vocational guidance can be worked into routine programs of the numerous permanent organizations of the church. However, special programs and planned group activities will likely make the greatest contribution in this area. Such planned activities need to take special account of the tremendous need for guidance in the realm of religious vocations. If guidance with regard to religious vocations is not given in or by church-related movements, it will likely not be given at all.

Young people expressing an inclination toward or interest in religious vocations need the counseling benefits of person-to-person interviews plus all the group guidance activities that can be provided. Such group activities could well take the form of a week of study of one of the books on religious vocations as published by denominational publishers. Or they could be encouraged to read such books as *Christ in My Career* by Allen W. Graves [1] and *God Calls Me* by J. Winston Pearce [2] and tracts on religious vocations from denominational sources. Having become familiar with such materials in their private reading, the young people will be better prepared to participate in the discussion periods of the study sessions or group guidance sessions.

These group guidance sessions could take the form of a regular study based on one of the above-mentioned books, or it could take the form of a special activity, finding its place in "Youth Week," "Dedicated Vocations Week," or an activity unrelated to any regular calendar event. The leader-counselor should prepare himself by making a study of such books as *I Find My Vocation* by Harry Dexter Kitson,[3] *Counseling for Church Vocations* by Samuel Southard,[4] and *Helping Youth Choose Careers* by J. Anthony Humphreys.[5]

The counselor-leader of such guidance in the area of church vocations should steer clear of the temptation to become an enlistment officer to recruit all young people into such vocations. His objectives should be to assist the young people in clarifying

[1] Nashville: Convention Press, 1958.
[2] Nashville: Convention Press, 1958.
[3] New York: McGraw-Hill Book Co., Inc., 1954.
[4] Nashville: Broadman Press, 1957.
[5] Chicago: Science Research Associates, 1950.

their own motivations, interests, qualifications, and knowledge pertaining to church-related vocations.

These suggestions have been made with specific regard to counseling for church vocations. Naturally all the young people affected by the ministry of any church are not inclined toward church vocations. Those interested in other vocations need help also. Much of what has been suggested above will also apply to vocational guidance efforts that are more general in nature. In such efforts a "Career Week" following high school graduation time would be an appropriate activity. During such a week of vocational emphasis profitable use could be made of available community resource personnel. Selected representatives of various types of vocations could make brief statements of facts concerning their respective vocations and participate in open discussion with the entire group. Willing members of the group of young people could be asked to make studies of vocations of their own interest, interview professional people, and report to the group to stimulate discussion. Field trips could be made to hospitals, schools, and industrial plants for occupational observation. Visual aids might well be employed.[6]

In many such efforts, particularly those characterized by freedom of expression, those with anxiety over their choice of a vocation and an obvious need for professional vocational guidance will be discovered. Within reach of most communities are vocational guidance specialists who are prepared to utilize valuable tests and give other helpful assistance. The National Vocational Guidance Association has prepared a directory of its professional membership. This directory lists, by states, those who can render professional vocational guidance services and can be secured at small cost from the National Vocational Guidance Association, 1534 O Street, Northwest, Washington 5, D. C.

Premarital and marital guidance and education.—Marriage counseling has been practiced in some form as long as there have been human problems. However, as a serious productive

[6] See list in Kitson, *op. cit.*, p. 265.

area of study and work, marriage counseling has existed for only a few years.

That there is need for help with regard to marriage problems needs no proof. Every person whose work is church-related has observed the clamor for help coming from the troubled victims of innumerable marriage problems. For a number of years there has been a growing concern about divorce and broken homes and the resultant moral, theological, psychological, and sociological facets. At last this concern has led to the realization that virtually all the causes of divorce are present in the form of personality, cultural, and environmental factors at the time of marriage. This means that with sufficient counseling and premarital preparation many family and marriage problems would be prevented.

The group approach to premarital counseling can be used to great profit in a local church setting. Such an approach affords the possibility of taking advantage of natural social inclinations. It provokes the sharing of ideas and the exposing and clarifying of feelings. Although it cannot fully take the place of personal, individual, or couple counseling, it does multiply the use of the counselor's time.

There are great possibilities of using the group approach, in certain situations, in contributing to the solution of marital problems which already exist. However, likely the greatest area of usefulness for this approach is with those who are not married. The aim of this approach is to prepare prospective marriage partners to the point that marriage problems can be prevented or can be competently handled.

Numerous churches are now conducting group counseling activities focused on engaged couples or those of an age group close to marriage. These activities utilize a wide spread of subject matter, techniques, and procedures. A typical example is one in which the group came together at the church every night for two hours for five nights. Each session began with a brief period of worship activity led by a young person. In this instance the subject matter and procedure was determined by the interest of the group. The week was characterized by freedom of expression. Open discussion consumed most of each session.

In other such efforts use has been made of personality testing, panel discussion, forums, discussion of assigned subjects by group members and resource personnel (including physicians, lawyers, psychologists, psychiatrists, sociologists, architects, home economists, and ministers) with assigned subjects, audiovisual aids, drama, role playing, and other activities utilized to provoke group discussion and participation. More extensive attention to this kind of group work is given by Wayne E. Oates in his book *Premarital Pastoral Care and Counseling.*[7]

Audio-visual aids can be secured from numerous sources. In instances in which the use of drama is being contemplated, plays or lists of plays can be secured from such sources as denominational book stores; Human Relations Aids, 1790 Broadway, New York 19, N. Y.; and Occu-Press, 479 Fifth Avenue, New York 17, N. Y.

In the realm of premarital counseling perhaps the richest, most rewarding opportunity of the pastoral counselor is in his counseling with engaged couples. The group counseling discussed above will not reduce the number of couples coming for more personal counseling but rather will increase the number.

Every counselor will develop his own program and procedure in counseling. A sample procedure which, with variations to meet the needs of each individual case, has been used many times is offered here solely for the sake of illustration and suggestion. This procedure ideally involves six routine interviews plus any other special sessions or meetings which may seem, during the progress of counseling, to be necessary. From the beginning, the purpose of the series is more to give opportunity for self-understanding than the impartation of knowledge, although in some areas this is also involved.

[7] Nashville: Broadman Press, 1958.

In this proposed series the first interview is characterized by informal discussion. There is abundant opportunity during the progress of this interview to employ, at least intermittently, the permissive counseling techniques. During this interview the counselor usually leads the couple to relate to him an account of the beginning and development of their romance. Usually they delight in doing this and often proceed into a permissive discussion of themselves in which they, often for the first time, give free expression and clarification of their feelings. The counselor also elicits as much discussion as possible regarding family backgrounds, family personality traits, family marital difficulties, cultural differences, educational differences, parent-child conflicts, sibling conflicts, the couple's previous courtship experiences and why and how they ended, their general ambitions for the future, and similar pertinent subjects.

Near the end of this first interview, which may last from an hour to an hour and a half, the couple often is given some personality tests. Many of these have been devised by the counselor himself. Others are of the better known professionally prepared variety. The Adjustment Inventory: Student Form (or Adult Form) by Hugh M. Bell and published by Stanford University Press, Stanford, California, is a usable test easily given and easily scored. If a counselor is interested in making a study of the simpler and perhaps less threatening tests, he will do well to look into the book *The Technique of Personal Analysis* by Donald A. Laird.[8] As far as this series of interviews is concerned, tests are never an end in themselves. As used in this series of interviews, the detailed score is of little importance. The tests are counseling tools. The very taking of the test arouses interest. Tests are excellent discussion promoters.

The early part of the second interview is given to the discussion prompted by the previously given tests. The remaining portion of this interview is given to an intense consideration of religious matters. In this period the couple look at the religion of

[8] New York: McGraw-Hill Book Co., Inc., 1945.

their two sets of parents, the place religion was given in their homes, the effect it had on their lives, the religion of their friends, their own personal religion and their regard for its importance, the difference in their religious beliefs (even if of the same denomination and church), and other matters pertaining to religion as could be introduced by the interest of the counselor or the couple.

The third interview is given largely to a general discussion of the physical aspects of marriage. No discussion of sex is forced upon a couple, but neither is it neglected with those who desire such a discussion. This consideration usually begins with the giving of two tests: Forms X and Y of the *Sex Knowledge Inventory*, available to doctors, ministers, and other professional counselors from Family Life Publications, Inc., Box 6725, College Station, Durham, N. C. Here again the mere taking of the test has great value.

At the conclusion of this interview the couple is presented a copy of the little booklet *The Doctor Talks with the Bride and Groom* by Dr. Lena Levine.[9] A copy of *Sex Without Fear* by Lewin and Gilmore [10] is loaned to the couple. They are also strongly advised—almost commanded—to see a physician before the next interview.

The fourth interview begins with a recapitulation of the previous interviews, reviewing the significance of the different phases of the discussion and pointing out possible new insights into the future. The couple tries to predict their own problem areas and the way they will handle them. This often develops into a very dynamic, self-searching, self-revealing session characterized in the end by personality growth.

The fifth interview is given to the young woman alone. It is entered without any previous structuring. If the previous session was particularly dynamic, she may wish to revive a portion of the discussion and expand it. She may have very personal mat-

[9] New York: Planned Parenthood Federation of America, Inc., 1950.
[10] New York: Medical Research Press, 1951.

ters about herself or her fiance which she would like to discuss when not in his presence.

The sixth interview is like the fifth except that it is with the man.

Family life education.—A program of family life education in the church will utilize every opportunity to minister to families in their homes, in the regular organizations and services of the church, and in specifically and purposefully planned extra activities. A church that is family-life conscious will attach special developmental significance to births, deaths, marriages, baptisms, new homes, special honors, and other events. Such a church will spare no means to promote a good educational program slanted toward family life development. Clinics and special educational and growth-promoting events will be provided for parents, prospective parents, grandparents, in-laws, and others. Special attention will be given to sex education. Parent-teacher relations, juvenile delinquency, and family recreation may well take places for discussion in such educational activities.

Mental hygiene.—Another area of activity demanding a relationship with pastoral counseling and the educational ministry of the church is that of mental hygiene.

Mental hygiene movements, organizations, programs, or activities have as their goal bringing about conditions which make possible the prevention of mental illness as well as the reaching of the optimal mental health potentialities and personal growth of the total population. Actually, it does not take much exploration or interpretation to see that this goal is also the goal of the church. The church, therefore, finds itself automatically in partnership with medical forces, psychiatric forces, psychological forces, social forces, educational forces, and all others interested in mental health. It finds that, because of this common goal, its workers are actually team members with physicians, nurses, and others in this significant work.

Aside from the possibilities of providing meetings and discussion groups to consider special mental hygiene subjects, and in addition to the possibility of distributing literature selected from the vast amount presently available, the church, as it carries on its usual program and conducts an efficient educational program, is in the very process of contributing to mental health. It is preaching and providing the love that is essential to healthy individual development. The church, in providing social and love opportunities, must also sometimes provide the controls which are lacking in some personalities.

The church, by affording opportunities for growth and development in love, security, sense of worth, autonomy, emotional maturity, and stability and by, at the same time, holding forth a religious faith and a religious objective for life, is helping the individual to acquire a religious maturity and an emotional maturity that actually come to be the same characteristic.

Alcohol education.—Aside from the moral, ethical, and strictly religious issues which may be involved in drinking, there are many other problems and areas of study. The alcoholic is a problem to himself, and his alcoholism grows out of his problem. He is a problem to his family, and they often are a problem to him and often contribute to his alcoholic indulgence. He is a problem to the industry or office where he works. He is a problem to all of society. He not only is a problem to society but a problem of and for society.

Counseling with the alcoholic requires more study than can be given in a limited space in this discussion. However, it can be said that, as in the case of the other areas of counseling which have been mentioned, the church can help the alcoholic by helping him to become a mature person. The church can be of assistance in helping him to arrive at his peak potential of personal competency and thereby enabling him to adequately handle his emotional problems before they manifest themselves in alcoholism.

One vital area, with regard to this problem of alcoholism, in which the church can work is that of preventive education. Naturally such an educational program is designed for and aimed at the youth of the church and community. Such a program utilizes study materials, discussion and discussional materials, visual aids, lectures, drama, and other aids for the purpose of assisting the young people to understand something of the dangers of alcohol, the whys of alcoholic addiction, the alcoholic as an individual, and his need for acceptance and love. The young people can learn to appreciate the therapeutic values of religion for an alcoholic. They can also learn the sources of help to which they can turn in behalf of their own loved ones who are victims of alcoholism.

Conclusion

Any discussion which relates to pastoral counseling and the educational ministry of the church is, of necessity, a very general discussion. Principles which are of value in pastoral counseling are important to parents as they exercise their ministry in the home. They have the same value to the teacher or worker with a small group in the church. Certainly, such principles do not apply only to the work of the minister, who happens to be called to lead the church. They apply to all who serve in the church, and all who use them are serving as pastoral counselors.

22. The Processes of Group Counseling

John M. Price

People have been gathering in groups throughout history. However, the study of the psychology of group life is fairly new. The effect of these studies on counseling, education, and church group life are of importance to the pastoral counselor.

Group work is a growing phase of counseling and psychotherapy. Counseling was primarily an individual process in its earlier, formative stages but has now advanced to include group counseling. This fact is of value to the person seeking some movement and growth in personality. Help through group activities is also given to those with extreme needs requiring group psychotherapy.

Group work is also a growing phase of education. Parallel to the use of group procedures in counseling has been increased interest in the therapy available through group education. Slavson implies that most "important education is derived from group experience; whether it is learning of facts or skills, training of character, or developing of personality, the educative process is a social one, for it occurs either in the family, the class, the gang, or the club." [1]

Although the groups in a church do not exist primarily for counseling and therapy, there are many direct and indirect results of group counseling available through them. The church leader feels the impact of Slavson's statement when he looks

[1] S. R. Slavson, *Creative Group Education* (New York: Association Press, 1937), p. 10.

about him and finds that he leads, influences, or is responsible for as great a variety of groups as any other leader in society. These include many age groups, as well as study, committee, planning, administrative, and prayer groups. Thus it becomes vital for anyone in religious leadership to know the psychology of group life in all its ramifications.

Since religious education is increasingly concerned with the total person, it is desirable that those involved will find satisfaction for their basic needs. Thus it will be possible for them to experience a spiritual and personal therapy while active in church group life.

Attention will be given in this chapter to the components of a group, group dynamics, and qualified leadership for church group life. Even if the religious leader does not find it advisable to organize special counseling groups in his church, he will still need to be aware of their influence in educational activities. He will find the group discussion method one of the best means for teaching important biblical and social truths.

Some Components of a Group

A group might be described as "a collection of organisms in which the existence of all (in their given relationships) is necessary to the satisfaction of certain individual needs in each." [2] Counseling groups become a reality when "each and every member believes that he can fulfill some need or needs in collaboration with other people that he cannot fulfill by himself." [3]

A counseling group attempts to accomplish the same purposes as individual counseling. The following might be listed as the ends toward which a counseling, or any other, group might work for the benefit of the individual in the group: a feeling of safety, acceptance, and freedom; a release of tension as common problems are verbalized; appraisal or analysis of problems;

[2] Margaret E. Bennett, *Guidance in Groups* (New York: McGraw-Hill Book Co., Inc., 1955), p. 97.

[3] Franklyn S. Haiman, *Group Leadership and Democratic Action* (Boston: Houghton Mifflin Co., 1951), pp. 78–79.

insight into the personality dynamics of problems, leading into an understanding and creative redirection of inner drives; learning to use the many types of information gained in the permissive group atmosphere; designs for a life plan, with a balance between immediate and long-range goals; a personal evaluation of actions when away from the group; and a more mature feeling and responsibility for others.

Group counseling affords a more economical approach to these ends than does personal counseling and often speeds up individual counseling that may be going on at the same time.

Beyond specific groups brought together for the purpose of counseling there are several other types of groups in which counseling and therapeutic activity can take place. Some church groups lend themselves very well to this type of activity. Educational or study groups have as their aim the sharing of information. Organizations of the church, such as Sunday school and training programs, are readily usable in the counseling process. When discussion is employed in dealing with the information at hand, personality interchange naturally follows. A skilful leader will use this interchange to bring about personal growth. Discussion groups seek to bring about fellowship and personal interaction while dealing with some topic. Socials, young people's discussion periods, parents' meetings, and informal planning meetings within the organizational structure are examples. They will contain many possibilities for group dynamics and personal growth.

Planning meetings usually seek to produce co-operative activity. Again, organizational meetings and deacons' meetings, committee work, church staff meetings, and others are examples. Often attainment of the primary goal by these groups will become impossible because of personality clashes. The religious leader who is aware of group dynamics and group counseling processes will take the time to deal with these personal emotional undercurrents. Thus he will be able to bring about constructive interpersonal movement while achieving the planning desired.

Personal growth groups are emerging and gaining identity in educational circles. These are found in social and club life and in religious schools and churches. Such programs are designed for the sake of personal growth and the advancement of mental health. They are fast losing the stigma of only being for the abnormal. The exploration of personality make-up and its effects on present interpersonal relationships is a major concern of these groups. Some of the processes of group counseling and psychotherapy are used. Many of these groups have been quite successful.

Counseling groups are organized for psychotherapeutic purposes to treat some of the emotional conflicts which provoke abnormal behavior. This is a specialized type of group work and requires the leadership of a trained therapist of mature depth. The ultimate aim of this group activity is the individual's achievement of a normal way of relating to others. It opens up avenues to a more healthy mind and soul. These achievements should increase the possibility of Christian conversion and assist in greater spiritual maturation.[4] Some churches have set up programs of counseling using trained religious and professional counselors.

As a group is formed, attention should be given to the variety of people that are present. Several things about each individual will be noted: the degree of maturity; age and sex differences; intellectual capacity; emotional health; economic position; and the desire to respond and to accept. At the group's first meeting the convener, leader, or counselor will lead the group to structure itself on certain limitations, such as time, place of meeting, and areas of concern. As the work of the group progresses, a determination of objectives gradually appears, and the problem situations of each member can then be viewed more realistically. As facts help to determine what is attainable and possible, solutions should evolve. After the possibilities are

4 William C. Young, "A Study of the Group" (unpublished manuscript, 1958), p. 6.

weighed and measured, then some experimentation and adaptation should follow.[5]

Attention should be given to the helpful processes found in group activity. A few of these are: emotional expression; the feeling of belonging and status; the protection from real or imagined threat; the enhancement of self-esteem; the loosening of the façade of defensive mechanisms; the curbing of infantile desires and behavior; the internalization of group standards in exchange for the love and protection received; the redirection of aggressiveness onto the real problems; and the process of identification.[6]

As the group is structured and proceeds through these processes, certain results will begin to emerge. Group life seems to become an enlargement of the family, and there is a tendency toward uniformity. There will be interstimulation (emotional involvement) among the members; interaction will begin to occur. There will be satisfaction of common needs. An atmosphere of equality will become more predominant. Shared ideals and interests will become commonplace. A feeling of loyalty and trust will develop. Both friends and enemies outside of the group will be excluded. A desire for cohesiveness will bring on a willingness to compromise.[7] As members of the group have these experiences, healing takes place.

Group Dynamics

The make-up of a group, as previously described, would be incomplete without a description of group dynamics and its meaning for counseling. Group dynamics, from a counseling and therapeutic standpoint, is an atmosphere or way of life in which a group allows the maximum participation of each member and produces for each person maximum growth and productivity. It might be further described as an atmosphere where

[5] Haiman, op. cit., pp. 159–64.

[6] Dorwin Cartwright and Alvin Zander, ed., Group Dynamics, Research and Theory (Evanston, Ill.: Row, Peterson & Co., 1953), p. 426.

[7] Young, op. cit., pp. 10–11.

acceptance is supreme. Acceptance produces a warm, safe, secure climate which encourages a deeper sharing, increases each person's desire to contribute, and brings about important attitude changes on the part of everyone involved. A person-centered rather than a material or content-centered climate should prevail, and certain attitudes rather than a set of techniques with which to manipulate others should exist for the leader. This atmosphere demands self-analysis and insight on the part of all participants. "Why do I react negatively or hastily to certain individuals?" and "What are my motives for being here?" are typical questions. This group-centered approach implies equality on the part of all present. Thus mutual respect will grow. "Did I 'pigeon-hole' that person before I really knew him?" and "How can I help him to grow?" are typical reactions.

Each person in the group has some worthwhile contribution to make. Some start out aggressively, some hold back, and others will assume a minority feeling. Some will show feelings of martyrdom. Still others will have strong dependency needs and will work at staying on the side of the leader. In each case, as they become involved, they do contribute. Each person can become more mature, responsible, and independent. Security needs can be satisfied through helping others rather than through manipulating others. Each person operates in a certain unique frame of reference and thus should not be hastily judged by the leader or others for his actions. The feelings behind his statements will be as important as the statements themselves.

The authority of the group will be accepted by the leader because of the respect for group opinion. Also, the group should accept responsibility for its actions and thus for the consequences that follow.

The leader can tell that progress is being made when he is accepted by the group as just another member and not someone to be watched and guarded against.

There are certain basic elements in group work. The physical setting should be attractive and comfortable, and there should be the sort of social atmosphere which produces a sense of well-being. Proper introductions will help. There should be direct interchange among the group members. By saying, "We have one point now. Are there others?" the leader will seek to promote interplay so that there is a flow back and forth between members. There should be a basic plan, but it should be flexible rather than static. The path of progress should be kept open and available to each person present. None should be pushed into participating but rather should be made to feel free enough to do so, and the experiences of the members should be the primary enriching ingredient of the discussion.

All of the members should feel a responsibility for the effective conduct of the group. By doing so they will improve their group performance through the achievement of acceptance of self and the acceptance of others. They should be helped to understand both the immediate and ultimate goals of the group.

Methods and procedures should vary as much as possible. Role playing, questions and answers, films, books, speakers, and critiques will be varied and useful.

These procedures in group dynamics may not all be applicable in a completely permissive counseling approach. Some or all might be engaged in at times in the process of group counseling and psychotherapy.

Only a brief statement will be possible in dealing with basic techniques and methods. Several of these processes will be helpful in creating a dynamic group atmosphere. Some of them would be used only to a limited degree in a group in which permissiveness is supreme and the group is allowed to set its own pace. Any or all of these procedures might be used at one time or another, however. Here are four major areas:

There are several ways of encouraging participation. Introduction and question and answer activities at the beginning of a group session will help to serve as ice breakers. They also provide an opportunity to give direction to the group. Discussion periods, informally arranged, or a panel from within the group can also be good starters. Round-robin opinion-giving is good if not pushed to the point of threatening individuals. It is also good at the summation time. Buzz groups help to get some members involved sooner than they would if they were required to speak out before the whole group. Small groups are easily arranged; the leader simply suggests that the two or three nearest each other turn and interchange ideas on some point at hand.

Role playing, one of the better involvement techniques, may be used as the group begins to feel safe. This is the process, discussed in another chapter in another context, in which some group member or members act out an event with specific implications to them and to the group. These are often planned in advance but can occur at a moment's notice when desirable and helpful. Resource materials may be brought in advance. These materials should not get in the way but may create safety for those who need to deal first with ideas rather than feelings. They usually lead to expressions of feeling, however. Refreshment time before, during, or after a meeting will be of help. It breaks the tension in the first stages as well as at a time of too critical an involvement. It starts the comments off again rather informally and serves as an excellent means of creating a social atmosphere.

Although there are many opinions as to the value of mechanical devices in a free, open, group counseling atmosphere, there are enough examples and testimonies to their value to warrant their being included. Recording, through disc or tape, the whole session helps to capture important ideas and can afford later personality insight both for the members and the leader. A microphone may be placed on the table with the machine out of sight. Long-playing tape will help to avoid interruptions. Usually the group is soon freed from any restraint caused by the presence of this device. It is a common practice today. Case records of someone outside the group may help the members to reach an objective appraisal of comparable problems. Psychological tests, including projective techniques, may be used within the group or with individuals. Only those trained in their use should attempt them, however. Taking inventory during the group meetings, especially in summary periods, may be attempted. Inventories are valid for research and study but should be controlled so as not to hinder cohesiveness. They should be short and simple but not planned to prove some predetermined point.

Questions could be raised as to the wisdom and value of any direct or coercive method in group counseling. If time dictates and the leader is able to divert these activities when they create anxiety, they are in order. If he can accelerate the counseling process for some member of the group, his method may be justified. An effort may be made to bring out negative responses. The leader may seek to direct these feelings toward himself by taking a particular point of view or allowing a brief display of temper or other similar activities. This technique must be carefully handled or more harm than good will result. Push or coercion is the procedure of drawing someone out beyond the point that he has felt safe on previous occasions. Support from the leader is very necessary at the right time if this method is successful. Quite often the response made by one member of the group to the related experiences of another reveals his own personal needs. Such responses also give the other members an awareness that some of their problems are not unique. This usually creates a spirit of sharing, concern, consideration, and understanding.

The leader or members may present a problem point or situation that is assumed to be one outside of the group. As an objective appraisal is made of this point, the discussion often leads to the mention of a similar and more personal problem on the part of someone present. It may indirectly help someone deal with an area of his life that may not come forth except through this association of ideas.

Whether in individual or group counseling, interpretation should be approached with skill and caution. All too often the one receiving the appraisal will resist, become hostile, or retreat from progress that has already been made. When interpretation is used, however, it ought to show an interest and concern for the one receiving the evaluation. The air of Christian love should be so evident that the individual can drop his defenses and still be accepted by those at hand.

Finally, some people in the group cannot respond until given a hand of support. Others find themselves going beyond intended revelations and becoming embarrassed. Still others become defensive about some thought of criticism which has been manifested. All of these situations will require tactful support in all types of counseling. If overloaded or misused, they can defeat the personality growth of the person involved.

Often summary and conclusion efforts are unwise and artificial. There are, however, several procedures that can be used if this technique seems best. Tests may be used at the end of a session for research data when agreed on in advance by the group. They may also be useful for further interpretations, individual reflections, and preparation for future meetings. The purpose of such a test should be to build better relationships. Group comments can promote personal revelations, both positive and negative, and will aid some to participate. The leader may say, "We seem to have better understood each other this time. We seem to be together more now." Failures may also be brought out at this point. In addition to the general processes previously described, a critical appraisal of one or more individuals may be made. Objective as well as subjective evaluations of an individual might be discussed. The leader may also find an opportunity to bring in general truths that have a bearing on demonstrations in the meetings. These should necessarily be interpreted. Finally, the group may try to see how much progress they have made in addition to planning other approaches for future meetings.[8]

[8] William G. Hollister *et al.*, *Education for Responsible Parenthood* (Raleigh, N. C.: Health Publications Institute, Inc., 1950), p. 45.

Among the traits of a good group leader the following may be emphasized. The good group leader attempts to understand all expressions of ideas and feelings in order to facilitate communication between members of the group. He accepts all viewpoints and feelings so that honest expressions of the group are brought out into the open. He clarifies feelings, ideas, meanings, and positions for the group as a whole as well as for each person involved. He listens with genuine concern to the group and to its members. He integrates, through reflection and other means, the contributions of individuals into the total group process. He allows the group to make decisions on as many points as possible. He encourages the feeling of responsibility and waits on the group to take the responsibility for its decisions. He seeks, when at all possible, to let the group interpret and evaluate. He seeks, as soon as possible, to be a resource person and not an authority. He reduces his individuality as a leader and becomes an equal member of the group.

Although the personal qualifications of a group leader are somewhat relative, they are all important. This list of traits may be used in an appraisal of the leader's ability to handle a group of people: psychological insight; a socialized personality; intellectual hospitality; respect for the views and personalities of others; broad social interests and an evolved social philosophy; the capacity to allow others to grow; emotional maturity; cooperativeness; resourcefulness; creativity and respect for creativity of others; love of people; cheerfulness and evenness of temper; knowledge; and humor.[9]

Some Results of Group Counseling

Just as it is difficult to draw specific conclusions in individual counseling, so it is difficult in group counseling. There are successes as well as failures. There are limitations as well as advantages.

Group counseling requires that a person be thoroughly aware

[9] Slavson, *op. cit.*, pp. 24–25.

of the qualifications above. The leader must be able to work for a considerable length of time without evidence of specific and lasting success. If he tries to force results, he may only promote failure. The leader must be prepared for several typical people to appear in the group process. The overly dependent person will insist on trying to be on the side of the leader. In nearly every group there is a Miss "Prim Rose," who seeks comfort and safety by leaning on the leader. There might also be Mr. "Bull Dozer," who tries to dominate the group. He does not care how fast and furious the action becomes as long as he is in control. It may be that he has been sports hero of the community and now attempts to regain the real and imaginary glories of school days. Mr. "Hiram I. Que" is safe in the group only when he can quote facts, figures, and authorities to the dismay of all others present. He has learned to lean on his mind and has difficulty facing his weaknesses in social interchange. It is the leader's task to help him come out from behind the façade. Miss "Ima Lonely" is also present. She tends to use every method and means to draw the attention of the men present. Mr. "Pair A. Noya" feels persecuted, yet experiences a strong need to be present. He attracts attention by coming late and indulges in other forms of resistance, showing many negative attitudes.

Mrs. "Sunshine Shaw" arrives bubbling over with enthusiasm and dedication to the cause at hand. She has probably left an unkept house, a disgruntled husband, and some confused children at home, but nothing is too good for the cause. Mrs. "Minnie Payne" comes to each meeting under great duress. She always suffers. Her introductory remarks include news of her latest nostrums and doctors. She rarely gets beneath the surface to see why she suffers. The leader and the group have as their duty the responsibility of helping her to do so, however. These and many more types of mild escape patterns will be demonstrated by group members. They are hazards as well as challenges to the leader and the group.

A person can meet many individual needs through proper

group life and group counseling. Some of them are: to accept himself for what he is and what he may become; to learn to live with his parents; to get along with others of his own age and sex; to develop happy relations with the opposite sex as a preface to normal, happy friendships and later marriage and homemaking; to learn to get along with and experience a feeling of kinship with all people; to become increasingly aware of the world of work and to prepare for an appropriate vocation; to develop an awareness of contemporary social issues and a deep sense of personal responsibility as a significant member of democratic society and of the world community; to lay the foundations for a philosophy of life, including the identity and choice of those values by which his future life will be governed; to cultivate interests and skills which will provide channels for recreational and avocational pursuits through the years to come.[10]

Starting a Group

For many people in the general field of social studies, beginning a group may pose a difficult problem. For the religious worker in a local church, however, it should not be difficult. There are many groups already in operation such as teaching organizations, staff meetings, and committees.

Many informal discussion meetings, especially with young people, are readily available. Meetings with parents concerning their children in the church are possibilities. Experimentation with group activities involved in group counseling can grow out of these and others. When the leader in a church becomes known as a successful counselor with individuals, he is in a position to arrange for groups. It is possible to begin meeting with the specific goal of group counseling announced in advance.

Group counseling processes can be most helpful for the pastoral counselor and will warrant his respect and attention in his busy schedule of serving people in the name of the Lord.

[10] Eugene C. Morris, *Counseling with Young People* (New York: Association Press, 1954), p. 32.

23. The Counselor Training
of Prospective Group Leaders

A. Donald Bell

Many privileges are enjoyed in the Christian life. These are earned by assuming certain responsibilities. These responsibilities constitute the stewardship of the Christian life and center on the task of presenting the gospel to others, which involves the initial testimony of the Word in soul-winning and continued spiritual help to those already regenerated. Since both tasks deal with human problems and personal relations, the Christian worker is always involved in the work which, even in this informal sense, can be designated as counseling. It has been said that every Christian is a teacher. In parallel, one can say that each Christian is also a counselor.

If Christians who are the lay leaders of groups in the church are dealing with other people in problem situations, the church should afford some training for them. These leaders are Sunday school leaders and teachers, those in training and missionary organizations, and chairmen of various committees and boards. Such training in counseling and mental health will of necessity be brief, informal, and limited. Most churches provide help in understanding many spiritual problems through training courses and promotional literature. Sunday school and other workers receive help on understanding people by age groups. Doctrinal studies aid in helping with specific problems of a spiritual nature. Training in fundamental counseling methods would supplement these basics and be invaluable. This is needed since the vocational staff members of the church cannot provide all of the problem-solving relationships needed in a typical church.

The lay leaders within the churches are key people—actually the vocationally called are in the minority in Christian forces. Since the first century, Christ has relied on lay leadership. He has endowed all kinds of imperfect human beings with wonderful talents and abilities which can be improved with training and experience. In God's divine wisdom and economy he saw fit to use human instrumentality—men must reach men. Part of the art of helping people in a counseling role is understanding people. The human aspect of the personality of Christ brought men closer to God. Therefore, today God still uses the human element in bringing divine help to mankind. There is someone in the church community each worker can reach and help.

The discussion to follow will cover counselor training with reference to the role of the leader, the personality dimensions of his role, situations which afford counseling opportunities, and in-service training programs.

The Role of the Group Leader

Any leadership situation is based primarily upon the position in which the leader finds himself. Involved in this position are the personality of the individual, his role in the situation, what his constituency thinks of him, the symbolism which he presents to his followers, and the contribution of all of his contacts with his constituency. Since the lay leader's position is less formalized than that of the paid staff member of the church, he must carefully study his own role and particularly what is expected of him in his position. True leadership can neither be studied nor improved in isolation because the leader must constantly be in the right relationship with his followers. Therefore, before the group leader can be trained, he must be properly positionized.

A significant factor of the group leader's role, in the first place, is that he himself has just come from the ranks of his followers. This proximity to them enables him to understand them better and them to feel closer to him. However, difficulties sometimes arise because of this intimacy, and additional guidance and help must be given to such a leader so that he can merit sufficient respect and followship from his workers without alienating himself from them. If, when he has been selected as a leader, he has difficulty in leading some who have been very close to him before he assumed the position, it may be that he will need additional help from staff members. Just as it is difficult for one to counsel with a member of his family about personal problems, so it may be between very close friends when one has been selected for leadership. In such a case the group leader should refer this problem to some staff member.

Actually, in a total church counseling program this may be the first step of referral. Thomas Wilson has been a member of a Sunday school class with John Smith. Mr. Wilson is selected to become the teacher of that class. Shortly after his friend has become teacher Mr. Smith gets into a situation in which he needs help. He goes to the new teacher, but because they have been on an equal level and intimate friends for such a long time, they find it difficult to create the right atmosphere for counseling between them. The new teacher is wise enough to see this because he has had some counselor training within the church, and he refers this member of his class to the minister of education of the church. As this person picks up the referral and deals with the class member, he soon finds that the person is worried about some of the deeper intricacies of church doctrines. After some orientation it seems wise to refer the person to the pastor.

Such a chain of referral is rather exceptional. Yet it does happen, and the first step in the chain can begin at the lay level. It will be remembered that the less formal the counseling situation and the less emotional the problem, the closer the counselor and counselee may be in their relationships. But the more formal the therapy and the more embedded the emotional conflicts are, the more professional distance there will be between therapist and patient.

Sometimes counseling can be kept at the lay level when the group leader refers the church member to some other member who in his professional life is trained in the field of guidance or counseling. Such a person might be a guidance worker in the local public school, an experienced physician or attorney, a social worker, a welfare worker, or some mature adult within the church membership.

A second aspect of the role of the group leader is that the group leader is more accessible to his fellow church members than a vocational staff member might be. At this point it is significant to remember that in all interpersonal relationships communication is most significant. Here the lay people are in good communication with one another. Sometimes a church member hesitates to go to a staff member with a problem which he considers to be of a minor nature. But since his contacts are almost day by day with his fellows, he will be more permissive with them. This communication is most significant and may be one of the assets of the lay counselor. In his recent book *The Communication of the Christian Faith* Dr. Hendrik Kraemer says,

The fields where the greatest possibilities of communication in the full sense of the word are realized are that of friendship, of the unity of man and wife in marriage, of the authentic community of the fellowship of believers as the body of Christ. Life is mostly filled with failing, frustrated, thwarted, or partly succeeding communication. . . . In this Biblical light it is understandable that intelligent self-observation tells us, communication between man is so often surrounded with mystery. We reach out toward one another, yet do not reach each other.[1]

Thus communication is helped because the group leader comes immediately from the ranks of the group. Another advantage

[1] Philadelphia: Westminster Press, 1956, pp. 58–59.

at this point is that the group leader understands the problems of his fellow workers better. He has so recently been close to them. Dr. Tralle writes, "The world's leaders come from the crowd . . . not from the clouds." [2]

In the third place, why are people motivated to come to the group leader? The group leader's followers will probably come to him for counseling for several reasons: They have psychological walls built up against clergymen. Many people have had unfortunate experiences with the church or with the ministry. Most cases like this are simply the results of unfortunate circumstances. Because of this fact, though the member may respect the clergyman, he will go to the lay group leader for help when the time of difficulty comes. Therefore, the lay counselor is in better rapport with the person than is the staff member. In fairness to the ministry the lay leader, in a circumstance like this, should be led to gradually break down this resistance in the thinking of the follower. In such a way the group counselor may graduate the person to a better attitude toward the pastor or minister of education. Slowly, pastor-member communication may even be structured.

Another reason the follower comes to the group leader is that this leader's position is more permanent. He is more durably related; that is, he sees his fellow church member as one who has perhaps lived in the community for a long time, is secure in the community, and is mature in his own personal contacts. These points give the follower a sense of security as he takes his problem to such a person. He may also anticipate a more intimate follow-up with such a lay person. This would be particularly true where there had been considerable change of local ministry in the church.

In the third place, a church member often goes to a group leader because that group leader is one who is in a respected position outside of the church. It may be that he is an older rela-

[2] Henry Edward Tralle, *Psychology of Leadership* (New York: D. Appleton-Century Co., 1939), p. 4.

tive, employer, or a superior person in a business or social circle.

A fourth facet of the role of the group leader in counseling is the development of a warm personality. Of necessity, this type of counselor will not have sufficient technical training for the most efficient level of counseling. This can be supplemented, however, with a warm and magnetic personality. The prestige of the lay counselor can be elevated when he has acquired this. In a given Sunday school two new teachers were assigned to classes of the same ages at the same time. After three month's teaching in these similar situations it was noticed that the pupils of the one teacher went to her for help and guidance while it never occurred to the pupils of the other teacher to do so. Neither of the teachers was trained in the field of counseling, and probably their technical knowledge was about equal. But the first teacher had a warmth of personality, a love and understanding of her pupils, and a sincere and evident desire to be helpful. Her personality was mature, and she herself was making a good adjustment to most of her life. These good personality characteristics were intangible invitations to her pupils to come to her.

A good personal inventory for the lay leader can come in response to the question, "To whom would a young person in my department go if he had a problem?" Later on in the chapter it will be seen that the first suggestion for in-service training is personality development. A well-integrated and mature Christian personality is the first requirement for a good group counselor. As in any other counseling situation this does not infer perfection, but at least the counselor ought to handle his personal problems with a reasonable degree of success. The more he matures emotionally and spiritually, the better he will be able to help others and the more readily they will be drawn to him.

The Group Counselor Understanding His Opportunities

The staff member ought to suggest to the group leader his many opportunities for counseling. Most lay workers enter their tasks with a rather clear understanding of the specific duties of the positions. However, many of them have not been led to look for opportunities for counseling as these permeate all of the specific duties of the place of service.

This might be called the counselor attitude of the lay worker. This evaluation of such opportunities will make him sensitive to them when they arise. The Sunday school teacher needs to be prepared for the opportunities for counseling in conjunction with his work. This involves some group counseling within the class period and, of course, personal contacts with pupils outside of the classroom and in their homes. Another instance would be the case of the superintendent who is always ready for counseling opportunities in his teachers' meetings. When the teachers ask him about the functions of the department or some classroom procedure, he will not only answer their questions within the group but he will also see them privately and encourage further discussion. Such opportunities will develop into teacher improvement. As long as such relationships are kept permissive they will be rather safe. It would, of course, be unwise for the worker to press advice upon his teachers or pupils. In summary, the group leader is going to do a better job of helping his followers when he is looking for opportunities.

Making the group leader aware of his opportunities should be balanced by a careful inventory of the leader's role in terms of its limitations and resources. He needs to properly positionize himself in terms of what his abilities are. This means that, as with professional counselors, lay workers will be stronger in some areas and weaker in others. Some people are able to make rather rapid and successful shifts in their positions and roles while it is difficult for others. One group leader may have to be Bill Jones, garage mechanic, on Monday and Bill Jones, Sunday school teacher, on Sunday. This role building is essential for all lay workers. This in contrast is not so much a problem with the vocational staff worker. The lay worker must constantly clarify his group position in the eyes of his followers, or he will be handicapped. Any sharing helpfulness will be difficult if his role is confusing in the sight of his followers. If to some of his followers he cannot shift from the role of mechanic to teacher, he will refer them to some other layman or staff member as indicated earlier in the chapter. Although in many instances the lay leader's intimacy with his followers is an advantage in counseling, it could, in this situation, be a partial handicap.

Closely related to this is a third problem which is difficult to handle—the possibility of emotional involvement. In his heart the Christian counselor must have a deep compassion for the people he helps. Yet he must not become too involved in their problems. This is a difficulty even to the trained church counselor. Therefore, it may create quite a difficulty for the lay person. This is one instance where the worker will not "feel with" his followers. Such objectivity is very difficult when dealing with someone with whom the counselor is intimate.

Leadership Opportunities for Counseling

The initial contact with the new member of the group affords one of the best opportunities for counseling. The new worker is seeking to make new allegiances with his fellow workers and his group leader. If the group leader in such a circumstance is a superintendent, then building a good friendship may be the opening to counseling opportunities.

In this context the lay counselor may ask, "How can I get my new workers to desire and accept my help?" Dr. Francis P. Robinson has four suggestions which can easily be applied to this situation in the church. First, he suggests that the leader simply make a specific appointment to talk to the new worker about the problem situation—which in this case would be assuming the responsibilities of the new job. Second, he suggests that the counselor maintain good relationships with his fellow workers so that they will make contact with him when they need help. A third suggestion is to provide situations away from the place of activity which will lead to the desire for counseling.

This would include contacts with the new worker in organizational meetings, social activities, and other functions, both inside and outside of the church. And fourth, the counselor will provide conditions within the working relationship which would lead the worker to bring out his problems.[3]

Another counseling opportunity can be found in dealing with the whole group but having the particular problem of one member in mind. This is one of the interesting techniques involved in group counseling which is discussed elsewhere. Every group leader—such as the Sunday school teacher—prepares specific help for individuals, which he gets across to the individual while he deals with the total group.

Dr. Wendell White suggests the following in his book *The Psychology of Dealing with People:*

Expressing one's idea without directing it specifically toward the person addressed avoids giving the impression of singling him out as being in need of information or guidance. Such a procedure is less likely to affront the individual than is a statement directed to him in particular. There are various ways in which one can keep another person from regarding the idea presented as being intended for him alone. Some are:
  a. Addressing one's ideas to the group.
  b. Presenting an idea as being a good policy.
  c. Stating that we should do a certain thing.[4]

A third opportunity for counseling is afforded when the group leader finds himself a member of a committee, board, or other planning group. In such a situation, though he has been a group leader in another position he holds, he is now thrown with his followers on an equal level. This definitely has its advantages in terms of counseling opportunities. On Sunday morning a person might be the superintendent of a department in Sunday school.

[3] Francis P. Robinson, *Principles and Procedures in Student Counseling* (New York: Harper & Brothers, 1954).
[4] Wendell White, *The Psychology of Dealing with People* (New York: The Macmillan Company, 1946), pp. 32–35.

On Sunday evening he might be a member of a training organization, along with one of the teachers in his Sunday school department. Such a different relationship might enable the group leader to help the teacher in some personal problem related to his teaching without the distance between the two positions in the Sunday school.

The function of a committee presents also an excellent laboratory for human relations. Perhaps a teacher and one of his pupils from the Sunday school might function on a general church committee together. In this relationship additional opportunities for counseling may be afforded. A slightly different possibility evolves when a group leader appoints a special committee. One example of this might be in the case of a director of a leadership training group who appointed a committee to plan a special program. After appointing the committee, the chairman and the director designated specific tasks within the general responsibility to each of the committee members. Then, as the members worked independent of the committee, the director had an opportunity to guide them in a unique and intimate way. One good plan relative to committee work is for the group leader to have a period when subcommittees meet simultaneously. Then the group leader moves from subcommittee to subcommittee and counsels with them as they plan their respective parts of the total task of the committee.

Of course, the most obvious opportunity for the counseling ministry is in dealing with members of the group in the time of difficulty or strife. Specific suggestions along this line will be given in the following chapter. But it is sufficient to mention that the group leader can be of distinct help in these times. If the group leader is experienced in counseling in his vocation, he can even deal with his group members in deeply emotional problems and personality difficulties.

Perhaps the most practical aspect of this type of counseling opportunity is that many of the workers' problems involve the organization in which they work. If there is friction between two teachers in a Sunday school department, the superintendent is in a good position to be of help. This situation is particularly safe for the untrained superintendent when these points of friction deal only with organizational difficulties. In other words, if the superintendent can deal with the problem and help the teachers by changing their rooms or helping them to better understand their particular task of teaching, he can be of service. If there are deep-seated emotional problems causing conflict, it would be best for him to refer them to the minister of education or the pastor of the church.

A more specific outgrowth of the fourth opportunity is the privilege of sitting down with group workers and helping them plan their work. If they are Sunday school teachers, the superintendent might take the opportunity of helping the inexperienced teachers with lesson preparation. Many problem-solving influences may be exerted by the group leader. A word of caution is in order here: the group leader would not continue this intimate counseling and help but would do it only to enable the group worker to later function on his own.

In-Service Training Programs

We have discussed the role of the group leader, the facets of his personality, and the help he can be given in seeing his opportunities for counseling. Now let us look at some specific things which the staff member can do in training the group leader in counseling methods, attitudes, and techniques. The following projected training programs could be utilized in most churches. In some situations additional training opportunities could be fostered. Most of these programs are general and in no way anticipate that group leaders in a local church would become technical specialists in counseling therapy.

First, a basic help is the institution of training courses and firsthand experiences in personality development. Religious publishing houses are producing some excellent materials in this field. Also, the average church member has at his disposal helps from magazines and newspapers. Some of this popular information is not too sound technically, but it has helped to make the average person better informed in developmental psychology. Further, as a Christian has been guided through the typical activities of church life, he has been helped in his own personality development, which is really more basic to a knowledge of the field. In short, this means that a typical church, by taking advantage of the training material and the laboratory opportunities of its program, will be able to educate its constituency in the area of personality development. Certainly a group leader will not be of much help to his fellows in the area of counseling unless he has the basic understanding of the dynamics of human personality.

In the second place, the in-service training program will include training courses and other helps in the areas of theological problems, philosophical concepts, doctrinal understanding, and biblical interpretation. Though the average group leader will probably not be highly trained in these particular fields, the one who is well informed in the distinctives of his beliefs is better able to help others. The better informed the leader is in these areas the less referral he will have to do to the pastor of his church. As the program of religious education advances in the typical church, the lay leaders become more informed; therefore, when the problems of their fellows deal with theological doctrinal questions, they can be of help.

A third part of a training program would involve the rudiments and fundamentals of counseling techniques. No church would be ambitious enough to attempt to make guidance specialists out of all of its group leaders. And yet there are some simple basic understandings of human relations and counseling techniques which are available even to lay leaders. Some authorities in the field believe that the nondirective or client-centered approach advocated by Dr. Carl R. Rogers is best for the lay counselor. Actually, the client-centered type of counseling can become very involved and technical. However, in its simplest form the permissiveness which is given makes it a good instrument for the nonprofessional.[5]

Again, during special emphases such as Christian Home Week, Sunday school clinics, and age-group conferences, excellent evaluation of materials and exhibits can be presented. In fact, it is impossible to train workers with the various age groups without helping them with the problems of those ages. Other helps are found in various denominational magazines and journals.

A fifth help would be the use of church libraries. Many churches are seeking to build up a section in the area of personal problems and counseling techniques. Leaders can be encouraged to use this material as supplements to some of the other suggestions given.

Encouraging group leaders to participate more in discussions of training and Sunday school programs and lessons about human problems is a sixth area of training. Needless to say, the counselor is not only trained by his acquisition of methods but also by his experience in discussing human problems and his acquaintance with human nature.

Growing out of this same idea is the use of biographies as training instruments for lay counselors. The biblical stories of great men of God seeking to solve their problems and to find new attitudes toward life are invaluable to church workers. Reading great biographies, both fiction and nonfiction, is helpful. The more acquaintance the group leader has with real life struggles, the better prepared he will be to utilize the counseling methods he has learned.

Finally, special counselor programs can be initiated. A church can invite an experienced school person or psychiatrist to present a special training program for the group leaders in the church. This worker would have to be well selected and have the ability to present the basic facts of the field in nontechnical

[5] Carl R. Rogers, *Client-Centered Therapy* (Boston: Houghton Mifflin Co., 1951).

terms. Along this same line help in the area of group counseling and group work will be particularly beneficial to Sunday school teachers and departmental leaders.

A final aspect of the counselor training program would be the initiation of a total church atmosphere of helpfulness, sharing, and ministry. In such an atmosphere the lay counselor is more likely to find his opportunities, take them seriously, and seek more help in the field.

24. Counseling the Discouraged Group Leader

A. Donald Bell

The volunteer leadership of the church constitutes one of its greatest assets. These men and women assume positions of leadership because of their desire to follow God's will and to project the gospel through the medium of Christ's church. The church staff member needs to remind himself of the fact that the dominant leadership of churches is in this constituency of volunteer workers. Usually the volunteer worker's responsibility is that of a group leader—chairman of a board or committee, superintendent or teacher of a Sunday school group, or leader of some smaller division of the typically organized church.

Such functions constantly involve a volunteer leader in human relations, and contacts between individuals are never perfect because human beings themselves are imperfect. In addition, the democratic approach to organization as expressed in a church of congregational polity allows much more freedom in the organizational processes, such as the selection, training, and tenure of workers. Further, such volunteer workers receive no financial remuneration for their service.

All of these conditions can contribute to periods of despondency and discouragement in the experiences of such volunteer group workers. The church staff member must, therefore, assume the responsibility of continued counseling with his group leaders.

The Significance of Good Worker Enlistment

If the counseling aspect of the enlistment of volunteer workers has been satisfactorily taken care of and if they have been well trained in the duties and responsibilities of their tasks, the chances of discouragement after they are functioning are smaller. However, in the finest church programs of worker orientation and in the best organized training programs there is still the human element. This means that every full-time staff member will need as much experience as possible in the area of counseling the discouraged group leader. As in other areas of dealing with people, preventive counseling at the time of enlistment and training is the ideal, and curative counseling after the person is already in trouble is only an emergency measure. Thus there will usually be a direct relationship between the time, effort, tactfulness, and thoroughness of the enlistment and training of the worker and the need for remedial counseling when the worker becomes discouraged. In other words, proper enlistment of the worker will reduce the possibility of discouragement later on.

Following these suggestions for proper enlistment might accomplish this.

1. The volunteer worker should accept the position only if he is motivated by a desire to serve.

2. The staff member ought to begin the invitation to serve in a given position with the statement that the person has been selected for the job after careful consideration.

3. He should express to the person the assurance that he can succeed in it.

4. The enlisted person should be told that others are depending upon him.

5. The rewards and satisfaction which he will receive should be emphasized.

6. All of the appeals in the enlistment interview should be expressed in positive language.

7. A spoken commitment should be obtained. This is natural if the staff member has in hand some pieces of literature that describe the responsibilities of the particular position and present it to the prospective worker as he gives verbal expression to his acceptance.

Problems May Be Minimized

The church staff member may be so involved in problems which he considers more significant that there is a tendency for him to minimize the importance of the worker's problems. A definite break of relationship occurs when such lack of understanding takes place. A pastor who is in the middle of an evangelistic effort or the construction of new buildings may feel that a problem of one of his Sunday school teachers is insignificant, and in contact with that worker he may attempt to shrug off the problem because it doesn't seem significant. This usually takes place when the staff member is not in good communication with group leaders.

In all church situations communication is most significant. However, it seems to be of unusual importance when it has to do with the members' understanding of one another's tasks. Everything which the volunteer worker does is important to him. Because of the fact that he does it out of love and devotion and on a volunteer basis, there is usually a desire on his part for recognition of its significance. The pastoral counselor needs to realize that none of his larger tasks could ever be accomplished without the secondary responsibilities of his volunteer leaders.

When the worker's tasks are minimized, he is easily discouraged. He is seeking for some recognition from his leaders, and naturally he becomes a better follower when this recognition is given. Too often, perhaps, church leaders wait until the group leader retires at the end of many years of service before they express appreciation for his service. If workers were consistently and regularly complimented and encouraged, there would be less discouragement on their part.

Lack of Prestige Causes Discouragement

Group leaders are frequently discouraged because the group to which they belong is not fully recognized. Just as public school teachers have lost group prestige in America, so in many church situations have Sunday school teachers. If the leaders maintain the prestige of such groups, then the workers within them—though voluntary—will have high morale. If the training and requirements for a position within such a group are standardized and made a little more stringent, the position is better appreciated and there is less possibility of discouragement.

An interesting psychological factor is involved here. Since the church worker is not remunerated for his services, he needs, in addition to his sense of responsibility to God, some other rewards. In the case of the church-related worker this is involved in his salary. With the volunteer worker this must be made up with group prestige and appreciation from his leaders. In a church where anybody and everybody is called upon at the last minute to teach a Sunday school class, it is obvious that there is little prestige for Sunday school teaching. Therefore, those who give themselves regularly to the task may become easily discouraged.

In the same area with group prestige is the feeling of the new church member. He has expected very high standards in the lives of the present church members. When he finds that they are imperfect human beings like everyone else, he is often discouraged. Therefore, if the church leader can properly orient the new member, he can prevent some of this disappointment. One of the best ways to accomplish this is for the pastoral counselor to have a class for the orientation of the new church member. This approach is particularly helpful to younger members who are easily disillusioned. Dr. Gordon Allport writes concerning this, "Common in these days, and especially among younger people, is the doubt engendered by visible hypocrisy and failure in institutional religion. Some select our doctrines or practices that seem *repressive* to intelligence." [1]

Problems Causing Discouragement

Some of the causes of discouragement growing out of poor enlistment, orientation, and training have been considered. Some specific worker problems which cause the group leader to become discouraged are the following.

Sometimes group leaders accept their responsibilities because they have been coerced into accepting them as a duty. Again, people accept such positions because of social pressures or because they will be able to exert some influence over others. Occasionally a person will accept a church position for the purpose of furthering his business enterprises in the community. These are unworthy motives, and wrong attitudes are immediately created. When a group leader accepts a situation because of such an unworthy reason, he is usually vexed with the following problems, which become a part of his discouragement in the task: disgruntlement, frustration, defeat, hostilities, a need for domination of his fellow workers, and negativism.

Another worker problem which brings on discouragement is failure in an initial attempt at some task. This problem again relates to the lack of training of workers, since so frequently failure is the result of poor preparation. Discouragement comes easily when a person begins his work and success is not forthcoming. This brings about particular conditions such as surrender, withdrawal, or depression. Sometimes an oversensitive conscience can also result from these initial failures. The staff member can be a particular help to the worker in this type of a discouraging situation.

Another cause of discouragement is the common conflict of personalities within the ranks of group leaders. The church counselor is constantly involved in such personnel problems.

---

[1] Gordon Allport, *The Individual and His Religion* (New York: The Macmillan Company, 1950).

When his workers are unable to work with one another in cooperation and alignment, several reactions may occur. A competitive nature between workers may develop; hostilities are sometimes seen; an attitude of blaming others is evidenced. Dr. Karl R. Stolz suggests the following:

A man may assume the infantile attitude of blaming others for the misfortune that has overtaken him. . . . So long as the delusion of martyrdom continues it is impossible for him to make the proper personality adjustment. In fact, it is likely to induce a chronic state of cynicism, captiousness, and discontent, if not active hostility and rebellion against others or what is denominated as fear. Another may keep reproaches upon himself for a misfortune in the precipitation of which he has had no part.[2]

A fourth reason for problems for the worker is simply failure at the task and lack of satisfaction from it. A typical reaction is blaming God for the failure. Many workers resort to this psychological dilemma, and counseling in this area involves both therapy and theological insight. They often develop deep depression and even will use physical illnesses as compensation in the situation. Dr. Carroll A. Wise says, ". . . such persons have a feeling that God is condemning and punishing them. They feel that physical illness is punishment for their sins, though intellectually they find it hard to believe in such a God. Others find that their guilt interferes with faith in God or any kind of close relationship to God."[3]

A fifth reason for discouragement of the worker is the lack of understanding of the total task of the church, that is, failure to fit into the organizational scheme. This comes again from a lack of orientation. When the worker does not have a grasp of the total church program, there is the likelihood of his seeing only his narrow facet of the work and becoming discouraged. If he

[2] Karl R. Stolz, *Pastoral Psychology* (New York: Abingdon-Cokesbury Press, 1932), pp. 113–14.
[3] Carroll A. Wise, *Psychiatry and the Bible* (New York: Harper & Brothers, 1956).

does not respond with some of the negative attitudes mentioned above, he may simply respond by a complete lack of co-operation. Resignations or something which is frequently worse to the health of the church, constant criticism, often comes. In his book *Mental Hygiene for Classroom Teachers* Harold W. Bernard writes, "Sharp criticism and repeated condemnations certainly are contributing factors (to discouragement). Belittling comparisons may cause the individual to feel that he is unworthy. Accidents involving injury to others for which the subject receives continued blame are known to have nourished feelings of guilt." [4]

Helpful Approaches

Initially the counselor must have a positive attitude and a genuine enthusiasm if he is going to help the discouraged group leader. This is to be carefully distinguished from a blind optimism which simply leads the counselor to slap the worker on the back and give him an artificial injection of courage. Real personal enthusiasm is one of the most significant characteristics of a good leader. When he is confident that his work is worthy of his energy and time, real enthusiasm is generated and a power radiates from his life. This enthusiasm is most contagious, and any leader is handicapped without it. It is such contagious enthusiasm that stirs up the emotions of followers so that the leader can lead such followers away from a feeling of discouragement.

Another thing which the staff member can do is to take an inventory of the other responsibilities which the worker has in the church. Many times the worker can be brought out of discouragement by simply relieving him of unnecessary pressures. Many group leaders are simply doing too much, and a wise adjustment in their responsibilities would be the best kind of help. Also, when a worker is overburdened, anxiety is frequently the

---

[4] Harold W. Bernard, *Mental Hygiene for Classroom Teachers* (New York: McGraw-Hill Book Co., Inc., 1952), p. 62.

cause of his discouragement. Leading him to take his tasks one at a time and doing a good job on each one may relieve such anxieties. The late Dale Carnegie emphasized the idea that over-concern for the future and neglect of the issues at hand brings discouragement to millions of people. In one of his books he wrote,

Years ago a penniless philosopher was wandering through a stony country where the people had a hard time making a living. One day a crowd gathered about him on a hill, and he gave what is probably the most quoted speech ever delivered anywhere at anytime. This speech contains twenty-six words that have gone down across the centuries: "Take therefore no thought for the morrow: for the mor-row shall take thought of itself. Sufficient unto the day is the evil thereof!" [5]

The unhappy worker can next be assisted by a clarification of his attitudes toward his particular task in church life. His coun-selor can listen patiently and seek to diagnose attitudes and feelings expressed by the group leader. If it seems wise to retain the worker in his present position and if the organizational setup cannot be adjusted, the alterations of his attitudes and feelings toward the task will prove to be the solution to the situation. This change may call for some rather intimate counseling pe-riods and therapy which delves beyond the immediate surface problems of the disgruntlement. At this point the counselor may find—as is often true—that the seemingly obvious problems causing the discouragement are not the basic ones. Often some deep-seated hostility has been involved without the worker's be-ing aware of it.

It is unwise for the counselor to allow the worker to reflect blame on his fellows. In attempting to bring the discouraged worker into a counseling relationship the staff member may be tempted to sympathize with him even to the extent of criticizing

---

[5] Dale Carnegie, *How to Stop Worrying and Start Living* (New York: Simon and Schuster, Inc., 1948), p. 3.

his fellows. In so doing the objective is to boost his morale with the lever of the imperfections of others. This is a negative approach which cannot be advantageous. In fact, the counselor, even if his method is nondirective, should guide the worker away from criticizing his fellows. Allowing the leader to build up his confidence artificially by pushing others down is only to give him false confidence. In fact, in helping the discouraged leader at all points the counselor must avoid quick assurances and false encouragement.

Finally, the counselor of the discouraged worker must remind himself again of the importance of keeping confidences. The danger zone is evident. The counselor is a staff member; he must therefore be particularly careful not to divulge any of the points of friction or difficulty involved in the particular worker's maladjustment and discouragement. When morale is high, workers minimize imperfections in fellow workers. When morale is low, imperfections are usually emphasized.

25. The Pastoral Counseling of Other Counselors

Wayne E. Oates

It is unmistakably clear to the experienced pastor that he has a major task in counseling others who themselves are carrying major responsibilities as counselors. In other words, he is a counselor of counselors. The pastor finds himself in a place of spiritual leadership similar to that of men of God in earlier days. Moses wore both himself and others out as he tried to be a counselor in all matters, great and small. His father-in-law Jethro wisely advised him to select others and train them to help him in the task. Likewise, at another time Moses became so exhausted himself that he lost patience with the people of Israel and asked God to remove him from this world! God answered his plea by endowing the seventy elders of Israel with the same spirit with which he had blessed Moses. They bore the load with Moses. However, Moses became a counselor to them in a special way; he became a counselor of counselors. Similarly, the pastor of today strengthens many counselors in order that they might become a comfort to those for whom they have responsibility as counselors.

The Pastor and the Official Family of the Church

Sunday school superintendents, training group directors, chairmen of official boards, and chairmen of important standing committees of the church carry heavy responsibility in the very life of the church as counselors to those who work with them.

318

These persons are often the willing horses who are worked to death in a volunteer effort such as the church. Their personal stresses and strains often find vent in church activities. They may even become open and running sores of personality difficulty, thereby confusing the objectives of the whole fellowship. One or two things need to be said as to practical ways of being pastorally meaningful to these church leaders.

First, the pastor himself is likely to lean so heavily upon them that they do not have a pastor to whom to turn when they need personal help. They may feel that to confess such need for help would be to break faith with him. Consequently, their own personal needs for counseling help may run far past the time when it will do any real good. A marriage conflict may become so far advanced as to burst into the divorce court before the pastor establishes counseling contact with it.

The pastor should look outside his own membership for his own needs for personal counseling and emotional support. He should turn to other pastors, physicians, or former professors rather than unload all his personal problems on the people of the church. He should not become so much a part of the family of his church people that they react to him as a kinsman and not as a pastor. This is particularly true of young pastors and other religious workers who still have strong needs for a parental home and have not yet developed their own home with a wife and children.

Second, the pastor is an administrative counselor to other paid workers on the staff of the church where he works as pastor. He may have no more than a part-time janitor, or he may have a large and complicated staff organization. However, those people who do work for the church, be they many or few, look to the pastor as a counselor and guide. Their economic problems, their difficulties in relationship to those with whom they work, and their problems in relation to the pastor himself can be perceived and understood by the pastor in such ways that their work is either enhanced or hindered, depending upon the pastor's skill as a counselor of counselors. Sometimes a pastor can spend an hour or two with one of these workers in carefully unraveling failures of communication, ventilating accumulated feelings of rejection and resulting hostility, and even in the simple impartation of information about "what the deacons decided last Wednesday after prayer meeting." Doing so increases the dedication and effectiveness of a worker to the purposes of the church and its larger ministry. Furthermore, it will save the pastor the many hours of hard work searching for a new staff worker which are occasioned by the all-too-frequent resignations of those working with callous and insensitive pastors.

A word of caution needs to be said about counseling with people with whom the counselor works every day. Even when the pastoral counselor does know enough to attempt to deal with the counseling needs of individuals holding prestige positions in the church's official family, he must bear in mind that longer-term and more intensive kinds of counseling with these people can best be done by persons other than himself. This holds true regardless of how well trained and qualified the pastor is as a counselor. His major task is helping these people find a counselor rather than conducting longer-term counseling himself. For instance, at the same time a pastor is interested in and committed to the personal growth and spiritual rehabilitation of a staff member who has stolen money from the church treasury, he also has to represent the larger interests of the church as a whole. Sometimes these two responsibilities will put him into an untenable position and expose the staff member to unbearable confusion. However, he as the executive officer of the church can on a confidential basis see to it that the staff member gets therapeutic help from another person. This frees his position as a representative of the church in this matter, and thus he may correlate the interests of both the individual and the church. Many such instances arise which reveal the counseling limitations of any administrative position.

The Pastoral Counseling of Other Pastors

The pastor himself often needs counseling. To whom shall he go? Experience reveals that he usually goes to another pastor. Hence every pastor is potentially the counselor of a brother pastor. A pastor can be of assistance to another pastor in several ways.

First, he can give support and affection in time of isolation and threat. He can usually do this best for fellow pastors who are his closest personal friends. Pastors can stand by each other and care deeply what is happening to each other. A friend can give unlimited time to a friend without counting the hours or the cost. He is totally committed on an all-out basis. He can do so without becoming directly involved in conflicts and losses such as a fellow pastor sustains when he is about to be dismissed from his pastorate or has gotten into a running battle with his enemies. But the latter takes great wisdom and much self-control.

Second, he can, if he is not too closely associated and does not have too deep and long personal ties with a fellow pastor, serve as a formal counselor for the troubled person. The close personal friend sooner or later hits his limitations. A friend can have the man and his wife and children as guests for three days, a week, or even a month if they are out of a job. But he cannot do so much longer. He can stay up one whole night listening to the man's troubles, or he even may be able to make it through two or three whole nights if necessary. But beyond this he begins to think that the man needs more help than he can render. Consequently, the man may have to turn to a formal counselor. If there is a pastor near who has been sufficiently trained to give this kind of help, then possibly he can help the troubled pastor. But it has to be someone who is not so well known to the pastor as his long-time friend. If another pastor is not available, it may well be that a medical doctor, a social worker, a psychologist, or a psychiatrist would be able to afford the pastor the anonymity and detachment needed for such help.

In the third place, he can help his fellow pastors by helping them find qualified professional help. The pastor needs particularly qualified people to help him with his problems when he becomes emotionally sick. He needs scientifically trained persons who at the same time can with sympathy and without prejudice appreciate his role as a minister in society today. Pastors need to have and to know such qualified professional people and be able to help fellow pastors make contact with them.

The Pastoral Counseling of Other Professional People

This last suggestion, however, points to the fact that the pastor is also deeply related to these "other professional people." Often they are the "lost sheep of the house of Israel" of secular America today. Particularly is this true of denominations who have neglected the professional people in the community as not being spiritual. These people also need friendship, comfort, guidance, instruction, and counsel. Pastors often overlook the pastoral needs of the doctor of a patient who dies. The family of the patient may reject him or even blame him for the death of their loved one. The doctor particularly needs the pastor's ministry at that time. The psychiatrist is an easy prey for legal suits thrown at him by unforgiving legalists known as paranoid personalities and certainly needs understanding and comfort as well as counseling help at such a time. The social worker deals with the down-and-out, the delinquent, and the bedraggled of the community so much and so long that he often becomes drained and bled white of inspiration. And these people have marriage difficulties, religious doubts, and confessional needs for forgiveness which often go unconsidered and therefore unmet by any pastor. In his community contacts, therefore, the pastor who establishes rapport and personal and professional ties with these counselors will rather regularly discover them turning to him as a counselor of counselors.

Obviously, the pastor who deals with such people must accord them the same acceptance, freedom from prejudice, and affirmation of worth as professional people which he would expect of them if he went to them for help. He cannot jokingly jeer about the "psychiatrists themselves needing help these days." No one knows better than a well-disciplined psychiatrist that he is not self-sufficient. Nor can the pastor, because this person is in dire straits, thereby write off the validity of his profession as a doctor, a social worker, or a public schoolteacher. It is no indictment of the Christian faith for a minister to admit that he needs help and is not self-sufficient. Nor is it a condemnation of the educational process if a public schoolteacher turns to another for guidance. Likewise, it is no invalidation of the hard-earned gains of medicine and particularly psychiatry if a psychiatrist himself needs pastoral care, counseling, and the unmerited grace of God. Such consideration shown to other professional people enables a pastor to reach out more readily for help when he himself needs it. For none of us lives to himself, and none of us dies to himself.

The Holy Spirit as the Counselor of Counselors

One can already detect the theme of shattered self-sufficiency that nurtures the need for counseling on the part of both those who seek help and those to whom they turn for it. The pastor himself must have a continuing Counselor at his side if he is to be "sufficient for these things." Such is the ministry of the Holy Spirit to the pastor as a counselor of counselors. The Holy Spirit is the gift of the Father God upon the specific request of the Son of God for the express purpose that we may have another Counselor who will be with us always. He moves with us as Comforter in times of our own desolation, making his home with us and refusing to allow us to remain as orphans. He stimulates us with new power and sends us into new directions when some great grief has caused us to lose our way and our strength.

The Holy Spirit moves over the face of the deep of our consciousness and brings up into clear awareness those hidden and forgotten recesses of our memory that we may be healed by the remembered teachings of our Lord. The Holy Spirit works in the processes of communication which become hindered and blocked through our sinfully distorted perceptions and enables us to understand each other, "each in his own language." The Holy Spirit even moves into the unutterable depths of our selves and articulates the groanings of our spirits to the Father when we ourselves have to admit that we cannot pray. The Holy Spirit finally convicts pastors that they, too, are sinners under the righteousness and judgment of God. The Holy Spirit reminds them that they have the ministry of counseling, as every other ministry, as a gift and not an earned right. This gift is held in earthen vessels, in order that the excellency of the power may be of God.

Appendix: Standards for Clinical Pastoral Education

Southern Baptist Association on Clinical Pastoral Education

I. Definition of Clinical Pastoral Education

Clinical pastoral education is an opportunity in a church, hospital, or other clinical facility for persons in church-related vocations to relate theological studies to interpersonal relationships through personal supervision by a pastoral supervisor within the framework of a theological education and in relation to the ministries of the church.

II. Qualifications of the Pastoral Supervisor

1. Graduation from an accredited seminary with a Th.M., M.R.E., D.R.E., or Th.D., when such degrees include
   a. Four full years of seminary education beyond the B.A. degree.
   b. At least sixteen semester hours of study described in Section V.

2. An adequate period of pastoral experience, with ordination or certification and denominational approval. Pastoral experience shall be a type of professional service for which persons are prepared in Southern Baptist seminaries.

3. At least one full year of seminary-related clinical pastoral education or its equivalent. This requirement may be met through the courses described in Section V.

4. A semester of supervised clinical teaching of seminary

students who are receiving credit toward an appropriate degree in an accredited seminary.

5. Personal qualifications to be appraised by the accreditation committee. The accreditation committee shall be governed by the above standards in evaluating the candidates for pastoral supervisor.

Note: It is anticipated that a number of men who hold the B.D. or M.R.E. degree and who have completed a semester of clinical pastoral education may be interested in opportunities to teach through seminary extension courses.

III. Requirements for the Clinical Training Center
1. The Training Center Committee shall determine the requirements for and eligibility of training centers.
2. The Association recognizes the requirements for the Clinical Training Center of the 1952 standards for general and mental hospitals.

IV. Minimum Essentials of Clinical Pastoral Education
In addition to the first six essentials of the 1952 standards, the Association adopts this statement in place of essentials 7 and 8 of the 1952 report:
7. A written evaluation of the student and his academic grade to be made by the supervisor to the seminary in which the student is enrolled.
8. If a student is not enrolled in a seminary, the supervisor shall send these records to the secretary of the Association, who may release them only to another clinical training center or seminary to which the person applies for further training.

V. Recommendations for Credit in Southern Baptist Seminaries
1. For B.D. or M.R.E. degree in any field:
a. Up to four semester hours' credit for courses related to clinical pastoral education which include some clinical orientation and practice.

b. Up to four semester hours' credit for advanced courses related to clinical pastoral education which include not less than ten hours weekly of clinical orientation and practice.

c. Four to eight hours' credit for a semester of courses in clinical pastoral education which include twenty hours weekly of supervised clinical experience, in addition to seminars, lectures, and reading.

2. For the Th.M. or M.R.E. degrees in the field of pastoral counseling or psychology of religion:

a. Four years of seminary education beyond the A.B. degree.

b. At least one semester or sixteen semester hours in clinical pastoral education which include twenty hours a week of supervised clinical training or the following:

c. Two semesters of graduate seminars in pastoral care, pastoral counseling, or psychology of religion which include a minimum of ten hours a week of supervised clinical training.

d. Proportionate semester hours' credit for full-time clinical pastoral education internship and/or residency training.

3. For the Th.D. degree in pastoral care, pastoral counseling, or psychology of religion: Satisfactory completion of the seminar requirements in 2c above.

For the D.R.E. degree in pastoral care, pastoral counseling, or psychology of religion (when such degrees consist of at least two years beyond the prerequisite degree): Satisfactory completion of the seminar requirements in 2c above. The vocational requirements for this degree can also be met through the satisfactory completion of 2d as described above.

Respectfully submitted,
STANDARDS COMMITTEE

About the Authors

A. DONALD BELL has been director of graduate studies in religious education and professor of psychology at Southwestern Baptist Theological Seminary since 1951. He studied at William Jewell College (B.A.), Southwestern Baptist Theological Seminary (M.R.E., D.R.E.), Central Baptist Theological Seminary, Menninger Clinic, the University of London, and Mississippi State Hospital. He is a contributing writer for several periodicals.

D. ALLEN BRABHAM is a native of Louisiana. He received the B.A. degree from Mississippi College and B.D. and M.R.E. degrees from New Orleans Baptist Theological Seminary; he has completed residence requirements for the D.R.E. degree. He is now chaplain and director of clinical pastoral education at Southern Baptist Hospital, New Orleans.

JOHN W. DRAKEFORD is professor of psychology and counseling at Southwestern Baptist Theological Seminary. Born in Sydney, Australia, he attended the University of Sydney (B.A., Diploma in Education), New South Wales Baptist Theological Seminary, Texas Christian University (M.A.), Brite College of the Bible (Th.M), and Southwestern Baptist Theological Seminary (D.R.E.).

JAMES LYN ELDER attended Louisiana State University (B.A.) and Southern Baptist Theological Seminary (Th.M., Th.D.). Having been pastor of churches in Louisiana and Virginia and chaplain of paratroopers during World War II, he is now professor of psychology of religion and pastoral care at Golden Gate Baptist Theological Seminary.

ALBERT L. MEIBURG is a native of South Carolina. He is a graduate of Clemson Agricultural College (B.S.) and Southern Baptist Theological Seminary (B.D., Th.D.) and is now associate director of the department of pastoral care at North Carolina Baptist Hospital, Winston-Salem, North Carolina. He is the editor of *Men at Work*.

WAYNE E. OATES is professor of psychology of religion at Southern Baptist Theological Seminary. He attended Mars Hill Junior College, Wake Forest College (B.A.), Duke Divinity School, and Southern Baptist Theological Seminary (B.D., Th.M., Th.D.). His publications include *The Christian Pastor, The Bible in Pastoral Care, Religious Factors in Mental Illness, Anxiety in Christian Experience, Where to Go for Help, Religious Dimensions of Personality, What Psychology Says About Religion, Premarital Pastoral Care and Counseling,* and articles in numerous journals.

JOHN M. PRICE was born in Fort Worth, Texas, and attended Baylor University (B.A.), Southwestern Baptist Theological Seminary (B.D., M.R.E.), and New Orleans Baptist Theological Seminary (Th.M., Th.D.). Having been pastor of churches in Texas and Louisiana, he is now director of the School of Religious Education and professor of Christian psychology, counseling, and clinical education at New Orleans Baptist Theological Seminary.

HAROLD L. RUTLEDGE came to his present position as assistant professor of psychology and counseling at New Orleans Baptist Theological Seminary after a number of years of practical experience as pastor and counselor. Born in Arkansas, he attended Ouachita Baptist College (A.B.), Southwestern Baptist Theological Seminary (Th.M.), New Orleans Baptist Theological Seminary (Th.D.), the University of Chicago, and Northern Baptist Theological Seminary.

SAMUEL SOUTHARD is associate professor of psychology of religion at Southern Baptist Theological Seminary. A graduate of George Washington University (A.B.) and Southern Baptist Theological Seminary (B.D., Th.D.), he is the author of *The Family and Mental Illness, Counseling for Church Vocations,* and *Religion and Nursing* as well as articles in various journals.

RICHARD K. YOUNG attended Wake Forest College (B.A.) and Southern Baptist Theological Seminary (B.D., Th.D.). He is now associate professor of pastoral care at Southeastern Baptist Theological Seminary and director of the department of pastoral care at North Carolina Baptist Hospital, Winston-Salem, North Carolina. He is the author of *The Pastor's Hospital Ministry.*